_FRED'S COL'
WINCHESTER

RESEARCH HIGHLIGHTS IN SOCIAL WORK 34

# Growing Up with Disability

*Research Highlights in Social Work series*

This topical series examines areas of particular interest to those in social and community work and related fields. Each book draws together different aspects of the subject, highlighting relevant research and drawing out implications for policy and practice. The project is under the general direction of Professor Joyce Lishman, Head of the School of Applied Social Studies at the Robert Gordon University.

## Social Work
### Disabled People and Disabling Environments
*Edited by Michael Oliver*
ISBN 1 85302 178 4 pb
*Research Highlights in Social Work 21*

## Developments in Short-term Care
### Breaks and Opportunities
*Edited by Kirsten Stalker*
ISBN 1 85302 134 2 pb
*Research Highlights in Social Work 25*

## Child Abuse and Child Abusers
### Protection and Prevention
*Edited by Lorraine Waterhouse*
ISBN 1 85302 408 2 pb
*Research Highlights in Social Work 24*

## Children and Young People in Conflict with the Law
*Edited by Stewart Asquith*
ISBN 1 85302 291 8 pb
*Research Highlights in Social Work 30*

## Effective Ways of Working with Children and their Families
*Edited by Malcolm Hill*
ISBN 1 85302 619 0 pb
*Research Highlights in Social Work 35*

RESEARCH HIGHLIGHTS IN SOCIAL WORK 34

# Growing Up with Disability

*Edited by Carol Robinson and Kirsten Stalker*

Jessica Kingsley Publishers
London and Philadelphia

*Research Highlights in Social Work 34*
Editors: Carol Robinson and Kirsten Stalker
Secretary: Anne Forbes
Editorial Advisory Committee:

| | |
|---|---|
| Professor J. Lishman | Robert Gordon University, Aberdeen |
| Ms M. Buist | Independent researcher, Edinburgh |
| Mr P. Cassidy | Social Work Department, Aberdeen City Council, representing the Association of Directors of Social Work |
| Ms A. Connor | Lothian Health Board, Edinburgh |
| Mr D. Cox | Robert Gordon University, Aberdeen |
| Mr M. King | Northern College, Aberdeen |
| Dr F. Paterson | Social Work Services Group, Scottish Office |
| Dr A. Robertson | University of Edinburgh |
| Ms C. Smith | Scottish Council for Voluntary Organisations, Edinburgh |

**Robert Gordon University**
**School of Applied Social Studies**
**Kepplestone Annexe, Queen's Road**
**Aberdeen AB15 4PH**

First published in the United Kingdom in 1998 by
Jessica Kingsley Publishers Ltd
116 Pentonville Road
London N1 9JB, England
and
325 Chestnut Street
Philadelphia, PA 19106, U S A

Copyright ©1998 Robert Gordon University,
Research Highlights Advisory Group, School of Applied Social Studies

**Library of Congress Cataloging in Publication Data**
A CIP catalogue record for this book is available from the Library of Congress

**British Library Cataloguing in Publication Data**
Growing up with disability. – (Research highlights ; 34)
1.Physically handicapped youth
I.Robinson, Carol II.Stalker, Kirsten
362.4'083

ISBN 1 85302 568 2

Printed and Bound in Great Britain by
Athenaeum Press, Gateshead, Tyne and Wear

# Contents

# Introduction

*Carol Robinson and Kirsten Stalker*

*Growing Up with Disability* encompasses a wide range of perspectives on childhood impairment and its social implications. Whilst there is a well established body of knowledge about the way parents experience life with a disabled child, children's own accounts of their lives are largely missing: their voices have not been heard. It is a central aim of this book to redress this imbalance.

The Research Highlights Series is known for bringing together the findings from a range of related studies around a particular theme. However, in this case, it was soon apparent that research about many aspects of disabled children's lives has simply not been carried out. We therefore took the unusual step (at least for editors of Research Highlights) of inviting original contributions from disabled young people themselves. Consequently, the book comprises a mix of chapters: some from academics, others from young disabled people. All authors were asked to ensure that the experiences of disabled children were kept uppermost in their contribution and some chapters include material gathered expressly for this book.

In approaching contributors, we identified three additional principles to which we hoped they would adhere. These were as follows:

1. Contributors should identify examples of progressive practice.

2. Contributors should, whenever possible, address issues of cultural diversity.

3. Contributors should base their chapters on the social model of disability.

The social model of disability, developed by disabled people, takes the focus away from individual impairment and places it firmly on the social barriers to inclusion. Unlike the medical model, which pathologises individuals, the social model locates disability in the social, economic and material world. We asked authors to use the terminology which is associated with this theoretical approach. The Union of the Physically Impaired Against Segregation (UPIAS) (1976) defines *impairment* as 'lacking part of or all of a limb, or having a defective limb, organism or mechanism of the body' and *disability* as 'the disadvantage or restriction of activity caused by a contemporary social organisation which takes no or little account of people who have physical impairments and thus excludes them from the mainstream of social activities' (pp.3–4). Within this broad framework there is a diversity of views and approaches, some of which are reflected in this volume.

## Structure of the book

The book begins with a theoretical and historical overview which provides a context for later chapters. The remainder of the book takes a broadly chronological approach beginning with the pre-school years and ending with transition to adulthood. At the same time, the chapters span a range of settings from home and school to foster care and residential homes.

The field of disability studies is emerging as a distinct and influential area of research. This work is based on the social model and is led by disabled researchers. In Chapter 1, Tom Shakespeare and Nick Watson, writing from this perspective, set out a theoretical framework for research with disabled children, drawing on disability studies and the sociology of childhood. They conclude with a set of principles for good practice with disabled children.

Chapter 2, by Maureen Oswin, provides an historical overview of the treatment of disabled children from Ancient Greece to modern times. She exposes the hostile and punitive attitudes which children have faced over the centuries and describes how these negative periods have been interspersed with more benign approaches.

Caroline Jones, in her chapter on early intervention programmes (Chapter 3), addresses two main issues. First, she emphasises the need to broaden the scope of existing intervention programmes to take account of the child's wider social sphere. Second, she focuses on partnership with parents and the importance of developing more flexible and responsive ways of involving them.

Other issues of concern for disabled children in their pre-school years are discussed in Chapter 4. June Statham and Janet Read provide a useful account of the legislative framework relating to education and daycare provision for under-fives. They review the research literature on families' experiences of using these services and draw out the implications for appropriate practice.

The theme of education is also taken up by Linda Shaw, who has wide experience of consulting disabled and non-disabled children about inclusion in mainstream schools. Chapter 5 provides the children's personal accounts of many aspects of school life, ranging from experiences of bullying to friendships. It also includes children's perspectives on special schools. She concludes with some pointers for structural change needed within schools to facilitate inclusion.

Chapter 6 draws on findings from research being carried out at Lancaster University which involved collecting personal accounts from disabled women about their lives. For the purposes of this chapter, Carol Thomas revisited her data to extract women's narratives about their childhoods, especially their relationships with parents. She concludes with some thoughts about the role of families as potential inhibitors or facilitators of social inclusion.

The focus of Chapter 7 is leisure and friendship for children and adolescents. Judith Cavet highlights the importance of leisure for all young people and documents the disadvantages experienced by disabled children and teenagers in accessing social opportunities afforded to their non-disabled peers.

Controversy surrounds definitions of disability, particularly when considering people who have chronic or recurring medical conditions which may be life threatening. Sometimes their conditions may have associated impairments which are invisible and the individuals may not consider themselves disabled. Nonetheless, such conditions would be encompassed within the UPIAS definition of impairment quoted above. As Alison Closs (Chapter 8) demonstrates, young people with serious medical conditions are likely to experience the same social barriers as other disabled people. Specifically for this book, the author conducted interviews with six young people to gain insights into their childhoods. The young people also speak about their ambitions and hopes for the future and the chapter highlights the restrictions they encounter in their everyday lives.

Recent research has highlighted the prevalence of abuse among disabled children. Helen Westcott brings together aspects of the ecological model of child abuse and the social model of disability to provide a framework for understanding why disabled children are more vulnerable than others. She underlines the significance of specific aspects of current policy and practice in the field of child protection and makes some suggestions for personal and organisational change.

Chapter 10 provides an account of the development of a self-advocacy group in a large residential setting. Sue Virgo, the group's independent advocate, presents material written by group members, their comments on life in a residential establishment as well as their personal concerns. Many of the young people involved had limited or no verbal communication: this chapter is a tribute to the group's (and Sue's) commitment to their being heard.

Whilst the majority of disabled children live at home with their natural families, some experience life with foster carers or adoptive parents. Rena Phillips, in Chapter 11, highlights the lack of research evidence about the lives of disabled children in alternative permanent homes and considers a range of policy and practice issues for such placements.

As editors we wanted to ensure that the views of some young people with learning difficulties were included in the book. We therefore invited a contribution from a group of young people attending the Leighton Project in North London. Their views, which appear in Chapter 12, were expressed during tape-recorded group discussions facilitated by Simon Grant and Daisy Cole. This chapter covers the young people's satisfactions and frustrations with their current lifestyles as well as their aspirations for the future. The chapter concludes with a commentary on these accounts, emphasising the disparity between the young people's current situation and their ambitions.

The final chapter in the book deals with the important theme of transition to adulthood. Here, Sheila Riddell discusses current economic and policy conditions which form the backdrop of young people's lives and the ways in which these impact on transitions for young disabled people. The author makes a distinction between the nature of the transition process for those with physical or sensory impairments which, she argues, follows a 'normal' pattern, and that for young people with a learning disability, for whom it may be 'arrested' or 'diverted'. She illustrates these points with two case studies.

This volume attempts to address a wide range of aspects of growing up with disability. However, one area which is not explicitly addressed is the process of consulting children. While many of the chapters involved consulting young people about their views, none of the authors were asked to explain in detail how they went about this. Communicating effectively with young people is an important issue both for practitioners and researchers. Readers who wish to explore this area further should turn to *Personal Accounts* by Bryony Beresford (1997, London: The Stationery Office) or *Seen and Heard* by Linda Ward (1997, York: Joseph Rowntree Foundation).

## Acknowledgement

Finally, we would like to thank all the contributors – both the authors and the young people to whom they spoke – for their thoughtful pieces. We are also grateful to Professor Joyce Lishman, Editor of the Research Highlights Series, for her advice and support, to Donald Ramsay for suggesting the book's title, and to Anne Forbes for her efficient secretarial support.

## References

Union of the Physically Impaired Against Segregation (1976) *Fundamental Principles of Disability*. London: Union of the Physically Impaired Against Segregation.

# CHAPTER 1

# Theoretical Perspectives on Research with Disabled Children

*Tom Shakespeare and Nick Watson*

It is our view that three major problems are presented by the existing literature about disabled childhood. First, like much of the prevailing research on disability, this is work where non-disabled people are discussing disabled people. Second, like much of the prevailing research on childhood, this is work where adults are discussing children. These two imbalances combine and reinforce each other. Third, this is work which defines disability as a problem, within a model which is individualist and medicalised.

We follow those who argue that disabled people are a distinct social group, in a similar way to black people, lesbians and gays. It is suggested that 'disability' is a structural relationship between people with impairment and a discriminating society. Consequently, it is not useful to separate various impairment groups – people with visual impairment, with physical impairment, with learning difficulties – as has been the practice of charities, schools and so on. This is an important insight into the collectivity of the disability experience: however, it should not be allowed to obscure real differences between disabled people, which may be about gender, 'race', sexuality and class. Nor should it be used to deny the individuality of disabled people, in the tradition of objectifying disability through terminology such as 'the disabled'. We argue the need for a balance between understanding disabled people as individuals and members of a disadvantaged group, and between realising the commonalities and respecting the differences.

In this chapter, we will briefly examine new research in the fields of disability studies, the sociology of childhood and children, and disabled children. We will also draw upon parts of our own research, in which disabled adults have discussed their childhoods, in the context of sexual politics (Shakespeare, Gillespie-Sells and Davies 1996) and health (Watson 1996). We conclude by suggesting better principles for exploring the lives of disabled children. It is our experience of discussing childhood with adults which has inspired us to undertake our current ongoing research project, an Economic and Social Research Council (ESRC) sponsored exploration of 'Life as a disabled child'.

We have a personal, political and academic commitment to enabling the voices of disabled children to be heard, and to developing a disability equality perspective on disabled childhood: we are both disabled people, and one of us has been disabled from birth and has two disabled children. We believe that better practice is dependent on better research, and that both the disability movement, and disability studies, have an urgent obligation to promote real change in this area.

### New approaches to disability

Since the 1970s, disabled people in Britain have been organising on the basis of a new understanding of disability known as the social model (Oliver 1983) and based on the ideas of the Union of the Physically Impaired Against Segregation (UPIAS 1976). This approach defines disability as the social restriction placed on people with impairment by society. People are disabled by discrimination and prejudice, not by their bodies. The problems that disabled people face are not the result of their individual impairments, but are the result of a society that fails to address their needs both in the delivery of services and its social organisation. The social model argues that rather than investing time and effort in medical or psychological efforts to correct the impaired body, it is more appropriate to remove the barriers in society which cause problems for people with impairments: these may be inaccessible physical environments, discriminatory employment or welfare policies, segregated education or transport, negative stereotypes or prejudiced attitudes.

The traditional or medical model of disablement sees the impairment as the root cause of the problems faced by disabled people. This results in services and research aimed at the individual level; the emphasis is placed on altering the individual rather than social processes. Impairment thus becomes the focus of service provision, resulting in the medicalisation of disabled people (Oliver 1996). The restoration, or generation, of 'normality' is prioritised; consequently disabled people are presented as a tragedy because of their inability to conform to this 'normality'. Disabled people are portrayed as victims of the biomedical tragedy that is their body. It follows that social policy adopts strategies aimed at 'compensating' disabled people for the tragedy that has happened to them (Oliver 1993). Whilst it is true to say that this is the dominant paradigm operated within the rehabilitation and medical services, it is also the approach adopted by those who write within mainstream medical sociology, such as Bury (1991), Pinder (1996) and Blaxter (1976).

This political shift in the definition of disability has led to an upsurge in the consciousness of disabled people, the formation of new self-organised groups and a campaign for anti-discrimination legislation and independent living. New techniques, such as direct action, and new forms of cultural expression, such as disability arts, have accompanied new ways of identifying and organising.

Alongside the growing disability movement has developed a body of academic and policy literature based on the new understandings of disability. Key figures such as Michael Oliver (1990), Colin Barnes (1991) and Jenny Morris (1991) have provided analyses of disabling social relations, evidence of discrimination, and accounts of disabled people's lives. Gradually, the literature has extended a social model approach into various areas of society and disability, and challenged pathologising or individualist traditions of analysis. Recent developments include new accounts of disabled sexuality (Shakespeare *et al.* 1996); a historical record of the origins of the disability movement (Campbell and Oliver 1996) and discussions of the relationship between disability and feminism (Morris 1996).

It has been suggested that the social model approach to understanding disability, a body of work which we would refer to as disability studies, has neglected to consider issues of impairment and physicality. Critics such as Liz Crow (1996) have pointed to the lack of analysis of impairment and the body, and argued that it is important to explore all dimensions of the disability experience. While the original statements of the social model were weighted towards structural and collective origins of discrimination, we would argue that disability studies can adequately conceptualise the social experience of impairment, as well as developing a causal analysis of disability itself. As the research develops and extends the radical model of disability, so new areas of life as a disabled person will be explored and understood. However, there are certainly tensions within disability studies between those who adopt a more materialist analysis, firmly in the UPIAS

tradition (such as Oliver and Barnes), and those who focus on individual experience (such as Morris and French (1996)). We argue that it is important to balance
an understanding of the individual experience, particularly in terms of identity,
agency and the body, with an analysis of the structural origins of disadvantage.
After all, both impairment and disability can only be understood as social
experiences.

The social model is the key concept underlying contemporary approaches to
disability. However, drawing on the politics of the disability movement, and the
disability studies literature, we can identify three subsidiary principles which may
be helpful in thinking about disabled children. While these ideas have largely been
developed as a result of disabled adults' political practice, they also have clear
relevance to the experience of disabled children and young people.

First, the principle of equality. The social model suggests that the social
experience of disabled people can be understood in terms of disadvantage and
restriction, not physical incapacity. The widespread poverty, unemployment and
marginalisation of disabled people is not explicable by physiological or anatomical
or psychological differences or attributes, but in terms of social policies and
economic priorities and physical barriers. Removing this inequality between
disabled people and non-disabled people is clearly an immediate necessity for
modern societies.

However, the concept of equality has a wider resonance than just economics: it
suggests that disabled people are entitled to full citizenship rights, and to equal
treatment with non-disabled people. Many states have initiated anti-discrimination
legislation, responding to disabled-led campaigns, in order to deliver this type of
fair treatment. Britain itself has gone some way towards this goal with the 1995
Disability Discrimination Act, but has a lot further to go if full civil rights are to
become a reality.

A second principle of the disability movement is for inclusion. This draws
attention to the ways in which environments and policies have been developed
which actively exclude disabled people, or do not consider the needs of the variety
of members of society. It has been argued that disabled people do not have 'special
needs', but have the same needs as everyone else: the difference is that these
ordinary needs are not normally met. Therefore structures and systems need to be
developed which do not single out disabled people for special (for which read

'segregated') treatment, but are open to the range of citizens. A particular example of this is education, where disabled children have been excluded historically and where the disability movement, and many parents of disabled children, are now demanding access. Inclusion is regarded as being a more appropriate concept than integration (Mason and Reiser 1994): the latter implies that society does not change, but that the individual is normalised or otherwise slotted in; inclusion implies that the barriers do not exist in the first place and that systems are designed explicitly to cater for all.

However, it must be observed that the rights-based educational principles which the Warnock report implied at the end of the 1970s have now been eroded due to broader developments in the education system centering on choice. Market mechanisms, competition between schools, league tables and other innovations promise to offer choice to parents, but in practice undermine the rights of disabled children to attend mainstream schools (Riddell 1996). From Warnock's liberal position that curriculum and teaching methods fail the child, we have moved to a position where the focus has returned to failing children: children who are not likely to perform well academically are not welcome in schools, because of their potential impact on league tables. Current 'choice' in education therefore denies the choice of inclusion to disabled people.

The third key principle arising from the practice and politics of disabled people is the idea of autonomy. This suggests that disabled people are the experts on their lives. It suggests that the legions of professionals, bureaucrats, clinicians, therapists and other authority figures can actually become a major obstacle to the self-development and liberation of disabled people. Wherever possible, disabled people should be in leadership positions, and in positions of power.

Rather than operating in the name of disabled people, service providers should adequately consult with disabled people: asking people what they want is so much more effective than giving them what the provider thinks they need. Where services are contracted out, as increasingly happens within community care, why not enable disabled-controlled organisations to deliver those services? Rather than having assessment procedures, why not introduce self-assessment? Self-help is better than professional help, and collective help and mutual aid are best of all.

The principle of autonomy does not mean that experts and professionals should be disregarded or dispensed with: the technical knowledge they possess and the assistance of committed workers in education, health and welfare is vital to disabled people, their families and their organisations. However, the key is for disabled people themselves to set the agenda, to dictate the priorities and to have a real voice in decision making about their lives.

## New approaches to childhood

While a major revolution has taken place with the arrival of the disability movement and the development of disability studies, a rather quieter paradigm shift has taken place within academic and policy approaches to childhood. For instance, the UN Convention on the Rights of the Child, adopted by the UK government, acknowledges children's rights to be consulted and to be heard on decisions affecting them. The Children Act 1989 again specified that any individual or organisation making plans for a child's future, including the courts, should consider the wishes and feelings of the child. This stress on children as free agents, capable of making decisions and entitled to be consulted, is reinforced by a new body of sociological work which originates from a children's rights perspective, or at least takes children's testimonies seriously.

Previously, exploration of childhood has been dominated by psychological accounts (for example, Piaget (1969) and Erikson (1968)), which have attempted to analyse the process of socialisation and child development, conceived as the way in which children become adults. The new approach considers children as children, and seeks to understand the experiences and feelings of children themselves (Butler and Shaw 1996; James and Prout 1990). Childhood is no longer being ignored by sociologists and left to the narrow, clinical and individualistic concerns of psychologists. Particularly, this involves regarding children as a social group, whose experiences are structured by wider policies and practices—such as state interventions in welfare, health and education – and whose everyday behaviour is policed and directed by adults.

Initial explorations of these new approaches originated in Scandinavia, with the 'Childhood, Society and Development' project; subsequently, sociologists in 16 industrialised countries collaborated on the 'Childhood as a Social Phenomenon' project, commencing in 1987 and led by Jens Qvortrup from Denmark. In Britain, Alison James and Alan Prout (1990), Shirley Prendegast (1992), Berry Mayall (1996) and others have developed the notion of children as social actors and explored particular settings (school, family and so on) and issues (menstruation, play, friendship). Most recently, the ESRC have funded 22 projects within a coordinated 'Children 5–16: Growing into the 21st Century' research programme.

An example of the new sociology of childhood is Priscilla Alderson's account of *Children's Consent to Surgery* (Alderson 1993). Challenging the developmental approach of Piaget, which characterises children as less competent adults, her research revealed the ability of children to understand complex clinical information and make informed choices about their treatment. She asks:

> 'Apart from certain physical differences, and the tendency to discuss ideas less elaborately and abstractly, how do school-age children differ from adults? This is the crucial question in any discussion of children's consent. Many children exceed many adults in, for example, intelligence, ability, prudence, confidence, size, strength, and profound experience of certain aspects of life ... Differences between adults and children lie mainly in social beliefs about childhood and behaviours affected by these beliefs, rather than in children's actual abilities.' (Alderson 1993, p.190)

In a comment which has implications for many professionals, she goes on to say:

> 'Ironically, experts who advise society on children's abilities tend to be those who would have most to lose if children's abilities and choices were more fully respected. It is in the interests of many experts to reinforce many myths about the inabilities of the 'normal' child. In doing so, they reveal their own, rather than the children's, limitations.' (p.190)

The new sociology of childhood, therefore, has implications for policy and practice. It counsels us against seeing children as 'objects' of welfare or clinical interventions, rather than agents actively negotiating systems. It raises questions of power, and focuses attention on the way that social structures and adult behaviours cause problems for children. It highlights the effect of different environments on children's lives. Finally, and perhaps most importantly, it encourages us to take children's own views and feelings about their lives far more seriously than either academic or professional 'experts' have ever done previously.

## Understanding disabled childhood

When we attempt to combine the new perspectives on childhood and on disability outlined above, we are immediately presented with a major problem. The voice of disabled children themselves is largely absent from disabled childhood research. Baldwin and Carlisle (1994), in their review of the literature, tell us:

'We found no studies focusing in detail on the disabled child's daily life and the way disability affects her.' (p.33)

and:

'We lack children's accounts of pain, discomfort, dependence on others for feeding, bathing and toileting. We do not know how they feel about the way doctors, social workers, therapists and other children treat them.' (p.35)

Whereas doctors, educationalists, parents and policy makers debate the problems of disabled children at length, we are unable to gauge the children's own perspectives.

Starting from a disability studies perspective, it seems fairly clear that a major problem for disabled children is that they live in a society which views childhood impairment as deeply problematic. We may no longer follow the traditional route of abandoning or killing disabled children (in most cases), but we are keen to invest immense amounts of money in developing techniques to prevent them being born (Bailey 1996; Shakespeare 1995). If by any chance an impaired child slips through this screen, an array of techniques is available to intervene surgically and attempt elimination of the physical abnormality. The word orthopaedics, we may want to remember, derives from the Greek for 'child correction'.

As Laura Middleton (1996) writes:

'All these efforts to make a child normal by stimulating brain waves, hanging them upside down, pushing, pulling and cajoling, mean that the child receives the very clear message that there is something about them that nobody likes. Chances are that they will learn not to like it either. Since it is likely to be something about which, realistically, they can do little or nothing, this over-emphasis is likely only to create a sense of failure or even of self-hate.' (p.37)

These approaches to childhood impairment combine with prejudiced cultural representations of disability to render disabled children as a highly negative stereotype (Integration Alliance 1995). Traditional stories – such as *The Secret Garden* or *Heidi* – reinforce these images. Charitable interventions – Children in Need, Action Research for the Crippled Child – seek to generate pity and sympathy for 'tragic but brave' disabled children who are in desperate need of public support. We – adults and children, and presumably also disabled children – are left thinking of disabled children as pathetic, in-valid, dependent and incapable.

The low worth accorded to disabled children, and the silencing of disabled children, may explain another starkly obvious feature of this experience: the increased exposure to physical and sexual abuse. Disabled children are more vulnerable to abuse than non-disabled children (Cross 1994; Sobsey and Doe 1991; Westcott, Chapter 9 in this volume). This provides devastating evidence that disabled children are seen as not mattering, as not being human.

'There are the ones who are chosen because they cannot speak of the horror. There are the ones who are chosen because they cannot run away, and there is nowhere to run. There are the ones who are chosen because their very lives depend on not fighting back. There are the ones who are chosen because there is no one for them to tell. There are the ones who are chosen because no one has even taught them the words. There are the ones who are chosen because society chooses to believe that, after all, they don't really have any sexuality, so it can't hurt them.' (Cross 1994, p.165)

In our research on disabled sexuality (Shakespeare *et al.* 1996), many respondents reported having experienced abuse. Mark said:

'I was sexually abused when aged six. It often happened, if I tried to resist I was hit very hard. Even these days I still have nightmares.'

Ruth told us:

'When I think about myself as a sexual being and having a disability there are two strands to it: one is about having a disability and the other strand is about previous experience of sexual abuse as a child and the two seem to go together and create what I think are enormous difficulties in my relationship.'

This last comment about the inter-relationship of disability and abuse is particularly relevant. There is increasing evidence that experience of abuse should be regarded as disabling in itself. Colleagues in child protection report that they are supporting children who could be defined as disabled because of their physical and emotional needs. This is recognised by the state in some cases, where the child is granted disability related benefits for their attendance and support. Again, certain 'normalising' interventions – for instance conductive education – have been described by some commentators as forms of physical abuse (Oliver 1993), showing how disabling factors may be better defined as abuse in particular cases.

From the evidence which we have set out, it is possible to begin to understand how many of the potential problems of disabled childhood are not caused by impairment, but are outcomes of social relations, cultural representations and the behaviour of adults. While abuse is the most extreme and distressing element of this social oppression, there are other insidious and highly common elements of life as a disabled child which contribute to shaping an identity which continues into adulthood.

For example, disabled children may be very isolated. This may be because there are no other disabled people in their family, no role models in the community, no positive images in the media or general culture. It may be to do with the fact that other children are prejudiced: it would be wrong to ignore the capacity for cruelty which exists in children. Kirsten told us:

> 'It is tough growing up different on a south London housing estate. The kids thought I was extremely snotty from a very early age, but I couldn't see them, I didn't know who they were, I couldn't see them and I couldn't explain. Maybe that would have made a difference. Maybe not, but they took the piss anyway. There was no one else on the estate with a disability. Not anyone who would admit to it anyway. So my peers assumed I was rude, snotty, stuck up and generally hideous and I believed it.'

Often, it is a product of the segregated education so many disabled children experience. This may mean being bussed off to a distant school early in the morning, and losing contact with local kids; it may mean that their only friends are other disabled children. Jeremy told us about this during our sexuality research:

> 'I used to go through such angst about not having any friends on my estate and seeing old friends going to schools that I could have gone to, but I wasn't allowed. They used to see me getting on this bus that came outside the house everyday to take me to my 'special' school. They changed, and I changed, and we grew in different directions and we didn't see each other. They just saw me as the cripple at the end of the road, being bussed off to school. It was quite traumatic.'

Other children live in residential schools, and may have little contact with their family or with non-disabled people. Phillippe, a deaf man, told us:

'I left home to go to school at two or three years old. My parents took me off to school, left me there and my father went first, then my mother, they never said goodbye. There were just communication barriers. They had gone and I couldn't understand why. I just thought they weren't interested in me, I felt totally confused, I had to stay there and mix with all these other people. It was really a terrible time.'

Maria said:

'Then, if any able-bodied person came into the children's home I'd always get round behind them to see where the key was. I couldn't understand how they could walk without crutches, sticks, callipers, so somebody had to wind them up in the morning, somewhere there had to be this key that turns. That's how I looked on it.'

Absence from mainstream schools and ordinary neighbourhoods may also mean that non-disabled children remain ignorant, and probably prejudiced, about disabled children.

Whether or not they attend local schools, many disabled children have their lives disrupted by regular time out for medical or therapeutic interventions: OPCS found that 20 per cent of children were absent from the classroom for long periods (Bone and Meltzer 1989). The same research found that nearly one-third of the most severely disabled children had no friends compared with only 1 per cent of the least severely disabled. The majority (55%) of disabled children had lots of friends, 27 per cent had two or three. Eleven per cent of parents reported that all of their disabled child's friends were also disabled.

An early account of disabled children by David Thomas (1978) focused on the problem of their isolation:

'Their cultural experiences differ from those of others in their age group because of prolonged periods in hospital, separate forms of schooling, institutionalisation, restriction on mobility or over-protection.' (p.99)

Almost 20 years later, many of the same factors still apply:

'A disabled adult is viewed as less than a full citizen, as dependent: in fact, as occupying a permanent childlike status. The preparation of a disabled child for full adulthood is therefore overridden by their preparation for life as a permanent child. As such, a disabled child is likely to experience neither a normal childhood, nor adolescence, and is conditioned into an adulthood of dependency.' (Middleton 1996, p.53)

## Conclusion

'The persistence of an ideology of childhood, which denies children an active social presence and articulate voice, means that, just as in traditional socialisation accounts, relatively little research has explored what the experience of disability or sickness is like from the child's point of view' (James 1993, p.83).

Given the absence of authentic and adequate accounts by children, it is difficult to do more than sketch out the disabling factors which operate in the lives of young people with impairment. To do so is not to argue that disabled children are necessarily victims, or are invariably damaged, or cannot be happy and successful. It would be very dangerous if the focus of disability studies on oppressive structures resulted in a view of disabled people as powerless or doomed. However, we need to have an understanding of the very real problems which may undermine the possibilities of fulfilment for disabled children and to realise that these factors are not fundamentally located in individual physical or mental impairments but in structural barriers.

What sort of principles might a consideration of disability studies and childhood literature suggest are appropriate for practice? The three elements of equality, inclusion and autonomy are a good basis. The following points arise as a consequence.

1. We would argue most strongly for inclusive, rather than segregated education, a position which is borne out by recent research (Alderson and Goodey 1996).

2. Rather than considering disabled children as having special needs, it is more appropriate to accept that all children and adults have the same basic needs. Disabled people, regardless of impairment, are first and foremost human beings, with the same entitlements and citizenship rights as anybody else. It is up to society to ensure that the basic needs of disabled people are met within the systems and structures of education, transport, housing, health and so forth. A first step would be to make all schools accessible to disabled people.

3. Much work on normalisation implies a refusal to accept difference. We argue that all children are different and that rather than ignoring or trying to eliminate the difference represented by disabled children, it is more appropriate to challenge notions of 'normality' and expand our understanding of human variation. Clinical interventions should be assessed in terms of their actual contribution to the quality of life of disabled children.

4. Disabled people and families with disabled children need access to appropriate resources and social support: this may include provision of personal assistants or support workers, aids and adaptations or financial assistance to recognise the extra costs associated with impairment.

5. Negative images of disabled people, especially disabled children, should be eliminated or at least balanced by positive images. Non-disabled people, especially children, need to be educated to respect the dignity and worth of disabled people, just as prejudice on the basis of race, gender or sexuality is challenged. Parents of disabled children may need the space to develop their own understandings of disability, as with the 'Parents in Partnership' model of equality training.

6. Professionals need greater awareness of the issue of disabled child abuse, and effective policies to counter this widespread problem need urgently to be implemented.

7. New policies – privatisation, the development of 'the market', increased competition – need to be audited in terms of their impact on disabled people. Many recent political changes have increased, rather than removed, the segregation and inequality of disabled people.

As we think about disabled childhood, we have to perform a delicate balancing act. While becoming aware of the ways in which children are isolated and oppressed, we must not end up thinking of them as victims or tragedies; while understanding that disabled children are a social group, we must also remember that they are individuals; while understanding the similarities, we must recognise the differences, including issues such as gender, race, class and the particularity of impairment itself. The social model should guide our analysis and the principle of disability equality should inform our values, but our ultimate commitment must be to the views of disabled children themselves. As researchers or as social workers, our task becomes clear: listen to what disabled children say about their lives, respect their wishes and support their choices.

## References

Alderson, P. (1993) *Children's Consent to Surgery.* Buckingham: Open University Press.

Alderson, P. and Goodey, C. (1996) *Integrated Education for Children with Physical and Learning Disabilities.* Report to Gatsby Trust. London: Social Science Research Unit.

Bailey, R. (1996) 'Prenatal testing and the prevention of impairment: a woman's right to choose?' In J. Morris (ed.) *Encounters with Strangers.* London: The Women's Press.

Baldwin, S. and Carlisle, J. (1994) *Social Support for Disabled Children and their Families: A Review of the Literature.* London: HMSO.

Barnes, C. (1991) *Disabled People in Britain and Discrimination.* London: Hurst and Co.

Blaxter, M. (1976) *The Meaning of Disability.* London: Heinemann.

Bone, M. and Meltzer, H. (1989) *The Prevalence of Disability among Children, OPCS Surveys of Disability in Great Britain.* London: HMSO.

Bury, M. (1991) 'The sociology of chronic illness: a review of research and prospects.' *Sociology of Health and Illness 9,* 3, 118–122.

Butler, I. and Shaw, I. (eds) (1996) *A Case of Neglect? Children's Experiences and the Sociology of Childhood.* Aldershot: Avebury Press.

Campbell, J. and Oliver, M. (1996) *Disability Politics.* London: Routledge.

Children Act (1989). London: HMSO.

Cross, M. (1994) 'Abuse.' In L. Keith (ed.) *Mustn't Grumble.* London: The Women's Press.

Crow, L. (1996) 'Including all of our lives: renewing the social model of disability.' In J. Morris (ed.) *Encounters with Strangers.* London: The Women's Press.

Disability Discrimination Act (1995). London: HMSO.

Erikson, E. (1968) *Identity: Youth and Crises.* New York: Norton.

French, S. (1996) 'Out of sight, out of mind: the experience and effects of a "special" residential school.' In J. Morris (ed.) *Encounters with Strangers.* London: The Women's Press.

Integration Alliance (1995) *Invisible Children: Report of a Conference.* London: Integration Alliance.

James, A. (1993) *Childhood Identities.* Edinburgh: Edinburgh University Press.

James, A. and Prout, A. (1990) *Reconstructing Childhood.* London: Falmer Press.

Mason, M. and Reiser, R. (1994) *Altogether Better.* London: Charity Projects.

Mayall, B. (1996) *Children, Health and the Social Order.* Buckingham: Open University Press.

Middleton, L. (1996) *Making a Difference: Social Work with Disabled Children.* Birmingham: Venture Press.

Morris, J. (1991) *Pride Against Prejudice.* London: The Women's Press.

Morris, J. (ed.) (1996) *Encounters with Strangers.* London: The Women's Press.

Oliver, M. (1983) *Social Work with Disabled People.* Basingstoke: Macmillan.

Oliver, M. (1990) *The Politics of Disablement.* Basingstoke: Macmillan.

Oliver, M. (1993) '"Conductive education": If it wasn't so sad it would be funny.' In J. Swain, V. Finkelstein, S. French and M. Oliver (eds) *Disabling Barriers – Enabling Environments.* London: Sage.

Oliver, M. (1996) *Understanding Disability: From Theory to Practice.* Basingstoke: Macmillan.

Piaget, J. (1969) *The Psychology of the Child.* London: Routledge and Kegan Paul.

Pinder, R. (1996) 'Sick but fit or fit but sick? Ambiguity and identity at the workplace.' In C. Barnes and G. Mercer (eds) *Exploring the Divide: Illness and Disability.* Leeds: Disability Press.

Prendegast, S. (1992) *This is the Time to Grow Up.* Cambridge: Health Promotion Research Trust.

Riddell, S. (1996) 'Theorising special education needs in a changing political climate.' In L. Barton (ed.) *Disability and Society: Emerging Issues and Insights.* London: Longman.

Shakespeare, T. (1995) 'Back to the future? Disabled people and the new genetics.' *Critical Social Policy 44,* 5, 22–35.

Shakespeare, T., Gillespie-Sells, K. and Davies, D. (1996) *The Sexual Politics of Disability.* London: Cassell.

Sobsey, D. and Doe, T. (1991) 'Patterns of sexual abuse and assault.' *Sexuality and Disability 9,* 3, 243–259.

Thomas, D. (1978) *The Social Psychology of Childhood Disability.* London: Methuen.

UPIAS (1976) *Fundamental Principles of Disability.* London: UPIAS.

Watson, N. (1996) 'Disabled people's perspectives on identity, health and the body.' Paper presented at Disability Studies Seminar, Leeds.

# CHAPTER 2

# An Historical Perspective

*Maureen Oswin*

This chapter looks briefly at historical aspects of disability from the time of the Ancient Greeks up to modern industrial society. Attitudes to disability have been influenced by a range of factors including humanity's struggle to survive, religious beliefs, economic change, literature and art, scientific discoveries, medicine, philanthropy, politics and laws. The development of services for children growing up with disabiity has a history steeped in vacillating attitudes: extreme cruelty alternating with protection, neglect alternating with enlightened provision, exploitation alternating with respect.

In early periods of history, disabled children were often abandoned or killed. Decisions and practices were based on the need for a society to survive, so those who were considered weak were cast aside in case they held back the strength of the group. The Ancient Greeks, aiming to create the 'perfect race', always killed deaf children; the Spartans threw children with impairments into pits.

More merciful religious ideals began to teach that people with impairments should be treated with compassion; the Bible and the Koran contain texts which say they should be protected. Protection could mean that a disabled child received special attention: for example, Bede (672–735) recorded that St John of Beverley taught a 'dumb youth' to speak. This is believed to be one of the first recorded examples of an aphasic child being educated (Pritchard 1963).

Blind people were the first to be systematically supported, largely because wars in which arrows were used caused blindness. In the fourth and fifth centuries, hospices for blind people were opened in Caesaria and Syria, and in 1260 an asylum in France housed 300 soldiers blinded in the Crusades. A hospice for 100 blind men opened in London in 1329. Attempts were made to help deaf children in the sixteenth century, led by the Italian, Geronomo Cardona, who recognised that they used their sight to compensate for their lack of hearing. However, the majority of deaf children were labelled 'deaf and dumb' until the present century (Pritchard 1963).

Other groups of disabled children did not evoke the same interest and sympathy. They were called 'cripples' and depicted as ugly and evil in art and literature. Fourteenth-century frescoes by Masaccio showed young disabled people manoeuvring themselves about on little wheeled sledges in Florence, their faces avaricious and threatening as they begged for alms.

Victor Hugo's early nineteenth-century novel *The Hunchback of Notre Dame* created a negative image of people with spinal disorders, and Robert Louis Stevenson's book *Treasure Island* suggested impairment was connected with evil and crime. *Rigoletto,* a popular nineteenth-century opera by Verdi, portrayed a man with a spinal impairment as a tragic lonely figure, embittered by negative attitudes towards him; this early portrayal of somebody with an impairment can be compared with the late twentieth-century film of Daphne du Maurier's story 'Don't Look Now' which reinforced the image of disability as evil, this time in reference to people of small stature. Indeed, children of small stature have historically suffered from the negative attitudes of others. Until the last 20 years they were often consigned to circuses, regarded as little figures of fun and not expected to have any 'normal' feelings nor to want a 'normal' life.

At different times in history, children with learning difficulties have both been regarded as possessed by the devil and, at other times and in some places, as 'blessed'; American Indians often called them 'Children of the Great Spirit' (Wallin 1917). Edward II of England (1307–1328) placed 'imbeciles' under his protection by law although in medieval palaces they were sometimes kept to amuse the family, but nonetheless attitudes continued to vacillate. Persecution flared up in the Reformation, when Luther and Calvin denounced people with learning difficulties as 'filled with Satan'. They were subsequently whipped, tortured and murdered.

This dreadful episode was followed by another period of protection. In the mid-seventeenth century a group of people with learning difficulties was gathered together in the Bicetre in Paris, a former chateau turned into a hospital. In 1801 the French physician, Itard, published an account of a boy with learning difficulties found living rough in the Aveyron woods. This story created interest in children's learning, inherited intelligence, and environmental influences. Séguin, a pupil of Itard's, then obtained some success in teaching a child with learning difficulties and was appointed to teach the children living in Bicetre. By the middle of the nineteenth century, interest in learning difficulties had developed in England. Due to the growth in institutions, there was then a captive population of children with learning difficulties who could be observed and described.

Urban society expanded as the Industrial Revolution developed. Poverty and diseases assumed shocking proportions in crowded unsanitary cities, and children stood little chance in the eighteenth and nineteenth centuries unless their families were rich. Terrible punishments were meted out if children were found thieving: as late as 1831 a 13-year-old London boy was hanged for theft, and in 1834 two Stafford children aged 10 and 11 were sentenced to transportation. There was little or no protection for disabled children and poverty made some families exhibit their children to get alms.

Poor Law workhouses built in the British Isles in the nineteenth century included infirmaries which accommodated people with diseases caused by poverty, frail elderly people, and children and young people with a variety of conditions. They had a roof over their heads, but no education or proper care. Many of them died.

There was no childcare service given by law and reform was bogged down by the Poor Law, but philanthropists like Captain Thomas Coram in the eighteenth century and Dr Barnardo in the nineteenth century rescued children from the streets and placed them in orphanages. The establishment of the National Society for the Prevention of Cruelty to Children in 1884 eased some of the worst excesses of cruelty, including the neglect and exploitation of disabled children. Due to philanthropic interest, blind children, deaf children and physically impaired children sometimes had opportunities for a basic education and training for a trade. But they had no rights, and they were not listened to nor given choices.

In the mid-nineteenth century, there was a rapid growth of asylums for people with learning difficulties as a result of the 1853 Lunatic Asylums Act which made it a duty for every local authority to provide asylums for people deemed to be 'idiots'. In 1855 a 'model asylum' was opened in Earlswood in Surrey to cater specifically for children with learning difficulties from rich families.

*Growing Up With Disability*

Starcross Hospital opened in Devon in the 1860s, under the Royal Western Counties Asylum provision. It was intended to accommodate all the people with learning difficulties from Devon and Cornwall. For over a century, hundreds of children grew up in Starcross toiling at menial tasks like knitting dishcloths, a stone's throw from beaches where able-bodied children played happily with families not knowing anything about the deprived children behind the walls on the other side of the road. The Royal Albert Hospital in Lancashire was a similar institution, serving the whole of Lancashire. Large places like Starcross and Royal Albert could each accommodate as many as 2000 people with learning difficulties from babyhood to old age. In 1867 the Metropolitan Asylums Board was formed to permit the institutionalisation of London's 'imbeciles and idiots' in two huge purpose-built hospitals – St Lawrence's in Surrey and Leavesden in Hertfordshire.

Similar institutions followed throughout the country. Sometimes large estates were purchased. The big house would be used for administration and villas would be built in the grounds for the people with learning difficulties. These estates became self-sufficient: the food was grown there, the laundry was done there. Living on such estates provided daily activities and the children who grew up on them had no idea about the outside world. The staff too became institutionalised and entrenched in their own patterns of work. By the turn of the century, thousands of adults and children with learning difficulties were living in large institutions far away from their families and communities of origin.

The Royal Commission on the Feeble-Minded was set up in 1904 and took evidence about people with learning difficulties who were still in workhouses because there was no other provision for them. Norah Fry, the West Country social reformer, gave evidence about 'feeble-minded' children. She described some living in workhouses with pauper women, some at village schools and mocked by other children, and one particular child whose parents kept him tied to the leg of a table. She thought parents should be compelled to send their children with learning difficulties to special colonies for education and training (Norah Fry's Verbal Evidence to the Royal Commission on 24th November 1905).

Norah Fry's recommendation of 'colonies' for children with learning difficulties seems shocking today, but it has to be seen in the light of the times: children *were* living in workhouses with pauper adults, and she wanted to 'rescue' them. Colonies were seen as an improvement; nobody realised that institutional care would create emotional and developmental problems for the children living in it.

Much of the work of the Royal Commission was concerned with terms and catgories (Hilliard and Kirman 1965). Time was spent on defining 'types of feeble-mindedness', and coining labels such as 'morons', 'idiots' and 'imbeciles' and describing their differences. These insensitive labels were used well into the 1960s. Following the Commission's report in 1908, the Eugenics Society was formed. Army officials in the Society, worried about the poor standards of army recruits, stirred up ideas about 'moral degeneracy' and there was an attempt to make laws allowing only intelligent, physically fit people to 'breed'.

Negative attitudes towards people with learning difficulties were particularly widespread in America in the early twentieth century. Immigrants from Europe were settling in America hoping to be part of a wonderful democracy, but some were singled out for shameful treatment by Americans who had long been settled there. A growing knowledge of genetics aroused feverish desires to weed out 'genetically unsound' people. Poor immigrant families struggling to learn a new language, find work and bring up children were at risk of losing their children if there was the slightest suspicion that they were 'retarded'. People with learning difficulties were blamed for a variety of urban ills: laziness, immorality, sexual promiscuity, crime, pauperism and prostitution. A wide range of ill-doings was considered hereditary and a learning difficulty was seen as a major threat to American society.

In 1914 a director of an institution for 'feeble-minded girls and boys' in America published a report on the 327 children and young people who were kept there. His photographs of them, often naked, as well as the publication of their personal letters, an investigation into their meagre belongings and criticism of their looks, behaviour and backgrounds is so cruel and ignorant that it beggars belief. His description of one resident, Mamie, who had been there for 17 years, since the age of 7, concludes:

> 'Mamie is a living and brilliant argument for the colonisation of all the children of defective ancestors. They need permanent segregation, to the end that that kind of defective human stock may cease to perpetuate itself.' (Goddard 1914, p.89)

The children of this institution grew up in total isolation from the rest of American society and the case histories in the report are each accompanied by complicated diagrams aimed to prove inherited 'degenerate' behaviour and backwardness, ideas which were accepted in the British Isles.

The Bill leading to the passing of the Mental Deficiency Act of 1913 was very harsh and actually included a clause prohibiting the marriage of people with learning difficulties. This clause was dropped, but a Board of Control was made responsible for all discharges from hospitals and there were few safeguards for the 'patient' or their families. By the 1920s the Board was recommending that every institution should take more people: not less than 800 and preferably up to 2000. By 1929 there were 25,000 people living in mental deficiency asylums in England and Wales. By 1952 this number was 60,000.

Big hospitals such as Leavesden, St Lawrence's and Darenth on the outskirts of London, Starcross in Devon and the Royal Albert in Lancashire, each had over 2000 patients. Thousands of children were growing up in these hospitals, many of whom were admitted as under-fives. As the numbers of patients increased the overcrowding worsened. Deprivations were severe. Some children were kept in large wooden pens like cages, their clothes often soaked in urine and excrement. Without occupation, they developed habits of rocking and self-mutilation.

The 1930s was a time of economic and political upheaval for Europe and North America. As always, economic crisis brought more vicissitudes to disabled people. The worst excesses of cruelty occurred in Germany where the Nazis, aspiring to create a pure master race, organised a euthanasia programme in the 1930s which emptied Germany's long-stay hospitals. Some hospital staff colluded with the children's mass murder by lethal injection or gassing.

In late nineteenth-century Britain, there were not only asylums for children with learning difficulties, but also a development of charity schools and homes for children who were deaf, blind or had physical impairments. Many of these were in use well into the 1970s, and some had been incorporated into local education authority or health authority provision.

Children with severe orthopaedic conditions resulting in chronic disability lived for years in long-stay hospitals; hospital schools were gradually developed for them. Provision was made by rich merchants, the churches and benevolent organisations. Chailey Hospital and School in Sussex was opened in 1903, inspired by Grace Kimmins, who in 1894 had set up the Guild of Poor Brave

Things in London to give 'crippled children' outings. William Treloar, a Lord Mayor of London, was the force behind a hospital and school which opened in Hampshire in 1908.

These schools, homes and hospitals for disabled children concentrated on training. Trades were taught according to sex and the children had no choices; for example, boys learnt shoe-making and tailoring, girls learnt embroidery and dressmaking. Blind children tended to be taught basket work. Their education was usually rigorous and unimaginative, but although amateurish, the work of the early teachers of children with special needs should not be dismissed. Their attempts to educate the children, and their records of what did and did not work, laid the foundations for today's care and education. Like Norah Fry and her wish to help children with learning difficulties, innovators such as Grace Kimmins and William Treloar aimed to rescue disabled children from ignorance, cruelty and exploitation. But the rights of the children were rarely considered, and some of the homes and hospitals became repressive and cruel.

Children's health problems in the first half of the twentieth century remained a cause of chronic conditions, for example, Stills disease, measles and fevers. Congenital hip dislocations and spinal disorders were not treated correctly and it was common until the 1940s to see children wearing a built-up boot to support a shortened leg. Chronic skin diseases often meant months and even years in skin hospitals. Fever hospitals were full of children with diphtheria and scarlet fever, illnesses which laid them low for months after discharge. Poverty exacerbated these problems. The children lost much education despite having bedside teaching.

Open-air schools were opened in the 1920s and 1930s, where frail and disabled children had a basic education and a regime of sunshine, fresh air and sitting quietly. Simple crafts were taught, such as weaving on little boards. Most open-air schools had open-sided classrooms.

With no cure for TB until after the Second World War, many children went to TB hospitals. The theory was that good food, bed rest and open air would cure them. So the children spent years lying in bed on open verandahs. Their bedside teachers strapped hot-water bottles under their own coats in the winter, and nurses went around putting cream on the children's ears, noses and finger tips to prevent the worst excesses of frostbite.

A strict classification of children's conditions influenced what sort of services were developed for them; for example, children with epilepsy were sent to 'epileptic colonies' (an ex-colony in Surrey is still in use). By 1945 thousands of disabled children were separated from their families because of rigid adherence to categories. They were sent hither and thither, like little parcels, to places thought appropriate to the needs of their condition or illness. But their emotional needs as homesick, lonely children were ignored. Opportunities for higher education, qualifications and jobs were rare.

Children with learning difficulties endured a lifetime of institutional care. Older children in 'mental handicap' hospitals were strictly segregated by sex, and there was no opportunity for making friends or getting married. As they grew older they sometimes worked in the hospital kitchens, laundries and gardens, earning meagre pocket money, the spending of which would be supervised by staff in a hospital shop.

Some teenage girls were admitted to long-stay 'mental handicap' hospitals from their own homes because they had become pregnant. They were labelled 'moral defectives'. Some may have had only a mild learning difficulty but were deemed unfit to be mothers. They were hospitalised for life and their babies were taken away at birth. Living in single-sex units, they worked in the hospital laundries, linen rooms and kitchen gardens and were never allowed to speak to the men within the institution.

Overactive children or those who were difficult were kept fastened to chairs, were heavily drugged, and were not allowed out of doors. Many children had all their teeth removed in case they bit somebody, a cruel decision which affected both their appearance and digestion for the rest of their lives.

Children in 'mental handicap' hospitals who had cerebral palsy or other physical disorders were separated from mobile children and called 'basket cases' or 'cot and chair cases'. These children never received help to improve their posture, so their bodies grew twisted. Those who survived to adulthood were kept permanently in large cots, usually naked because of the difficulties of getting clothes on to their bodies. This widespread neglect of hundreds of people with cerebral palsy was one of the worst of the many scandalous things that happened in 'mental handicap' hospitals. The wards accommodating these people were known as 'back wards', and were rarely seen by outsiders (Oswin, personal notes on visits to mental handicap hospitals 1963–1983; Oswin 1971, 1978, 1984).

Following the Second World War steps were taken to improve education for all children, with the aim of building a new prosperous Britain. The National Health Service had already been blue-printed and was ready to go. The 1944 Education Act listed 11 categories of childhood impairment which would require the children to be educated in Special Schools. Children classified as 'educationally subnormal' were entitled to special education under their local education authorities, but those labelled 'severely subnormal' or 'ineducable' were given occupations in centres run by local health boards or voluntary organisations.

These were very distressing times for parents of children with learning difficulties who wanted to keep their children out of 'mental handicap' hospitals; the staff of the local occupation centres were often very choosy about whom they accepted. If children had severe impairments, were overactive or had fits they could be refused. The parents were frightened that this would force their children's admission to hospitals. Children with severe learning difficulties did not come under the responsibility of local education authorities until 1970, and this was achieved because parent groups such as MENCAP campaigned for their children's rights. Sadly, by the time the 1970 Education Act was passed, many of the children of the first campaigning parents were over school age and so did not themselves benefit from the campaign.

In 1944 the Curtis Committee reported on conditions for children living away from home. Their recommendations resulted in the 1948 Children Act, but this Act did not protect children with physical impairment and learning difficulties who were living permanently in long-stay hospitals. The Committee had noted the deprivations suffered by children living in tuberculosis, orthopaedic, skin disease and 'mental handicap' hospitals, but it was considered that the needs of these children were outside the Committee's scope. Its few references to children in long-stay hospitals were concerned only with improving their educational and recreational needs, not with improving childcare – and certainly not about getting the children out of hospital and setting up community services. By 1950, there were over 10,000 children living in long-stay hospitals, 6000 of whom had learning difficulties and were in 'mental handicap' hospitals. The others were in orthopaedic hospitals and one-time tuberculosis hospitals.

Under the NHS there was a takeover of private hospitals, a change of use of the Poor Law workhouses, and an increase in the population of large 'mental handicap' hospitals. Many of the old asylums were given a facelift, and new wards were built in the grounds. These wards were called 'houses' or 'cottages' and given fancy names such as 'Acacia' or 'Lilac' or 'Lindens', but the same repressive regimes continued (Oswin, personal notes 1963–1983). Some wartime emergency hospitals, mere collections of huts put up to house air-raid victims or wounded servicemen, were used to accommodate children with learning difficulties. This was said to be only a temporary measure, but many children grew up in them and continued to live in them as adults.

As cures were found for fevers, tuberculosis and skin diseases a new generation of children filled the empty hospitals; they had impairments caused by thalidomide damage and conditions such as muscular dystrophy, cerebral palsy, Still's disease, polio and spina bifida. The physiotherapy and provision of modern aids may have been of a high standard, but the children led strange, abnormal and deprived lives in these isolated long-stay hospitals. For example, a small group of children with polio continued living in Queen Mary's Hospital in Carshalton throughout the 1960s because there was not enough support for them at home. At weekends they wandered about the grounds on their crutches, talking to other children's visitors, bored and cut off from mainstream society. Another ward accommodated boys with muscular dystrophy from the age of five to late teens. They spent their childhood years watching each other getting older, and eventually dying. Some of these children were brothers.

In the 1960s and 1970s professionals started to listen to parents of disabled children who formed organisations to campaign for their children's right to education and treatment. In order to get recognition for their children, the parents often described them in popular style, for example, children with Down's syndrome were 'loving, happy, musical', autistic children were 'fairy children, mysterious and highly intelligent', children with cerebral palsy had 'intelligent brains imprisoned in helpless bodies'. Collection boxes outside shops depicted 'spastics' wearing callipers, or angel-like blind children with closed eyes, and MENCAP had a logo of a vacant waif-like little boy. The parents at that time were fighting for recognition of their children's needs, and were not aware that their publicity methods were causing negative images.

In the 1960s and 1970s Professor Jack Tizard became an inspirational figure regarding reforms for children with a variety of impairments who were growing up in institutions. He was the first person to prove that children with learning difficulties could achieve more if they were brought up under normal childcare practices (King, Raynes and Tizard 1971; Tizard, Sinclair and Clarke 1975). Such research was not well received by medical authorities who saw any criticism of hospital care as a threat.

In 1974 the Harvie Committee Report (DHSS 1974) was published. This Committee had been set up to make recommendations concerning responsibilities for children with severe learning difficulties who were in residential care. At the time there were 6500 children living in mental handicap hospitals, 1000 in local authority homes, 600 in voluntary homes, 300 in private homes and schools and 100 being fostered. This total of 8500 children was assessed as being 'severely subnormal'. The Harvie Report disclosed neglect caused by children with learning difficulties falling between the two stools of medical care and local authority responsibility, but no action was taken.

In 1976 the Committee on Child Health Services, chaired by Donald Court, published its report. This comprehensive report went far beyond the health of children. It set out a far-thinking philosophy of child-centred services including responsibilities to be taken by GPs, paediatricians, teachers, social workers and local authority planners. It drew special attention to the deprivations suffered by disabled children growing up in institutions. If the recommendations of the report had been acted upon swiftly, reforms would have come quicker, but the politics of the medical world caused a mixed reception to its findings.

Observers in long-stay hospitals in the 1970s recorded a continuation of appalling deprivations; for example, children were growing up without ever seeing shops or food being cooked; they never mixed with children outside hospitals; they were denied affection; they were got out of bed at 4.30 am and were left half naked in cots for many hours; some spent hours sitting on potties on concrete floors with cockroaches crawling around their bare feet; some were tied to chairs all day (Oswin 1971, 1978).

Campaigns to get children out of institutions and into small units provoked opposition from nursing unions, notably COHSE, who saw the closure of 'mental handicap' hospitals as a threat to their livelihoods. This occurred particularly in areas where local employment depended on the institution. People who said that hospitalised children were deprived met opposition and personal abuse (Oswin, personal experience during campaigns in 1970s for changes in 'mental handicap' hospitals). In the late 1970s, COHSE vehemently opposed all reforms recommended by the Jay Committee aimed at making mental handicap nurse training more child-centred (Jay Report 1979).

By the mid-1980s fewer children were growing up in hospitals because families were being supported by better community care. Nonetheless, long-stay hospitals retained a function in providing short-term care and many children continually went in and out of inappropriate wards which provided a style of care which could only be described as 'kennelling' (Oswin 1984). However, good practices in providing family support were pioneered in Somerset and Leeds, with family placement schemes providing short-term care for disabled children; by 1988 family placement schemes existed all over the country (Stalker 1990; Robinson 1991).

Finally, the 1989 Children Act was passed, followed by the Children (Scotland) Act 1995 and the Northern Ireland Children's Order 1995, which gave children rights and choices and encouraged better services for all children growing up with disability. A belief in children's rights now exists in all areas of their services, and professionals are generally accepting that children should be listened to.

With hindsight it seems as if throughout history terrible wrongs have been inflicted on disabled children. Ironically, many of the wrongs were actually initiated by people who were enlightened and trying to help them; for example, the reformer Norah Fry recommended more asylums. However, it has to be remembered that a philosophy of *rescue from something worse* ran through all the early provision of services for children growing up with disability: the hospices set up in France for young people blinded in battles in the thirteenth century to save them from begging in the street; the homes set up by Victorian philanthropists to rescue children from exploitation in cities; the boarding schools set up by the Spastics Society in the 1970s to prevent children from growing up in long-stay hospitals.

Nobody can possibly understand how it really was for the children and young people over many centuries who have grown up with impairments. For the twenty-first century it remains to be seen how society will support and respect children with severe impairments who are now surviving babyhood due to advances in medicine; how the new form of hospice care will develop for these children, and whether children who cannot communicate and move will be given real choices.

## References

Children Act (1989). London: HMSO.

Children (Scotland) Act (1995). Edinburgh: HMSO.

DHSS (1974) *Mentally Handicapped Children in Residential Care (Harvie Report)*. London: HMSO.

Goddard, H. (1914) *Feeble-mindedness: Its Causes and Consequences*. New York: Macmillan Co.

Hilliard, L.J. and Kirman, B.H. (1965) *Mental Deficiency*. London: Churchill.

King, R., Raynes, N. and Tizard, J. (1971) *Patterns of Residential Care*. London: Routledge and Kegan Paul.

Oswin, M. (1971) *The Empty Hours*. London: Allen Lane, The Penguin Press.

Oswin, M. (1978) *Children Living in Long-Stay Hospitals*. London: Spastics International Medical Publications.

Oswin, M. (1984) *They Keep Going Away*. London: King Edward Hospital Fund for London.

Pritchard, D.G. (1963) *Education and the Handicapped 1760–1960*. London: Routledge and Kegan Paul.

*Report of the Committee on Child Health Services (Court Report)* (1976) CMND 6684. London: HMSO.

*Report of the Committee of Inqury into Mental Handicap Nursing and Care (Jay Report)* (1979) Cmnd 7468. London: HMSO.

Robinson, C. (1991) *Home and Away: Respite Care in the Community*. Birmingham: Venture Press.

The Royal Commission on Care and Control of the Feeble-minded (1908) *Report of the Radnor Commission*. Cd 4125. London: HMSO.

Stalker, K. (1990) *Share the Care: An Evaluation of a Family-Based Care Service*. London: Jessica Kingsley Publishers.

Tizard, J., Sinclair, I. and Clarke, R.V.G. (1975) *Varieties of Residential Experience*. London: Routledge and Kegan Paul.

Wallin, J.E.W. (1917) *Problems of Subnormality*. New York: Yonkers-on-Hudson.

# CHAPTER 3

# Early Intervention: The Eternal Triangle?

## Issues Relating to Parents, Professionals and Children

*Caroline Jones*

My sister is different
because she is handy - caped.
She can't see that much,
But she likes her food very much,
She likes biting toes,
She likes biting your arm and your fingers,
And once she bit my neck.
My sister thinks I am funny,
And she starts to laugh.
And at night-time she gets MAD!!!!

by Christopher, age 7

### Introduction

This chapter sets out to explore the complexity of 'growing up with disability', recognising that what happens to the youngest children at the earliest points of intervention is of paramount importance both to the child and to the family. It aims to move the debate surrounding early intervention a step forward and help create a firmer grip on some of the issues which influence the functioning and effectiveness of service delivery. The chapter is divided into two sections. The first part outlines the background theoretical framework and suggests that early intervention services could be broadened to take account of the child's wider social context.

The second part takes up the specific theme of partnership with parents, highlighting moves towards more responsive and flexible approaches which involve the whole family.

The focus of the chapter is on early interventions involving children under statutory school age being monitored mainly in a non-school setting, usually the home. This includes those children identified as 'in need' under the Children Act 1989, the Children (Scotland) Act 1995 and the Northern Ireland Children's Order, 1995, or identified as having 'special educational needs' as defined in the Code of Practice on the Identification and Assessment of Special Educational Needs (DfE 1994). The grounds for intervention under these new childcare laws are if a child is unlikely to achieve a 'reasonable standard' of health or development, or health or development could be impaired without access to services, or if the child is disabled. The definition of 'disabled' incorporates physical, sensory and 'mental disorders of any kind'. The Act explicitly places intervention within the remit of social services as well as education. The Code of Practice (DfE 1994) adopts a relative definition of 'special educational needs', ranging from those who 'need a little extra help' to those with more severe and complex learning difficulties, and places early intervention within a multi-disciplinary context. The Children (Scotland) Act 1995 clearly defines the responsibilities of parents and others towards children and reiterates the need to provide services which minimise effects of disability on children, allowing them the opportunity to 'lead lives which are as normal as possible'. The Children (Scotland) Act also points out that services should be designed to consider children who may be adversely affected by the presence of a disabled person in the family.

As Carpenter and Herbert (1995) acknowledge, families of disabled children are 'first and foremost families' (p.2) and 'it is the family who will bear the main responsibility for the child with disabilities throughout their childhood, their transition to adulthood and beyond' (p.3). The emphasis in both sections of this chapter is on the fundamental role played by an intricate web of professionals in identifying and responding to the needs of young children and their families. The term 'professionals' is used to describe those with an input into policy and practice at local level within the three major providing departments, namely health, social services and education.

Social services departments, district health authorities, NHS trusts, schools, LEAs and all other agencies involved in identifying and assessing children with special educational needs must have regard to the Code of Practice (DfE 1994). Identification and assessment, in turn, become the assumed grounds for intervention. A broad definition of intervention is offered by Wolfendale (1994) as 'an action and/or provision which aims to meet a child's special educational needs'. Wolfendale outlines a continuum of intervention practices which includes home- or centre-based teaching programmes with parental involvement, aiming to promote early learning and specific skills. 'Early' intervention is generally understood as an umbrella term used 'to describe programmes of education or therapy designed to accelerate the development of children with disabilities in the pre-school years ...', and 'commonly used to describe general early education programmes such as those based on the Portage model' (Buckley 1994, p.13). The increasingly popular Portage model, originally developed in Wisconsin, USA, involves a planned approach to home-based pre-school education for children with a variety of developmental delays, impairments or any other special needs.

At local level, services have developed their own 'personalities' in response to local circumstances. Although early intervention for under-twos tends to be home-based, centre-based services often run concurrently. Such intervention may begin shortly after 'diagnosis' and aims to give parents skills, confidence, activities and strategies they will need to help their child.

For the purposes of this discussion, it is assumed that most children requiring 'early' interventions by professionals are identified and supported at any time from shortly after, or in some cases even before birth, to the developmental check which usually occurs around the third birthday.

However, early intervention does not stand isolated from the wider social and political context. It is closely linked with the notions of identification and assessment and the roles, as some see it, of classification, labelling and exclusion. The influences of early intervention strategies upon children, families and the education system as a whole may not be neutral. While, on the one hand, early intervention can be seen as enabling, in that it ensures appropriate provision for particular children, on the other, it can be seen as a potentially divisive practice separating the 'normal' from the 'special' and leading to dependency.

## Early intervention – policy and purpose

It is almost two decades since the Warnock Committee identified early intervention as a priority in policy and practice for disabled children and special needs (DES 1978). It is now widely accepted that education in the first five years of life is crucial and should begin as early as possible. Legislation such as the 1981 Education Act introduced the concept of special educational provision literally from birth and DES Circular 1/83 states that 'Special educational provision' for a child under two means 'educational provision of any kind including support and advice to help parents help their children'. This formal recognition of the need for early intervention services for the under-fives was re-emphasised in the 1994 Code of Practice alongside the need for early identification and the need to inform, advise and support the parents during and after the assessment process:

> 'Because early identification should lead to a more timely assessment and intervention which in turn should avoid the escalation of a difficulty into a significant special educational need, it is important that any concern about a child's development and progress should be shared at the earliest possible moment.' (DfE 1994, para. 5:16)

However, Tomlinson (1982) suggests that the idea that special education is in the best interests of the child provides a moral framework from within which professionals and practitioners can work. This includes assumptions concerning access to expertise, skills and centralising resources for the benefit of the child. She concludes that the professional imperative is to compensate for perceived inadequacies of individual children. Tomlinson contends that this point of view sustains the impetus and maintenance of a separate system of provision for children with physical impairment or learning difficulties as an 'instance of the obligation placed upon civilised society to care for its weaker members' (p.5). In relation to early intervention, Wood (1988) asserts that the provision of Portage and other home-based early intervention programmes have specifically extended special education into the previously private world of the home. The value of this extension of special education is rarely questioned, the justification being to maximise the child's potential and compensate for his or her difficulties as early as possible. As Lindsay (1995) points out, at first glance, the argument is straightforward and superficially persuasive:

> 'In order to help children...we should identify their difficulties as soon as possible. By so doing we shall then be in a position to provide intervention

which will remedy the problem, or at least provide amelioration, or prevent the development of more serious difficulties.' (p.7)

Both policy and practice need to move beyond this level of argument to take account of the wider social context within which a child 'grows up with disability'.

## Early intervention – professionals and theory

Official documents have consistently stressed the importance of social integration. The Warnock Committee (DES 1978) adopted the approach of The United Nations Declaration of the Rights of Disabled People (1975) which stated that whatever the origin, nature and seriousness of their condition, disabled people have the same fundamental rights as their fellow citizens. This referred to rights in education, work and quality of adult life. More specifically, children's rights were highlighted in the United Nations Convention on the Rights of the Child (1989, quoted in Newell 1991, Appendix A). This confirmed a consensus regarding the right of a 'mentally or physically disabled child' to access education and other services conducive to 'achieving the fullest possible social integration and individual development' (Article 23).

Herbert and Moir (1996) extend the principle of social integration contending that it is the right of *all* children to be given the opportunity to grow, socialise and learn alongside their friends in the local community. They acknowledge that the community itself needs to have the desire to include and support such children. In my current research (Jones, in progress), which explores issues relating to early identification, assessment and provision for children with special educational needs, one parent's experience illustrates this point:

'Selfish as it may sound, it's hard on me because I feel...I don't feel embarrassed because he's my son...but some people do stare. I mean I have had people comment to me and as good as say he needs a good smack. It's always in supermarkets, I'd say 99 per cent of the time, always in supermarkets someone will make some comment. And most of the time it's at the checkout. People at the checkout, because when you get to the checkout he has to put the alarms on, he's pulling the straps across, he's fiddling around with the trolleys. I mean, don't get me wrong, I try my hardest to keep him away from shops but I know he's got to go in a shop, he's got to do it'. (Tom's mother)

Herbert and Moir (1996) further assert that, 'It is the role of the professional teacher, healthcare worker and social worker to disseminate information and conviction so that the community is empowered to offer this support' (p.57). This implies that professionals working in early intervention services are in a unique position to review provision, to articulate and promote an inclusive philosophy, to become 'change agents'. This latter role is crucial and is one which Havelock (1973, cited in Jeffs 1988, p.65) defines as 'a person who facilitates planned change and planned innovation'. One of four associated roles is that of a 'process helper' who can, for example, assist by showing the client how to recognise and define needs, diagnose problems and set targets, access resources, create and evaluate solutions to determine if they are satisfying his or her needs.

Professionals involved in the planning and delivery of services need to consider adapting and developing existing schemes, beyond the meeting of children's developmental goals, to take further account of the family and child within a broader social and political context. As Wood (1988) asserts, by viewing a scheme such as Portage as a model to be replicated, the focus is drawn to a standardised service and away from providing choice from a range of services which would allow parents more direct control as consumers. Cunningham (1983) reflects the danger of falling into a standard response which may not take account of wider considerations: '...we (professionals) recognise some increasingly familiar cue and are likely to produce an increasingly familiar recipe for action' (p.97).

If professionals fail to respond, the view that early intervention serves to accentuate differences and fosters the marginalisation of disabled children and their families from a very early age is reinforced. It has been argued that the professional approach to special education is clearly influenced by the medical model of disability.

'Special' children are given a special curriculum designed to compensate for their 'deficiencies'. Children become categories separate and different from 'normal' children (Vincent *et al.* 1996, p.483). Calling them 'special' does not necessarily comfort their parents:

> 'I'd love him to be..., I'll be crying in a minute...I mean...I mean I love him to bits but I'd love him to be normal, I would, I'd love him to be normal but...' (Tom's mother)

The Warnock Report (DES 1978) stressed the importance of early intervention as a preventive measure and as a means of supporting and involving parents, warning that: 'If adequate arrangements are not made for these children when they are young, more severe difficulties in learning, motivation and behaviour may arise...' (para. 11.49). Two decades later the question is – does the Code of Practice have a preventive and inclusive function? Or does it, by emphasising early identification via stages of need and intervention, work structurally in the same way as any category-based system, legitimating various kinds of exclusion policies and encouraging alternative provision for large numbers of children?

## Early intervention – professionals, parents and practice

Undoubtedly, early intervention has moved a long way in a relatively short space of time. Until the 1970s the usual experience of families was little or no support at all (Buckley 1994). They were told the 'diagnosis' by a doctor and then often left to cope as best they could. Over a period of two decades the growth of early intervention schemes has resulted in a significant shift from giving parents little incentive to stimulate or teach their child and offering low expectations, towards an apparent desire to empower parents to make informed decisions about their children from a position of strength. These principles have been enshrined in the phrase 'partnership with parents'. The potential benefits of joint efforts between parents and professionals to enhance learning and development are repeatedly sanctioned by official documents. Warnock claimed a widely accepted philosophy of parents 'rather than teachers' as the 'main educators' of their children and recommended that '...reinforcement and skilled support should be provided for parents of children with disabilities or significant difficulties in the earliest years' (DES 1978, para. 5:31), and that such support should be available in every area.

The Code of Practice supports early intervention schemes and suggests that Local Education Authorities (LEAs) should consider home-based programmes such as Portage (DfE 1994, para. 5:5) or peripatetic services for children with sensory impairment. The Code views professional collaboration with parents as of crucial benefit to the child:

> 'Children's progress will be diminished if their parents are not seen as partners in the education process with unique knowledge and information to impart. Professional help can seldom be effective unless it builds on parents' capacity to be involved and unless parents consider that professionals take account of what they say and treat their views and anxieties as intrinsically important.' (DfE 1994, Section 2:28, p.13)

On the surface, partnership with parents appears to be a straightforward concept. However, the process is complex and problematic and needs to be set against the wider political context of changing relationships in the new education 'market place' where the parent is increasingly regarded as the consumer with 'choice'. The rhetoric of parent–professional partnership is often based on shared stereotypes of what families should be like and how they relate to their children.

It is recognised that disabled children and those with significant difficulties may need to be taught skills which other children learn spontaneously. Children can learn and progress but may need special help in order to do so (Buckley 1994). This apparent need for small specific steps influenced the majority of early intervention programmes towards using structured behavioural methods to teach new skills. The Portage programme, for example, requires tasks to be set out in a highly structured way, stating precisely how to teach the child and how to record tangible progress and errors.

A common and central feature of early intervention, whatever the setting, is the key notion that parents are willing and able to undertake regular teaching of their child at home. The responsibility of care and teaching often falls on the mother with an assumption that she is automatically able to become the child's first educator. The mother may therefore feel responsible for the child's failures as well as the successes. What if the mother is depressed, isolated or living in poverty? How are fathers involved or other children's needs identified and supported?

A complex array of models has developed during the last two decades. Cunningham and Davis (1985) looked at the ways in which parents participate in intervention programmes and identfied three distinct models. First, the 'expert model', exemplified by the professional taking control in making the decisions and the parent as the passive recipient of services. In practice, parents and children may become increasingly dependent on professionals and the partnership element remains minimal. Second is the 'transplant model' whereby professionals transplant skills and expertise but this is still not a full partnership because ultimately the professional retains control. This model could promote an unhelpful emphasis on the parents as having to absorb 'teacher skills' instead of strategies for communicating with their child in a more natural manner. It could also, as Hornby (1995) points out, overburden the parent. The third model is that of parent as 'consumer' and is based upon the assumption that the parent has considerable knowledge to be shared. The consumer model acknowledges the parents' rights to make decisions regarding services and resources and parents are accorded equiv-alent status in the relationship. Appleton and Minchom (1991) developed an empowerment model which takes account of the wider family dynamics. This developing model starts with the parents' natural style of interacting with their child and takes account of the needs, resources and uniqueness of each individual family. It rests on the assumption that further progress in developing services for young and disabled children is dependent on professionals' ability to understand and take account of the range of different ways in which families function.

A home-visiting project or service plan may be restricted to precise aims and objectives, but this model acknowledges a fundamental need to appreciate that parents may have different and changing expectations. Carpenter and Herbert (1995) affirm the contribution not only of parents but siblings, grandparents, other relatives, colleagues, neighbours and friends.

More recently, Dale (1996) has introduced the 'negotiating model', which she describes as:

> 'a working relationship where the partners use negotiation and joint decision making and resolve differences of opinion and disagreement in order to reach some kind of shared perspective or jointly agreed decision on issues of mutual concern.' (p.14)

A key element, which distinguishes it from previous models, is that both professional and parent are recognised as having valuable contributions to make. However, it is not uncommon for parents of disabled children to have at least five 'professionals' involved at any one moment in time and effective early intervention is closely linked to cooperation between disciplines. Cunningham and Davis (1985) explain:

> '...In principle such partnerships should be the same as with parents. A prerequi-site is that each member of the team brings his/her own expertise and complementary skills and has equal status.' (p.158)

The Children Act 1989 stresses the importance of a corporate approach and implies a need for agreed strategies across all key departments. The Act places a duty on social services departments to assist local education authorities with the provision of services for children with special educational needs. The potential overlap and common interest between the departments is reiterated in the Code of Practice (DfE 1994) which asks LEAs and social services departments to agree on procedures to be followed when the LEA notifies a social services department of its proposal to assess a child's special education needs. Social services may combine an assessment of a child 'in need' under the Children Act 1989, with a statutory assessment under the 1993 Education Act. The Code suggests that if a child is referred before the age of two he or she is 'likely to have a particular condition or to have a major health problem which has caused concern at an early stage' and 'it is probable that any special needs will have been identified by his or her parents, the child health services or social services' (DfE 1994). The Scottish Office report (H.M. Inspectors of Schools 1994), which sets out the principles to be followed by education authorities, describes inter-professional teamwork as 'a cornerstone of effective pre-school provision' (para. 3.16). Statutory arrangements in Scotland for assessing and recording needs are advised in Circular 4/96. Effective comm-unication through formal and informal contact between every person involved, including social workers, doctors, health visitors, teachers, therapists and parents, is again seen as crucial (Scottish Office 1996, paras. 39 and 40).

Families of children growing up with impairments require a complex range of services embracing a number of different professional disciplines. Combined approaches reduce the high potential difficulty for parents in knowing which need should be met by which service. Sloper and Turner (1992) investigated service contacts and perceived helpfulness of services, gathering information from a sample of 107 families of young children with a severe physical impairment. They reported that 73 per cent of parents thought that the most helpful aspects of professionals were approachability, openness, honesty, giving information and listening to parents. On initial contact with professionals parents may be adjusting to their own feelings:

> 'Well, I was worse when I was first told...I was absolutely devastated. I felt as though my heart had fallen out. It was horrible. I don't know. It just felt like death. I was grieving for absolutely months and months and months. But after the space of 18 to 20 months you just get, you know you've just got to get on with things. It is hard though, terribly hard...' (Tom's mother)

Although primarily a home teaching model, it has been suggested that the Portage system has important lessons for inter-disciplinary team organisation (Dale 1996). It has been run by health authorities, social services, education authorities and voluntary agencies. In this way, professionals from different disciplines develop a joint approach and Dale reports that regular team meetings combine individual autonomy with team accountability. Coherent and well coordinated access to ongoing support for families can only be achieved by close dialogue and collaboration between disciplines.

## Conclusion

This chapter allows a number of conclusions to be drawn about future developments in early intervention. First, the definition of need is still predominantly based on addressing what is viewed as an individual problem. This pervades the teaching process, the categorisation of children, assessment and the professional practice. The rhetoric of 'partnership' and legislation may leave underlying value judgements unchanged. As Wills (1994) concludes:

> 'Negative attitudes towards disability have strongly shaped what we do to people who are disabled, how it is done and the consequences for their families.' (p.249)

Young disabled children are cocooned by the parent and professional, creating an eternal triangle of early intervention, which largely ignores the wider social, economic and political issues.

Second, the effects of early intervention have not as yet been systematically evaluated within the UK. As Buckley (1994) points out, critics are not saying that early intervention is not effective, but that its effectiveness remains to be scientifically demonstrated with reliable and valid research studies. There is an urgent need for further qualitative and quantitative research to determine more precisely the immediate and long-term social, political and educational consequences of early intervention and family support.

Third, in policy and practice, high priority should be given to developing a system which enshrines what Cunningham and Davis (1985) describe as 'transdisciplinary' cooperation, whilst maintaining individual autonomy. As Davie (1993) succinctly states:

> 'An underlying rationale for interdisciplinary work is that the child or young person is seen as a whole individual, whose needs and characteristics overlap and interrelate. He/she is neither a pupil, a patient nor a client but a person.' (pp.140–141)

There is a need to develop new, flexible initiatives and extend combined packages of care from education, social services and health authorities. Such schemes could be developed in negotiation with parents and in response to the changing needs of families. Early intervention is not only concerned with organising and administering provision for disabled children, or providing tangible, measurable outcomes, but plays a crucial role in altering underlying values, beliefs and attitudes towards disability.

## Acknowledgements

I would like to thank Elaine Herbert for her help with references and confidence in my abilities. Also thanks to 'Tom' and his family for sharing their experiences. Finally I would like to thank Christopher for the poem.

## References

Appleton, P.L. and Minchom, P.E. (1991) 'Models of parent partnership and child development centres.' *Child: Care, Health and Development 17*, 27–38.

Buckley, S. (1994) 'Early intervention: the state of the art.' In B. Carpenter (ed.) *Early Intervention: Where are We Now?* Oxford: Westminster Press.

Carpenter, B. and Herbert, E. (1995) 'Fathers - are early intervention strategies meeting their needs?' Paper presented to the International Special Education Congress, Birmingham, UK.

Children Act (1989). London: HMSO.

Children (Scotland) Act (1995). Edinburgh: HMSO.

Cunningham, C.C. (1983) 'Early support and intervention: The HARC Infant Project.' In P. Mittler and H. McConachie (eds) *Parents, Professionals and Mentally Handicapped People, Approaches to Partnership.* Beckenham: Croom Helm.

Cunningham, C.C. and Davis, H. (1985) *Working with Parents: Frameworks for Collaboration.* Buckingham: Open University Press.

Dale, N. (1996) *Working with Families of Children with Special Educational Needs.* London: Routledge.

Davie, R. (1993) 'Interdisciplinary perspectives on assessment.' In S. Wolfendale (ed.) *Assessing Special Educational Needs.* London: Cassell.

Department for Education (1994) *Code of Practice on the Identification and Assessment of Special Educational Needs.* London: Department of Education.

Department of Education and Science (1978) *Report of the Committee of Enquiry into the Education of Handicapped Children and Young People* (Warnock Report). London: HMSO.

Education Act (1981). London: HMSO.

Education Act (1993). London: HMSO.

Herbert, E. and Moir, J. (1996) 'Children with special educational needs – a collaborative and inclusive style of working.' In C. Nutbrown (ed.) *Respectful Educators - Capable Learners: Children's Rights and Early Education.* London: Paul Chapman Publishing.

Hornby, G. (1995) *Working with Parents of Children with Special Needs.* London: Cassell.

H.M. Inspectors of Schools (1994) *Effective Provision for Special Educational Needs.* Edinburgh: Scottish Office Education Department.

Jeffs, A. (1988) 'The appearance and reality of change within special educational needs.' In L. Barton (ed.) *The Politics of Special Educational Needs.* Lewes: Falmer Press.

Jones, C. (in progress) 'How are special needs identified and met in the early years?' Doctoral thesis, Department of Education, University of Warwick.

Lindsay, G. (1995) 'Early identification of special educational needs.' In I. Lunt and B. Norwich (eds) *Psychology and Education for Special Needs.* London: Arena.

Lindsay, G. (1995) 'Early identification of special educational needs.' In I. Lunt and B. Norwich (eds) *Psychology and Education for Special Needs.* London: Arena.

Newell, P. (1991) *The UN Convention and Children's Rights in the UK.* London: National Children's Bureau.

Scottish Office Circular (1996) No. 4/96. *Children and Young Persons with Special Educational Needs: Assessment and Recording.* Edinburgh: Scottish Office Education Department.

Sloper, P. and Turner, S. (1992) 'Service needs of families of children with severe physical disability.' *Child: Care, Health and Development 18,* 259–282.

The Stationery Office (1995) *Children (N.I.) Order 1995.* Belfast: The Stationery Office.

Tomlinson, S. (1982) *A Sociology of Special Education.* London: Routledge and Kegan Paul.

Vincent, C., Evans, J., Lunt, I. and Young, P. (1996) 'Professionals under pressure: the administration of special education in a changing context.' *British Educational Research Journal 22,* 4.

Wills, R. (1994) 'It is time to stop.' In K. Ballard (ed.) *Disability, Family, Whanau an Society.* Palmerston North, New Zealand: Dunmore Press.

Wolfendale, S. (1994) 'Policy and provision for children with special educational needs in the early years.' In S. Riddell and S. Brown (eds) *Special Educational Needs Policy in the 1990s: Warnock in the Market Place.* London: Routledge.

Wood, S. (1988) 'Parents: Whose partners?' In L. Barton (ed.) *The Politics of Special Educational Needs.* Lewes: Falmer Press.

# CHAPTER 4

# The Pre-School Years

*June Statham and Janet Read*

## Introduction

The first five years of a child's life are a crucial time, for children growing up with disability as much as for any others. A great deal of children's learning takes place in these early years, and the foundations are laid for their later attitudes and behaviours. They are important years for parents too. The way parents are told about their child's condition, the kind of support that is offered and the attitudes which they meet in these early years will all have an impact on their subsequent lives. This chapter begins with an outline of the legislation governing services to disabled children, followed by a description of the range of services that are available for young children and their families, with a particular focus on pre-school education and daycare. It then considers what is known about families' experience of using services, and finally draws out some of the implications from the research for social workers and others working with young disabled children and their families.

## The law and disabled children

Two major pieces of legislation have particular relevance to the provision of services for young disabled children. The first is the 1993 Education Act, which replaced the 1981 Education Act and was later incorporated into the consolidating 1996 Education Act. It introduced a new Code of Practice to guide schools and local education authorities (LEAs) on how to identify, assess and meet a child's special needs (Department for Education 1994). The Code emphasises the need for LEAs to share information with other statutory agencies and with voluntary groups such as playgroups and day nurseries, and to carry out assessments of young children in settings where they and their parents feel comfortable. A distinction is made between children under two and those aged two to five. LEAs may assess a child's educational needs before they reach two, but are unlikely to issue a formal statement (i.e. a record of need), although they should still provide services where required. From the age of two, the statutory procedures for assessing and meeting special educational needs apply. The Code of Practice emphasises the importance of LEAs working in partnership with parents, and gives parents the right to appeal to a tribunal if they are unhappy with the way their child's needs have been dealt with.

The second major piece of legislation is the Children Act 1989, which gave local authorities a new opportunity to develop appropriate support services for disabled children and their families. The Act came into force in England and Wales in 1991, and similar legislation was passed in Scotland and Northern Ireland in 1995. It sets out the following principles on which work with disabled children should be based:

- The welfare of the child should be safeguarded and promoted by those providing services.
- Children with disabilities are children first.
- Recognition of the importance of parents and families in children's lives.
- Partnership between parents and local authorities and other agencies.
- The views of children and parents should be sought and taken into account.

(Department of Health 1991)

The Act introduced the concept of 'children in need' for whom the local authority has to provide services, and it included disabled children within the definition of children in need. Local authorities are expected to provide a range of services to minimise the effects of disability and enable children to live as normal a life as possible. They are also required to maintain a register of disabled children for planning purposes, and to consider a child's religious persuasion, racial origin and cultural and linguistic background when providing services.

Other legislation which applies to adults may also govern the provision of services to disabled children. For example, Section 2 of the Chronically Sick and Disabled Persons Act 1970 places a duty on local authorities to provide a range of practical support services to disabled children as well as to adults (although this is not always recognised by practitioners), and under the Carers (Recognition and

Services) Act 1995, parents of disabled children may be able to be assessed as carers with an entitlement to additional services.

## Services for disabled pre-school children: what is available?

Services for disabled pre-school children and their parents may be provided by a range of agencies, including social services departments, education and health authorities, voluntary organisations and the independent sector. Excluding purely clinical and medical services, the different forms of provision and support available in the early years include:

- social work and counselling
- family centres
- daycare and childminding
- nursery education
- home liaison teachers/Portage schemes
- opportunity groups
- short-term breaks (respite care)
- toy libraries and equipment loan schemes
- child development centres
- physiotherapy, speech therapy and occupational therapy
- parent befriending schemes (e.g. Contact-a-Family)
- information and advice services
- financial assistance from the Family Fund.

Not all of these services will be equally available everywhere, nor may they be equally accessible to all families. For instance, some parents may find it difficult to use services because of language differences or because the provision is inappropriate. Baxter *et al.* (1990) found that many voluntary organisations working with young children with learning difficulties had little understanding of the needs of black and minority ethnic groups, and wrongly assumed their services were accessible and welcoming to them. We return to this issue later, when looking at the experiences of parents and children.

Services can be provided in different ways, with varying degrees of inclusivity. Nursery education, for example, may be offered to disabled children in ordinary nursery schools and classes with the provision of additional support such as an extra nursery assistant, specialist peripatetic teaching and special equipment. Disabled children may be able to attend full time rather than part time, and from the age of two rather than three or four. Nursery education may also be provided in special units attached to ordinary schools, in opportunity classes (which usually involve parents and are staffed by volunteers, but with a qualified teacher paid for by the education department), or in nursery classes that are part of special schools. LEAs have a duty to include children in ordinary schools so long as the child's needs can be appropriately met, other children's education is not adversely affected, and resources are being used efficiently, or unless the parent specifically requests a place in a special school.

Similarly, day nurseries or playgroups for disabled children may be provided by social services and health authorities, or disabled children may qualify for priority places in council day nurseries as children in need. However, disabled pre-school children may also attend local daycare services which are open to all children in their neighbourhood, run by voluntary and private groups. In some cases, their place may be paid for or 'sponsored' by the local authority. The use of sponsored places in community provision is increasing, and surveys have shown that most independent daycare providers are very willing to offer places to children with impairments and other 'special needs' (Cameron and Statham 1997). However, it is important that such providers are given appropriate training and support and not exploited as a cheap resource. Sometimes this can best be achieved through an organised scheme, for example, the Special Needs Referral Scheme, which is operated by playgroup associations in most counties in Wales, funded by the Welsh Office and local social services departments. Scheme coordinators find places for children with learning difficulties in local playgroups, arrange and pay for extra helpers, provide special equipment where needed, and support parents and playgroup staff. It is widely regarded as a successful and non-stigmatising way of providing support, although there are often too few places to meet demand (Statham 1996).

Despite the potentially wide range of provision for young disabled children, there are a number of problems with the current delivery of services. A lack of coordination between agencies has long been recognised as a particular problem in the pre-school field (Moss and Penn 1996, Pugh 1992), with different agencies tending to focus on only one aspect of children's needs, for instance education, childcare, health or protection from harm. A few local authorities have integrated all care and education services for young children within one department, usually education. Strathclyde, for example, set up a Pre-Fives Unit in 1986 which unified pre-school services within the education department, and adopted a policy that gave disabled children equal access to services:

> 'Services should be organised in such a way that any provision can accommodate and meet the needs of children with a handicap or chronic illness however severe the condition. The emphasis should be on directing extra resources and support to the community where the child is. No child should be denied access to a service on grounds of health or disability.' (Strathclyde Regional Council 1988)

Such integrated, inclusive policies are still rare. In most local authorities, services for young children are still fragmented and uncoordinated (Pugh and McQuail 1995). However the Children Act 1989, while not addressing the basic split between pre-school care and education services, does attempt to encourage local authorities to adopt a more coordinated approach, by requiring social services and education departments jointly to carry out a review of the services available for children under eight. These 'Section 19' or 'daycare' reviews should be carried out every three years, and can provide a valuable source of information about local authority policies and services for young children, both universal and specialist. For this chapter, we analysed 70 daycare reviews produced by English local authorities in 1995 or 1996, and found that a number of issues concerning the provision of services for disabled children were raised time and time again. The daycare reviews are concerned with provision for children under eight, but many of these issues will also be relevant to families with older disabled children. They include:

- the need for improved access to mainstream daycare services for disabled children
- insufficient respite care to meet parental demand
- lack of publicity and information for parents
- difficulties in establishing a register of disabled children and using it as a planning tool

• lack of coordination between different agencies working with disabled children.

## The experience of parents and children

We consider next what research has to tell us about parents' response to learning that their child has an impairment, the needs of parents caring for such children and their views about the services that are provided in the pre-school years. There has been growing resistance to the ways in which, in professional literature, disabled children have sometimes been misrepresented exclusively as tragedies or burdens (Beresford 1994; Goodey 1992; Read 1991). Although much of the research cited here highlights the difficulties, it is important to remember that with the right support and high quality services, the pre-school years can be rewarding for both parents and children, often in unanticipated ways (Russell 1991). The challenge for social and medical workers is to learn from families how to help them acquire the support they need.

### The early days

Research findings on the experience of families with young disabled children echo many of these concerns. There is consistent evidence that the process of discovering that they have a disabled child, whether at birth or later, is experienced as highly stressful by many parents. A substantial proportion express great dissatisfaction with the services that they receive from professionals at this crucial time. Apart from the importance of developing humane and sensitive practice, it must also be recognised that those parents who have what they experience as unhelpful treatment at the hands of the professionals at this stage, may carry the hurt and disillusionment with them for some time to come.

A number of studies highlight the fact that parents are frequently the first people to suspect that there is something unusual about their child's development, and report that their concern and anxiety is exacerbated by a lack of appropriate help, information and support from the professionals who become involved. Parents often believe strongly that their concerns about their child were not taken seriously (Audit Commission 1994; Baldwin and Carlisle 1994; Hall 1997; Quine and Pahl 1986).

There is evidence that the process of disclosure and encounters with professionals and organisations at this time can be particularly hazardous for some parents and children from minority ethnic communities (Shah 1992, 1997; Sheik

1986). Shah points out that it can be very difficult indeed for those who do not have English as a mother tongue to gain access to essential information verbally and in writing. They may never be provided with appropriate counselling or other support sensitive to their needs (Shah 1997). It is not only a question of language, however. Baxter *et al.* point out that research in the UK on cross-cultural counselling is in its infancy and little attention has been given to matching counsellors and clients on the basis of ethnic origin and gender (Baxter *et al.* 1990). It has also been argued that there is widespread ignorance among service professionals about conditions such as sickle-cell anaemia and thalassaemia, which predominantly affect people from black and minority ethnic communities. It is suggested that this, combined with the allocation of very limited resources, has resulted in the needs of these disabled children and their families being neglected both at the point of identification and later (Dyson 1992).

## A new way of living

It is the parents of disabled children, particularly the mothers, who shoulder the main responsibility for their care and during the pre-school period many feel isolated and even abandoned (Haylock, Johnson and Harpin 1993). While the upbringing of all small children can be very hard work, it has to be recognised that the care of a disabled child frequently makes demands that go well beyond what is required of parents of young, non-disabled children (Baldwin and Carlisle 1994; Baldwin and Glendinning 1982; Glendinning 1983; Powell and Perkins 1984; Sloper and Turner 1992). The volume of work to be undertaken directly with the child on both a routine and non-routine basis tends to be greater. It is not uncommon for the caring tasks to be more complex than with other children and in the early days at least, more unfamiliar and anxiety-provoking to parents.

The demands may be greater now than in the past, because over the past 20 years, developments in medical technology have brought about a shift in the population of disabled children. Greater numbers of low-birthweight babies and those with severe and complex disorders are surviving and are being cared for at home. This has a very significant effect on families' lives as well as implications for services attempting to meet their needs (Baldwin and Carlisle 1994; Hall 1997; Lawton 1989; McConachie 1997).

There is also a great deal of evidence that bringing up a disabled child has a significant financial impact upon the household. Raising a disabled child involves substantial additional expenditure (Baldwin and Glendinning 1982). Simultaneously, however, the demands of caring reduce the options that parents, particularly mothers, have for gaining income by undertaking paid work outside the home (Baldwin and Glendinning 1983). The combination of this double squeeze leaves households with disabled children with fewer financial resources than those in the general population and this can have a substantial negative effect on standards of living. Research indicates that lone parent households are particularly vulnerable in this respect. Also, the more severe the child's impairment, the greater will be both the expenditure and the restrictions on earning (Baldwin and Carlisle 1994; Smyth and Robus 1989).

There is growing concern about the ways in which increased childhood poverty, the restructuring of the labour market, higher levels of unemployment and greater incidence of lone parenthood may impact particularly harshly on households of disabled children, adding to their pre-existing economic disadvantage (Baldwin and Carlisle 1994; Blackburn 1991; McConachie 1997). The Family Fund, for example, which gives financial assistance to families with a severely disabled child, has reported that these trends are clearly reflected both in the increased numbers of grant applications received and in the often extremely disadvantaged circumstances of the parents and children applying. The Family Fund has reported that the single most significant trend is the increase in applications from such parents of children under the age of two years, many of whom have complex and severe impairments (Williams 1992).

Parents of young disabled children not only manage these new and difficult circumstances but they may also have to balance them with competing demands such as the need to look after other children. They may also find that the measures which most parents of young children use to offset the demands of childrearing are less available to them. Their social lives may become more restricted: babysitting and other informal supports are not always easy to find for the parents of a disabled child (Meltzer, Smyth and Robus 1989; Read 1991; Russell 1991).

Given such circumstances, it is not surprising that there can be an impact on the physical and psychological health of those doing most of the caring (Russell 1991). Parents of disabled children, particularly mothers, have been found to experience higher levels of stress than comparable people in the general population. Again, lone parents are found to be particularly at risk (Meltzer *et al.* 1989).

There is also some evidence that there are links between stress levels and the severity of impairment in the child and the availability of support from a partner (Baldwin and Carlisle 1994). It is argued, however, that the factors which generate stress or promote personal well-being are complex, suggesting the need to be cautious about generalisation (Russell 1991). Beresford's recent work, for example, focuses specifically on the ways in which parents manage stressful circumstances by actively developing their own personal coping strategies in order to create an equilibrium in their lives (Beresford 1994).

In reviewing research on the impact on marital relationships between parents, Baldwin and Carlisle (1994) argue that the evidence suggests that the risk of breakdown is greater when there is a disabled child and that this risk increases with the severity of the impairment. They also point out that mothers of disabled children are more likely than others to become lone parents and less likely to remarry, this being particularly so for older women and again, those with children who have severe impairments.

Baxter *et al.* (1990) suggest that while the pre-school years represent a difficult time of adjustment and change for many parents of children with learning disabilities, the circumstances of black and ethnic minority parents may be 'particularly bleak'. They argue:

> 'Most of the research carried out amongst black women carers points to their ex-treme isolation. The myth of the cohesion of Asian communities belies the lone-liness and isolation faced by many carers. Black and ethnic minority people may have a greater need for support than their white peers. Migration may have severed their traditional networks of support. Even where there are relatives in Britain, they may live in other cities. Many black and minority ethnic carers to whom we spoke felt isolated and desperate.' (p.60)

*Parental satisfaction with services*

A common source of frustration and difficulty for parents is the need to deal with a multiplicity of different agencies and professionals. As described above, services are delivered through complex organisational arrangements and by an increasing range of specialists. There are problems associated with coordination and joint planning between key agencies and disciplines at all levels, and an ever-present danger that disabled children and their parents fall through the gaps or become marginalised (Appleton *et al.* 1997; Audit Commission 1994; Baldwin and

Carlisle 1994; Baxter *et al.* 1990; Beresford 1995; Butt and Mirza 1996; Court 1976; Glendinning 1983 and 1986; Hall, 1997; Haylock, Johnson and Harpin 1993; McConachie 1997; Sloper and Turner 1992, 1993; Social Services Inspectorate 1994; Warnock 1978; Wishart, MacLeod and Rowan 1993; Yerbury 1997). The research also shows that parents have to be extremely active and persistent in order to gain access to what they regard as appropriate information and provision, especially if parental and professional views on needs differ. The families under the greatest pressure because of a combination of stressful life events and very limited resources are often least likely to be able to take on these formidable tasks (Sloper and Turner 1992).

A number of other studies have highlighted children and families from black and minority ethnic communities, lone parents and those on low incomes as having unmet needs for support (Baxter *et al.* 1990; Beresford 1994; Shah 1992, 1997). The under-representation of poorer children and their families and those from black and minority communities among users of the generally successful family-based short-term break schemes has been a cause for concern (Robinson and Stalker 1993). Research has drawn attention to the ways in which predominantly white service professionals may misunderstand the needs of Asian parents and stereotype their lifestyles in ways that are damaging to theirs and their children's interests (Baxter *et al.* 1990; Shah 1995; Sheik 1986).

The picture that emerges from research on parents' views is very consistent: they would like better access to information especially in the early years, an approach from professionals which treats them as partners (the characteristics which parents particularly value in professionals are empathy, warmth and interpersonal skills), and a wider choice of services, including access to mainstream provision with appropriate support (Haylock *et al.* 1993; Russell 1991; Sloper and Turner 1992; Stallard and Lenton 1992).

### Developing services to meet need

In this final section we identify some of the main messages from the research for professionals involved with young disabled children. The research stresses the importance of:

- partnership with parents
- a key worker

- interagency working

- pre-school provision

- short-term breaks

- information and advice.

*Partnership with parents*

Parents generally know the most about their own child, and professionals need to work together with them to provide the services which families need. Since the needs of young children and their parents are so closely tied together, outcomes for the child are likely to be more successful if attention is given to supporting the whole family rather than focusing exclusively on the disabled child. It has been argued that the most effective services aim to support, directly or indirectly, parents' own personal styles and strategies for managing their lives (Appleton *et al.* 1997; Beresford 1994).

*A key worker*

Research has repeatedly emphasised that one of the most effective and valued provisions is the allocation of a single key worker to parents and their child. The recommended tasks (Beresford 1995; Glendinning 1986) for such a worker vary from providing information and guidance through to much more active facilitation, advocacy or care management. Such individuals are not only well-placed to fill the information deficit so often described, but also to act as a guide through the maze, to take some of the strain of negotiation from parents and to help them access services that they need and want. Key workers may also be effective in tackling the problem that those most in need are least well-placed to gain support.

*Interagency working*

Linked with the notion of key working is the importance of coordination and cooperation between the services and personnel involved. At a strategic level, this could involve an integrated early years service, or an interagency group developing joint assessment procedures (such as the Oxfordshire Joint Commissioning Reference Group for Children with Special Needs, described in Russell 1995). At the service delivery level, it could be a centre bringing together community health, social services, the education authority and the voluntary sector, to provide parents with a single access point to a range of facilities. These might include pre-school playgroups, home visiting, clinics and primary healthcare as well as flexible short-term residential support and information and guidance for parents.

### Pre-school provision

There is consistent evidence that many parents value and feel supported by provision aimed at aiding the child's development either through work with parents or that undertaken directly with the child. Examples include opportunity groups and nursery classes, early intervention or teaching programmes such as Portage, home-teaching services and conductive education as well as speech therapy and physiotherapy (Cameron 1997; Hall 1997; Haylock *et al.* 1993; Read 1996). Apart from the valued aims in terms of the child's development, there is evidence that contact with a centre or professional providing such a service frequently facilitates access to other information, support and benefits.

### Short-term breaks

Schemes which offer parents and children a range of short-term breaks are also valuable and popular, although not widely available (a national disability survey carried out in the late 1980s found that although nearly half of families with a disabled child had heard of respite care, only 4 per cent had actually been offered or used it (Bone and Meltzer 1989)). Again, it needs to be recognised that what is acceptable and useful varies from household to household and from child to child. For example, some parents find the link with another family providing short-term breaks immensely supportive. Other parents prefer a regular sitting-in service provided in their own home. Whatever the arrangement, however, it is increasingly clear that parents, as well as good professional practice, demand that the break should be seen as a positive experience for both the child and the rest of the family (Robinson and Stalker 1993).

### Information and advice

Information and advice services are an important source of support for families, especially when their child is young and they need to find their way around the system and discover what is available. Clear information needs to be available in an accessible, usable form about a child's condition and other crucial matters, including entitlements to benefits and practical support services. Parents' need for information as well as their ability to absorb it varies across time and in different circumstances. In the very early days, for example, the unfamiliarity of the situation combined with probable stress and anxiety will require particular attention to be paid to ways of ensuring that parents do not feel cut adrift. This may require repeated follow-up sessions, a willingness to go over material again, the availability of counselling, contact, where appropriate, with support networks of other parents, and immediate link-up with community services. Information and advice needs to be culturally appropriate and translation or interpreting facilities available for those whose mother tongue is not English. There is often a particular need for advice, information and personal support at other critical stages such as the transition to nursery or primary school, and during the statementing process.

## Conclusion

The pre-school years clearly offer many challenges to disabled children, their families and the agencies that support them, especially as increasing numbers of children are surviving with severe and complex impairments. A family's earliest experience of life with their disabled child is a crucial time, and is likely to affect not only their long-term well-being, but also the extent to which they view professionals as partners with whom they can work to obtain the support they and their child need. Running through the research studies reported are several key factors associated with the provision of an effective service for young disabled children: respect for the views of parents and children and a willingness to work with them, good coordination between agencies, the avoidance of unneccesary multiple assessments, the provision of a range of support services including pre-school daycare and education and short-term breaks as well as access, where appropriate, to specialist services such as physiotherapy and speech therapy. The pre-school years set the base upon which the later experiences of disabled children and their parents will build. Social workers have an important part to play in ensuring that these early years provide a solid foundation for future growth.

## References

Appleton, P., Boll, V., Everett, J., Kelly, A., Meredith, K. and Payne, T. (1997) 'Beyond child development centres: care coordination for children with disabilities.' *Child: Care, Health and Development 23*, 1, 29–40.

Audit Commission (1994) *Seen But Not Heard: Coordinating Community Child Health and Social Services for Children In Need.* London: HMSO.

Baldwin, S. and Carlisle, J. (1994) *Social Support for Disabled Children and Their Families: A Review of the Literature.* Edinburgh: HMSO.

Baldwin, S. and Glendinning, C. (1982) 'Children with disabilities and their families.' In A. Walker and P. Townsend (eds) *Disability in Britain: A Manifesto of Rights.* Oxford: Martin Robertson.

Baldwin, S and Glendinning, C. (1983) 'Employment, women and their disabled children.' In J. Finch and D. Groves (eds) *A Labour of Love: Women, Work and Caring.* London: Routledge and Kegan Paul.

Baxter, C., Poonia, K., Ward, L. and Nadirshaw, Z. (1990) *Double Discrimination: Issues and Services for People with Learning Difficulties from Black and Ethnic Minority Communities.* London: King's Fund Centre.

Blackburn, C. (1991) *Poverty and Health: Working with Families.* Buckingham: Open University Press.

Beresford, B.(1994) *Positively Parents: Caring for a Severely Disabled Child.* York: Social Policy Research Unit/HMSO.

Beresford, B. (1995) *Expert Opinions: A National Survey of Parents Caring for a Severely Disabled Child.* Bristol: The Policy Press.

Bone, M. and Meltzer, H. (1989) *The Prevalence of Disability Among Children: Report 3.* London: HMSO.

Butt, J. and Mirza, K. (1996) *Social Care and Black Communities.* London: HMSO.

Cameron, R. (1997) 'Early interventions for young children with developmental delay: the Portage approach.' *Child: Care, Health and Development 23,* 1, 11–27.

Cameron, C. and Statham, J. (1997) 'Sponsored places: the use of independent day-care services to support children in need.' *British Journal of Social Work 27,* 85–100.

Carers (Recognition and Services) Act (1995). London: HMSO.

Children Act (1989). London: HMSO.

Chronically Sick and Disabled Persons Act (1970). London: HMSO.

Court, S. (1976) *Fit for the Future: Report of the Committee on Child Health Services.* Cmnd 6684. London: HMSO.

Department for Education (1994) *Code of Practice on the Identification and Assessment of Special Educational Needs.* London: DfE.

Department of Health (1991) *The Children Act Guidance and Regulations: Volume 6, Children with Disabilities.* London: HMSO.

Dyson, S. (1992) 'Blood relations: educational implications of sickle-cell anaemia and thalassaemia.' In T. Booth, W. Swann, M. Masterson and P. Potts (eds) *Curricula for Diversity in Education.* London: Routledge in association with the Open University.

Education Act (1981). London: HMSO.

Education Act (1993). London: HMSO.

Education Act (1996). London: HMSO.

Glendinning, C. (1983) *Unshared Care: Parents and Their Disabled Children.* London: Routledge and Kegan Paul.

Glendinning, C. (1986) *A Single Door: Social Work with the Families of Disabled Children.* London: Routledge and Kegan Paul.

Goodey, C.(1992) 'Fools and heretics: parents' views of professionals.' In T. Booth, M. Masterson, P. Potts and W. Swann (eds) *Policies for Diversity in Education.* London: Routledge in association with the Open University.

Hall, D. (1997) 'Child development teams: are they fulfilling their purpose?' *Child: Care, Health and Development 23,* 1, 87–99.

Haylock, C., Johnson, A. and Harpin, V. (1993) 'Parents' views of community care for children with motor disabilities.' *Child: Care, Health and Development 19,* 209–220.

Lawton, D. (1989) 'Very young children and the Family Fund.' *Children and Society 3,* 3, 212–225.

McConachie, H. (1997) 'The organisation of child disability services.' *Child: Care, Health and Development 23,* 1, 3–9.

Meltzer, H., Smyth, M. and Robus, N. (1989) *Disabled Children: Services, Transport and Education.* OPCS Surveys of Disability in Britain. London: HMSO.

Moss, P. and Penn, H. (1996) *Transforming Nursery Education.* London: Paul Chapman Publishing.

Powell, M. and Perkins, E. (1984) 'Asian families with a pre-school handicapped child – a study.' *Mental Handicap 12,* 50–52.

Pugh, G. (ed.) (1992) *Contemporary Issues in the Early Years.* London: Paul Chapman Publishing.

Pugh, G. and McQuail, S. (1995) *Effective Organisation of Early Childhood Services.* London: National Children's Bureau.

Quine, E. and Pahl, J. (1986) 'First diagnosis of severe mental handicap: characteristics of unsatisfactory encounters between doctors and parents.' *Social Science and Medicine 22,* 53–62.

Read, J. (1991) 'There was never really any choice: the experience of mothers of disabled children in the United Kingdom.' *Women's Studies International Forum 14,* 6, 561–571.

Read, J. (1996) *A Different Outlook: Services Users' Perspectives on Conductive Education.* Birmingham: Foundation for Conductive Education.

Robinson, C and Stalker, K. (1993) 'Patterns of provision in respite care and the Children Act.' *British Journal of Social Work 23,* 45–63.

Russell, P. (1991) 'Working with children with physical disabilities and their families–the social work role.' In M. Oliver (ed.) *Social Work, Disabled People and Disabling Environments.* Research Highlights in Social Work 21. London: Jessica Kingsley Publishers.

Russell, P. (1995) *Positive Choices: Services for Children with Disabilities Living Away from Home.* London: Council for Disabled Children.

Shah, R. (1992) *The Silent Minority: Children with Disabilities in Asian Families.* London: National Children's Bureau.

Shah, R. (1997) 'Services for Asian families and children with disabilities.' *Child: Care, Health and Development 23,* 1, 41–46.

Sheik, S. (1986) 'An Asian mothers' self-help group.' In S. Ahmed, J. Cheetham and J. Small (eds) *Social Work with Black Children and their Families.* London: Batsford.

Sloper, P. and Turner, S. (1992) 'Service needs of families of children with severe physical disability.' *Child: Care, Health and Development 18,* 259–282.

Sloper, P. and Turner, S. (1993) 'Determinants of parental satisfaction with disclosure of disability.' *Developmental Medicine and Child Neurology 35,* 816–825.

Smyth, M. and Robus, N. (1989) *The Financial Circumstances of Families with Disabled Children Living in Private Households.* London: HMSO.

Social Services Inspectorate (1994) *Services to Disabled Children and Their Families: Report of the National Inspection of Services to Disabled Children and Their Families.* London: HMSO.

Stallard, B. And Lenton, S. (1992) 'How satisfied are parents of pre-school children who have special needs with the services they have received?' *Child: Care, Health and Development 18,* 197–205.

Statham, J. (1996) *Young Children in Wales: an Evaluation of the Implementation of the Children Act 1989 on Day Care Services.* London: Thomas Coram Research Unit.

Strathclyde Regional Council (1988) *Pre-Five Unit: Progress Report 1987–88.* Glasgow: Strathclyde Regional Council Department of Education.

Warnock, M. (1978) *Special Educational Needs: Report of the Committee of Enquiry into the Education of Handicapped Children and Young People.* Cmnd 7212. London: HMSO.

Williams, E. (1992) 'One hundred thousand families to support.' *Search* 13, September.

Wishart, J., MacLeod, H and Rowan, C.(1993) '"Parent" evaluations of pre-school services for children with Down's syndrome in two Scottish regions.' *Child: Care, Health and Development 19,* 1–23.

Yerbury, M. (1997) 'Issues in multidisciplinary teamwork for children with disabilities.' *Child: Care, Health and Development 23,* 1, 77–86.

# CHAPTER 5

# Children's Experiences of School

*Linda Shaw*

## Disability as a social process

By defining disability as a social process rather than an individual defect, the disability movement has taken disability into the realms of everyday life, affecting everyone, regardless of whether they have an impairment, either physical, mental or emotional (Rieser and Mason 1990). This chapter is about children with and without impairments, and their experience of schools where they can learn together. It therefore concentrates on children's experiences of what have come to be known as 'inclusive' schools and is mainly based on interviews with pupils at 12 schools which I conducted for the Centre for Studies on Inclusive Education (CSIE) (Shaw 1994, 1997).

The first part of the chapter looks briefly at the current educational landscape in which children are growing up and some of the latest developments and research regarding their learning. The main part of the chapter then covers children's experience of school, including their views on arrangements for learning support and on how their schools respond to diverse needs for accessing the curriculum, accessing the physical environment, preventing communication difficulties, and nurturing emotional well-being. It also looks at the children's experience of what helps learning and what makes learning difficult, including comments on bullying, and children's views on friendship and special schools.

## Moving towards the mainstream

The 'social' model of disability began to be developed by disabled people during the late 1970s and is a relatively new approach. Many children are growing up today served by an education system which is still largely dominated by a 'medical' model which sees disability as an individual defect to be cured or managed, rather than as a barrier created by society to be prevented or tackled. The sections of the 1996 Education Act concerned with disability and education (formerly the 1993 Act and the 1981 Act) have at their heart a concept of special needs based on notions of normality and abnormality, rather than a process of school development, increasing accessibility, and the outlawing of discrimination. The Code of Practice on Special Educational Needs (DfE 1994), although containing helpful guidance for schools, cannot legally depart from the special needs framework.

The disability movement has done much pioneering work in introducing the social model of disability to schools, particularly in making the distinction between 'integration', mainly a locational matter, and 'inclusion', a process which recognises that

> 'impairment and disablement are a common experience of humanity, and should be a central issue in the planning and delivery of a human service such as education.' (Mason and Rieser 1994, p.1)

Yet the common experience for many children is still that disability sets individuals apart. This experience is perpetuated and reinforced for the 88,800 children in England still segregated in special schools for their education (Norwich 1997). Other children with impairment are isolated in specialist units in mainstream schools or by full-time attachment to mainstream welfare assistants who act as barriers rather than links. Nevertheless, inclusive practice is growing, as demonstrated by the children's and young people's accounts later in this chapter.

Over the last few years there has also been a gathering of national and international support for inclusive education evident in such influential documents as the UNESCO Salamanca Statement (United Nations 1994), the UN Convention on the Rights of the Child (United Nations 1989), and the UN Standard Rules on the Equalisation of Opportunities for Persons with Disabilities (United Nations 1993) (CSIE 1995).

A growing number of national bodies are backing inclusion, as illustrated by signatories to The Integration Charter (CSIE 1996) and by the statements of support compiled by The Alliance for Inclusive Education (1997). There is also an increasing body of research documenting that the more people are included, the greater their likely achievement and that the damage done to young people in traditional, segregated provisions is considerable (Baker, Wang and Walberg 1995; Carson 1992; Gartner and Lipsky 1987).

Most of the children's accounts of inclusive education practice to which this chapter now turns were drawn from many hours of discussions with children and young people with and without impairments, in groups and individually. The aim was to provide a platform for young people's views, trying to focus on the issues which they identified as important (Shaw 1994). Other accounts are based on interviews which were part of a detailed inquiry into inclusive practice, focusing on how support was delivered and received by individual pupils (Shaw 1997).

## Classroom support

Disabled children learning in the mainstream invariably have support in the form of aids and equipment, building adaptations and alterations, differentiated access to the curriculum and curriculum development, individual learning programmes, help from specialist teaching staff and from educational assistants.

A main point which emerged from the pupils' accounts was the matter-of-fact attitude they took to the provision of the various supports which made inclusion possible and how easily these supports fitted into everyday school life. What might on first impression seem to be sophisticated and complicated equipment, highly personal forms of support, or unusual approaches to learning, became part of routine school arrangements.

The following edited extracts are general descriptions by children and young people of the kind of help their schools provide.

'When the school found out I was going to have an operation they started arranging things for me. I had a supply person to help me. She would push the wheelchair around and help me down the stairs with the wheelchair. They had a lift type thing which they put my wheelchair on and it would take it up the stairs and down. They borrowed it. The school also let me come later into lessons. In one of the buildings they've got a ramp so I used that. Sometimes I used to have to disturb classes to go through but they didn't mind. Nobody suggested to me that I couldn't keep coming to the school.' (12-year-old pupil who was unable to walk temporarily after an operation and used a wheelchair for six months)

'I like doing maths, writing and playing [an instrument]. I write stories, and if I get a chance, I publish a poem in the publishing book. In my class, first of all it's got a blackboard, after the blackboard there's my teacher's desk, after the teacher's desk there is our desks, after our desks there is displays. There are black and white pictures and publishing books. I've got my own desk and there are other people on it. The other thing I want to say about my school is about the hall. First of all there is a door and when you go in that's where you sit when we have assemblies and when we have PE. We sing and tell people about books and there is displays and talking about displays. I haven't heard of disabilities but I have heard of special needs. There are children with special needs here and the teachers teach them nicely.' (10-year-old pupil who has Down's Syndrome)

'I've improved a lot since I've had my helper. She was my friend. She wasn't just my teacher. She helped me to understand life. I can take it now. I don't get in a huff and a puff when people call me names. I don't run out of the class and hide or something like that. I tell my teacher or I sort it out myself. She helped me to understood why I shouldn't be doing this or I should be doing that. She understands what I was going through so she knew how to stop it.' (Pupil with emotional and behavioural difficulties)

'If somebody sits by me it disturbs me and then I forget. I'm trying to learn and people start messing about and I get irritated and stop my work. I get mad and that's when I get told off. Since I have had a helper it's better. She says even if she is not there she is there helping me. It stops me doing things like wandering around the class and disturbing other people.' (Pupil with emotional and behavioural difficulties)

'I come to school in a taxi with a friend. Once I'm at school people help me around the place and in lessons I have a brailler. It's easy to carry around and it has a printer with it as well. I learn like anybody else.' (Pupil with visual impairment)

'If I can't see something my special needs assistant goes to the office and makes it bigger on the photocopier. She spends some time with me in the class and she also does jobs for the teacher. The mobility officer comes to school to see me. He's helping me to cross the road so that when I get a bit older I can come to school on my own. He gave me a cane as a symbol so when the cars see it they will stop and let me cross.' (Pupils with visual impairment)

'The social welfare lady helps me to go to the toilet. It's a good arrangement. Another lady comes to do a check up with my hearing aid and what batteries and stuff like that. I use a hearing link as well so I can hear the teacher.' (Pupil with kidney problems and hearing impairment)

'In mainstream lessons I have an interpreter using signs. I can't understand the English on the board. The reason deaf pupils sign to one another and don't use English is because it is our language. English and signing are very different. When you use English you use a sentence to describe what you have to say. With sign you can do it very clearly and very simply. For example when you are describing *Star Trek* and Mr Spock's ears you have to use three words in English – "Ears point upwards". In Sign you just do this [points fingers to stick upwards out of ears]. It is so simple and everyone knows what you are talking about.' (Pupil who is profoundly deaf speaking through a sign language interpreter.)

## Support teachers and educational assistants

Support teachers working in mainstream schools support disabled children in a variety of ways. They act as consultants to class teachers on how to extend teaching styles and adapt classroom organisation to cover a wider diversity of children. They co-teach alongside subject teachers to make lessons more accessible. They develop the curriculum to make it more easily understood, and they design and monitor individual programmes where necessary. They also work with individual pupils on specific learning tasks and advise educational assistants on ways of working.

Educational and general assistants also have a variety of roles (and often as many names) supporting disabled children in the mainstream. The most common roles include providing physical support to pupils to move around the school, helping to set up, use and maintain various types of specialist equipment, and providing personal care. Educational assistants support children when difficulties in learning occur by working with support teachers on implementation of individual learning programmes, achieving targets and offering strategies to make the curriculum accessible. They serve as facilitators to help pupils develop relationships and offer themselves as mature, adult friends to children with emotional difficulties. Training staff and pupils about disability equality issues and providing information about different impairments are further ways educational assistants help disabled children to participate in mainstream schools.

## Working with educational assistants

While children appreciate the contribution of specialist support teachers, particularly if the latter support them on an individual basis, it is educational assistants who feature most prominently in pupils' conversations about school placements.

Children have all sorts of views about how they like assistants to work with them and the level of support which they feel they need. Pupils' views can sometimes clash with adults' views. Two possible areas of tension are how to achieve appropriate levels of support for pupils without undermining their independence and how to ensure pupils do not harm themselves or others without becoming overbearing or imposing unnecessary supervision and monitoring. Children worry that their assistants might be too obtrusive and hinder their ability to make friends, and they also worry that they will not be able to participate with everybody else because their assistant is not available.

'Sometimes you don't like the supporter that you are working with and it brings trouble. That's why I don't really like having the supporter to work because other kids go "Look you've got a supporter. You can't work by yourself". So I really try to make the best out of myself and when I get any trouble I just come here to this room and you work in here for reading and spelling. But I'm none of that. I'm just trouble, that's all that I got.' (Pupil with emotional and behavioural difficulties)

'There is just a little thing I just want changed a little. My assistant, she keeps scampering off to other classes. I know it's part of her job but it's a bit annoying. It happens every single week. She's only with me Thursday afternoons and Fridays so that isn't very long is it?' (Pupil with cerebral palsy)

'Person must not want job for power. Person must be able to listen to child. Person must understand limits of safety. Person must be able to help friendships. Person must be strong and able to lift. Person must not get ill regularly. Person must listen to my Mummy.' (Job description for an assistant by pupil who has brittle bones)

## Learning problems and solutions

Bullying was identified by many children as a main factor making school life difficult. They pointed out that impairment was only one attribute which could become a focus for bullying. Children might also get bullied because of skin colour, background or personality-type and it happened in special schools as well as in mainstream. Children might get 'picked on because they are not well off', particularly in relation to their clothing.

'His problems are that his parents are not as well off as some other children and because he hasn't got brand names on his trainers. Maybe the children think he can't afford it and he's a tramp and there's something wrong about not being as well off as other people. They'll pick on him because he's trying to act like they are and he can be doing the exact same but they will pick on him.'

'You have to be strong because there is a lot of bullies in this school – and I have been bullied at one point. The one thing you don't have to beware of is there are a lot of people who haven't got any friends and they'd like to be your friend.'

'They would say I was a baby and I was in a pram and things because I was in a wheelchair. I told them to shut up and I told the teacher and they stopped it. They were not used to seeing people in wheelchairs in the school and they didn't really think about what they were saying.'

These pupils saw the presence of children with physical impairment or learning difficulties as a civilising influence and a way of preventing bullying because people 'get used to having them around the school'. Children who had moved into mainstream from special school said it was upsetting to be 'called names' but that didn't make them want to go back to special school. They coped with name-calling by walking away or telling the teacher.

Other problems with learning, according to the children, were schools which preferred children who could do well, lessons which moved along too quickly and lessons which were repetitive.

'The kids that are brainy and can keep up, the teachers carry on at their pace and anyone who – say they are ill or they haven't been at school for a long time – just loses track and they can't get back on. I just couldn't keep up with the amount of work they wanted. The school is supposed to cater for everybody but it doesn't. They tend to aim for the kids that can do well and they just keep them going and the kids that can't they don't give them any encouragement at all.'

'I was doing better then it ended. I had learned everything you really could. It's like a computer game. You learn it and then once you can complete it you get bored with it. I just kept doing the work over and over again. They kept putting me back and back.'

Pupils complained about residential schools which 'closed children out of the real world'. Nor were they happy with special needs units in mainstream schools because children had to ask permission to attend which drew attention to their special needs. At the same time, going to a unit made children miss favourite lessons:

'They take you out of the lessons and bring you to a different unit called the special needs unit. It's a bit annoying because sometimes they take you out of your favourite lessons. A lot of people, if they don't like the lessons, they don't want to work. I don't think it's fair taking you out of your favourite lessons and not doing the good work.'

Interesting lessons, a relaxed atmosphere, friendly and encouraging teachers and strict policies on bullying all helped make learning easier, according to the children and young people:

'You need teachers that will keep you going and cheer you on. You need people to tell you that the people [who are picking on you] are wrong and that there is nothing wrong with you, otherwise you start believing it and get upset. There might be a few teachers that aren't as good as the others but there's always one good teacher in the school or one good friend.'

'I think I'm learning a lot here. It's better here because you get more time to complete assignments and it's a more relaxed atmosphere.'

'At this school the teachers are more considerate and show more attention to you. They don't just do something and help you but they let you know they are helping you. You do more activities. You learn more interesting things. You don't do the same things over again. You can have a laugh with the teachers. You can speak to the teachers, have a joke in the lesson and then start work. It's not too strict and it's strict on bullying.'

## Separation and friendship

The strongest comments about placement in special schools came from able-bodied pupils who widely condemned it as an injustice and denial of opportunities:

'It's like cruelty. Like for example say my best friend was here and we were separated then that would be cruelty to the people.'

'I don't think we should keep special schools because we should keep everybody together. When you know the difficulties a disabled person has they can learn from other people and do the same with them.'

'I think it's wrong. If you said that, you are just pushing him out and not helping him to deal with his problems and to learn.'

Pupils also found it difficult to understand the benefits of separate, specialist education, saying they could see no reason for special schools because what children needed was already in mainstream or could be provided there.

Many of the disabled young people and children who were interviewed had moved from special placements to mainstream with classmates, some had moved on their own and others had always been educated in mainstream schools. In general, their response was to remain neutral about comparisons between mainstream and special school placements and to stress that it was important to be with friends and with people who understood disability and the implications of different impairments. Some children expressed feelings of isolation in the mainstream and regretted that other disabled children were not there. None of the disabled children said they wanted to return to special schools or move from mainstream.

Discussing friendship, children spoke of how they 'think differently now' after getting to know children with learning difficulties. They described how at first they had felt silly talking to disabled classmates, had been frightened to touch them or had felt sorry for them. Later they realised they had much in common:

'I used to think I'm not going near him because there is something wrong with him, but now I know he's a good friend. He hangs around with us and messes about like all the others. He's just like all the others, he's just got learning difficulties.'

'I felt right sorry for him and I was helping him and then I thought he's got to learn something and I didn't help him as much. He's getting used to it now. He's getting better.'

'When he came to school no one liked him that much. He kept being lonely but we learned to be friends with him and try and give him a chance. He's got one kidney, or one liver – something like that – but inside he's quite good.'

'I help him, give him spellings, ask friends if he can play football with us, I just know it's not his fault about why he smells. I know that nothing will happen to me if I touch him.'

Pupils were fiercely loyal in response to any suggestion that disabled classmates should return to special schools:

'It's good having them here because we can learn more having them with us.'

'If they are going back I'm going with them, and I think everybody in school would be behind me as well. If they're going, we're going. Without them it wouldn't be right. It never would be right because we are used to having them around.'

'They're doing all right here. There's no point sending them back to special school because they have got friends here.'

'I think that would be wrong because they will be much better off in a proper school like our school because people are around them to help them.'

## Conclusion

The pupils' comments about inclusive education on which this chapter is based show that the experience of growing up with disability has changed for them in profound ways. Pupils with and without impairments who would have been separated in the past are now growing up together, equal and different. Friendships and acquaintances which would have been denied are flourishing. Impairment is becoming an integral part of the diverse mosaic of needs, difficulties, abilities, influences and understandings of all kinds which make schools richer, more challenging and more humane places.

The children's experience suggests that, in order for such relationships to flourish on a wider scale, schools need to work towards inclusion by restructuring to accommodate different ways of learning and to value and respect different types of accomplishments.

The pressing human rights considerations involved in bringing children together call for greater priority to be given to making the necessary changes and developments in the mainstream. As well as upholding civil rights, putting learning support at the heart of school development and aiming to tackle the full range of needs in ordinary settings has been shown to improve the learning environment for everybody. As one pupil put it: 'They can learn from us and we can learn from them. Our education isn't lowered when disabled people are here: we are getting more of it.'

Planning for inclusive education based on a social model of disability involves accepting impairment and learning difficulty as part of the everyday experience of ordinary schools. Appropriate arrangements and equipment to support impairment and difficulty need to be seen as central and extensive, rather than intensive and exceptional additions for 'special' pupils.

Greater role flexibility for all staff, including support teachers and educational assistants, as well as improved cooperation and teamwork appear to be vital for inclusive practice. Staff selection, training and supervisory arrangements need to reflect this. Educational assistants especially need to be trained to understand children's sometimes ambiguous feelings about supporters who have the potential to hinder as well as help, by providing too much or too little support. Getting the right balance to ensure adult interventions are truly enabling seems to require a high level of awareness and sensitivity as well as continuing negotiation with children on an individual basis.

## References

Alliance for Inclusive Education (1997) *Campaign Pack*. London: Alliance for Inclusive Education.

Baker, E., Wang, C. and Walberg, H. (1995) *The Effects of Inclusion on Learning*. Philadelphia: Centre for Research in Human Development and Education.

Carson, S. (1992) 'Normalisation needs and schools.' *Educational Psychology in Practice 7*, 4, 216–222.

CSIE (1995) *International Perspectives on Inclusion, Four Summaries of International Documents*. Bristol: Centre for Studies on Inclusive Education.

CSIE (1996) *The Integration Charter*. Bristol: Centre for Studies on Inclusive Education.

Department for Education (1994) *The Code of Practice on the Identification and Assessment of Special Educational Needs*. London: Department for Education.

Education Act (1996). London: HMSO.

Gartner, A. and Lipsky, D. (1987) 'Beyond special education, towards a quality system for all students.' *Harvard Educational Review 57,* 4, 367–395.

Mason, M. and Rieser, R. (1994) *Altogether Better.* London: Charity Projects.

Norwich, B. (1997) *A Trend Towards Inclusion: Analysis of English LEA Statistics for Special School Placements 1992–1996.* Bristol: Centre for Studies on Inclusive Education.

Rieser, R. and Mason, M. (1990) *Disability Equality in the Classroom: A Human Rights Issue.* London: ILEA.

Shaw, L. (1994) *Talking Inclusion.* Bristol: Centre for Studies on Inclusive Education.

Shaw, L. (1997) *Inclusion in Action.* Bristol: Centre for Studies on Inclusive Education.

United Nations (1989) *The Convention on the Rights of the Child.* Geneva: United Nations Children Fund.

United Nations (1993) *The Standard Rules on the Equalisation of Opportunities for Persons with Disabilities.* New York: United Nations.

United Nations (1994) *The Salamanca Statement and Framework for Action on Special Educational Needs.* Paris: United Nations Educational, Scientific and Cultural Organisation.

# CHAPTER 6

# Parents and Family

## Disabled Women's Stories about their Childhood Experiences

*Carol Thomas*

### Introduction

As adults we tell stories about our childhood to others and to ourselves. We do this, in part, to make sense of where and who we are now. Narratives about our childhood – about parents, home, family, school days, friends and neighbourhoods – help us to give meaning and structure to our lives. This is, perhaps, particularly true for those of us who grew up with the knowledge that we were 'different' because our bodies were 'not right' and that this difference mattered in ways which went far beyond not being able to walk, to see, to hear, to talk or whatever. Difference in this second sense refers to the social reactions to impairment which, with the emergence of the disabled people's movement and the development of the social model of disability, can now be understood as manifestations of disablism, social exclusion and oppression (Morris 1989, 1991, 1996; Oliver 1990, 1996; Swain *et al.* 1993; Zola 1982a, 1982b).

This chapter considers some of the stories disabled women have told about their experiences of living with impairment and disability as children (all names have been changed to protect identities). It focuses on family experiences, especially on relationships with parents. I draw on a subset of data collected as part of an ongoing programme of research on women and disability which involved personal communication with 68 disabled women in 1996 and early 1997 (see Thomas 1997; Thomas and Curtis 1997). These women shared their experiences of living with disability with me through the media of letters and self-made tapes or in interviews, after finding out about my research through a press release I sent to disability organisations. My method of 'data collection' is outlined below, but what resulted is a body of material which offers a wealth of personal narratives about disabled lives. Of the 68 women who entered into communication with me, 34 had been impaired since birth or had acquired an impairment, or multiple impairments, before the age of 16, and many of these women included recollections of growing up with disability in their accounts. It is this subset of personal experience narratives which I draw on here.

In keeping with the original Union of the Physically Impaired Against Segregation (UPIAS) 1976 statements informing a social model approach to disability (cited in Oliver 1996, p.22), I make a clear distinction between impairment (relating to the body) and disability (relating to the social): *impairment* is defined as lacking part or all of a limb, or having a defective limb, organ or mechanism of the body, and *disability* is defined as the disadvantage or restriction of activity caused by a contemporary social organisation which takes no or little account of people who have physical or sensory impairments and thus excludes them from participation in the mainstream of social activities.

The construction of a new story out of those belonging to many others is inevitably informed by the narrative I would tell of my own experiences. I was born without a left hand, an impairment which I began to conceal at some point in my childhood (probably around 9 or 10 years of age). This childhood concealment strategy has had a long legacy: I still struggle with the 'reveal or not to reveal' dilemma, and more often than not will hide my 'hand'. Like some other women in the study, I learned the advantages of 'hiding' my impairment at a young age. As Goffman put it, the rewards of 'passing' are so great that most people who can pass will do so (Goffman 1963), or so it was. However, as the narratives testify, concealment carried and continues to carry considerable psychological costs and has real social consequences. In this and other ways childhood experiences cast long shadows forward.

## Growing up narratives

My press release did not explicitly invite accounts of childhood experiences, not least because it was addressing disabled women in general and not just those who had experience of living with impairment and disability as children. However, in telling their stories many of the women did refer to their childhoods, and in some of the interviews it seemed 'natural' to 'start at the beginning'. In their narratives, some dwelt on their childhoods whilst others merely noted events or features of their earlier years in passing. This suggests that childhood experiences are of varying significance and meaning for disabled adults, as for everyone. One could embark on a long discussion about the psychodynamic and epistemological status of these narratives. Why are some events in childhood remembered and/or selected whilst others are not? What is 'fact' and what is 'fantasy'? What is the nature of the knowledge embodied in these narratives? What is the status of 'memories' as sources of information about life events? It would be inappropriate to move into a detailed discussion of these questions here but a few points need to be made. The women's narratives cannot give us direct access to their life experiences as disabled children – they are not exact records of what happened. Rather, narratives are *representations* of past events and how they were experienced and constructed at the time. They inevitably involve interpretation and selection in their construction (the 'telling'), in their consumption (my 'reading'), and in their reproduction (my 're-presentation') (Riessman 1993). In using narratives, reality is always represented partially, selectively and imperfectly (Riessman, p.15). However, reality is being represented, and the insights we can gain from first-person accounts of growing up with disability are of great value. We have access to 'truths' about living as children with disability as constructed by active subjects and this draws our attention to those childhood experiences which have lasting meaning and effect. This can be an important guide to policy and practice in the disability field.

One of the striking features of the narratives is the way in which living with impairment and disability is gendered. Disability was woven into lives that were very conventional in terms of gender roles, or is written or talked about with reference to the norms of other women's lives. In their experiences both as girls and women, gender and disability have been inseparably connected. Growing up with disability meant growing up as a girl with disability.

After a brief review of my data collection methods, I turn to some of the themes and issues relating to parents and family which emerged in the women's childhood narratives.

## The data

Disabled women volunteered to tell me about aspects of their lives in response to a press release I sent out in January 1996 to over 150 disability organisations (mainly national ones) listed in the Disability Rights Handbook 1995/6. The press release told women that I was undertaking research for a book on women and disability, that I was a disabled woman myself, that I was looking for some first-hand accounts of living with disability so that 'women's voices' could be represented in my work. It listed 15 areas of social and personal life; however, 'childhood experiences' was not listed as a distinct category and no explicit reference was made to 'growing up with disability'. The items on the press release listing did not play a prescriptive but a facilitating role, and I am certain that by naming areas such as 'sex, sexuality, sexual relationships' and 'abuse – physical, emotional, sexual' the women were 'given permission' to communicate about very private or painful personal experiences that they may otherwise have kept to themselves.

Women were invited to write to me, to send a self-recorded tape, or to communicate in some other way. In all, I received written material from 49 women, self-made tapes from five more, and conducted 14 interviews.

In a statistical sense, the 'sample' of participating women is not representative of disabled women in our society. However, ages were fairly even distributed through the 20s, 30s, 40s and 50s, with a few in the 60s and 70s. There was also a very wide range of physical and sensory impairments represented (my research does not extend to learning disability). Among the 34 women who had grown up with disability, impairments were very variable and were associated with the following conditions: cerebral palsy, spina bifida, polio, asthma, chronic eczema, Still's disease, multiple extostosis, Rieger's syndrome, Friedreich's ataxia, a rare hyper-mobility syndrome and autism. Visual and hearing impairments were also represented. The variable geographical location of the total sample of women was pleasing, as was their differential socio-economic, educational and familial experiences. Sexual orientations were varied and personal circumstances differed enormously. However, it is important to note that none of the women who communicated with me by letter or tape told me that they were black or from a minority ethnic group (and those that I met were white), so the 'sample' might be exclusively white. I may have failed to reach and engage such women and the absence of their stories is a major omission (the press release was purposively sent to 'black' disability organisations). Nevertheless, despite its shortcomings, the sample of women who entered into dialogue with me constitutes a hugely variable yet at the same time 'ordinary' cross-section of disabled women.

## Parents and family

Parental figures loomed large in many of the women's childhood stories. This was particularly the case when a parent was seen, perhaps only in retrospect, to have been at fault in some way or was viewed with considerable ambivalence. For some, writing or talking about one or both parents was something they wanted to do despite its emotional toll – it re-opened wounds and meant revisiting painful territory. For others, a mother, father, or both were viewed as sources of support, caring, love and self-sacrifice. In fact, whilst family relationships are inevitably complex and multi-faceted, parents tended to be represented as figures of authority who were either allies in a difficult and sometimes hostile world, or as people who had to be resisted, often at great personal cost. This is well illustrated in the contrasting experiences of Sally and Nicole on the one hand, and Fiona and Janette on the other.

'My mum and my dad have been brilliant and have always fought for me against all odds. They never felt that they had to protect me. They said that they found it very hard when I went to University but that they had to let me go. My disability has never been a 'tragedy', 'embarrassment' or 'nuisance' to them ...They always had faith in me and say that they've never once felt restricted by my disability. I have never found it hard to talk about my disability to my family. However, my mum is the person I talk to most. She completely understands and always listens...Without their attitude and constant belief in me I wouldn't have come as far as I have.' (Sally, with cerebral palsy)

'Born with cerebral palsy, I am severely disabled. I was fortunate to have parents who brought me up absolutely as normal, encouraging me to think for myself and giving me opportunities to experience life to the full. Apart from six years at boarding school I lived at home nearly 36 years. During this time, I used to go into homes for people with disabilities to give my parents breaks from caring for me. I didn't enjoy the times in these homes, as they were run on institutional lines...After one of these breaks I came back to my family home depressed. The reason for this was I thought I had glimpsed the inevitable life I would lead in a home when my parents could no longer look after me. This didn't enthral me, and I used to beg my parents to allow me to enter a home just to get the dreaded business over with. However, my parents didn't listen to my pleas, and I am mighty glad, as the future has turned out very different from the one I imagined.' (Nicole, with cerebral palsy involving non-verbal communication)

'Parents: This has not been easy. My father always blamed my mother for my disability and I imagine that it must have been tough for him to have a disabled girl as his first born instead of a healthy boy. After my paralysis at the age of 13 my father never touched me again, not even to help me cross the road. I still don't feel that he is as proud of me as he should be – or maybe he just can't bring himself to admit it. I know that he is very scared by me and what I represent and possibly what I have the potential to do. He finds it much easier to relate to my able bodied sisters and is quite happy to hug them...I had major problems with my mother, partly because she has been a toxic parent to all four daughters, I just got more of it than they did. She always pushed me to be better than everyone else – I couldn't just be average, I had to be superhuman. The problems really began after my hospitalisation. She denied that things were as serious as they were and insisted that the doctors and physiotherapists were all wrong and that I would walk again – there were many stand-up rows at the end of my bed between her and the medical profession. It was made quite clear to me that I was not wanted at home until I could walk again (the underlying feeling being that as a wheelchair user I was no longer acceptable).

I did learn to sort of walk again. However as I was still housebound and too young to drive I ended up trapped at home with her for long periods of time. Thus I became her unwilling confidante. She continually denied what was physically wrong with me and also claimed that my hospitalisation had had no psychological effect on me – she was the only one who had really suffered during that time. After several years my parents' marriage broke down and again I had to support her. I ended up feeling that as I was the failed daughter, I was only good for looking after her. Also my own depression and problems were always denied and ignored. In addition to this, any disagreement with my mother's point of view always led to her threatening to kill herself or dumping us on the street or in a home. I was so scared of having to live on the streets (which would physically kill me) that I never dared contradict anything. My sisters did fight back a bit because these threats were less scary to them – they could have got jobs in bars etc. to support themselves. I now have no contact with my mother because of her continual denial of my condition – I have problems coping with my deterioration, I don't need someone else implying that it is just my laziness causing it. She also still tells people about how tough it was for her to bring up a crippled child – she fails to mention that this crippled child had a good degree, good job and her own car and house. I think that Mum thought that as I was disabled I would never leave home and would thus always be there to support her – it was quite a shock when she (and I) discovered that I could live an independent life.' (Fiona, with spina bifida)

'I was five when I contracted polio and the disability in those days was seen in a very different light from how it is seen today. Both my parents were devastated when I contracted polio and the disability it left. They realised the effect it would leave on my life and from the very beginning they pursued a protective environment for me. Although they meant well and worked to see I had a good quality of life and a good education, they actually thought I would not be able to choose and follow a 'normal' lifestyle. They thought I would not be able to have normal relationships with the opposite sex and never encouraged me to get involved with men friends. They thought a career was the best way forward and actively encouraged this, by sending me to private school and making sure I would be trained in the ultimate career – teaching. This career would give me a regular income and pension at the end of my life. Unfortunately, I was never allowed to forget this and had to pay for their sacrifice in lots of ways. My parents educated me and gave me what they thought was essential to make me happy. My father died and this had a devastating effect on my mother, from then on she demanded my company. She did not want me to break away from her and have a life of my own, she had very powerful ways of making me feel guilty and at times feelings of inadequacy. This was really an act to suit her own needs and she saw me as a servant and to be at her beck and call at all times. It was interesting to see my mother go into 'keep your hands off my daughter' drive. She would manipulate everyone into thinking how dependent I was on her because of my disability and put them off by telling them of past tales of my struggle with my disability. Always after a meeting like this my relationships would change, especially with those who were unsure about disabilities.' (Jeanette, with polio)

These extracts testify to the profound and continuing impact for good or ill that parents, particularly mothers, have on disabled peoples' lives. Sally and Nicole use words and phrases like 'fought for me', 'faith in me', 'completely understands', 'listens', 'encouraging me', 'giving me opportunities'. Fiona and Janette talk of 'blame', 'guilt', 'scared by me', 'denial', 'not wanted at home', 'failed daughter', 'crippled child', 'devastated', 'never encouraged', 'never allowed' and 'manipulate'.

How different are these childhood experiences and how important for these women's psychological well-being and life trajectories.

Parents are certainly a primary conduit for messages about the social meaning of one's difference, and thus play a crucial role in the formation of our self-identity. They can buffer and challenge or reinforce the stigmatising cultural meanings attached to most impairments in our society with very variable consequences: feelings of confidence, self-acceptance, shame or self-hatred. This has great significance for our behaviours and well-being as children and adults. Like Fiona, Sarah (now in her fifties) talked about her long and ongoing struggle to accept her body and to value herself. She rooted her difficulties with self-acceptance in her early years at home:

> 'I guess I received many of the messages common to a girl brought up between the mid-1940s to early 1960s about what a young woman should look like and be like. I had two aunts who had been to university, however, and great store was put on my academic ability. It was viewed, at least in part, as a blessing that would to some degree compensate for my lack of physical desirability (as perceived I think – though it was rarely overtly expressed – by my family). At least this was a message I picked up quite strongly from my total environment.' (Sarah, polio at one year of age)

The narratives suggest that being treated as 'normal' within a family can either be empowering or disempowering. There is, perhaps, a fine line between too much or too little emphasis on 'being normal'. If normality is stressed to such an extent that a child's experiences of impairment and disability are not acknowledged or discussed, the consequences may be damaging. In Jane's family, for example, 'being normal' was taken to an extreme. She talked in an interview about life in a very competitive family, growing up alongside a non-disabled brother who was 'good at everything'. Her pronounced limp and narrowed right leg (the effects of polio) were not spoken about. She pretended her impairment did not exist and strove to live up to her parents' expectations to succeed like her brother. By the age of 17, she had some serious psychological problems: she could not accept her appearance, felt very insecure, judged herself a failure and contemplated suicide. Her family's inability to acknowledge and engage with her physical difference and the wider disablist social reaction to this did not facilitate her acceptance of self.

There were echoes of these experiences in many of the women's narratives. This suggests that whilst parents and the wider family grouping can provide emotional security, promote a sense of self-worth, assist in opening up opportunities, and encourage social inclusion rather than exclusion, they can also do the opposite. Relationships with parents may be problematic without the presence of impairment and disability, but these add new twists and can become a vehicle for the expression of emotional abuse and the erection of barriers. The narratives also suggest that the form this takes is highly gendered – for example, the expectation that a disabled daughter will not attract a male partner, marry or have children. Learning to resist a stifling, controlling or abusive parent who aids and abets social exclusion is, thankfully, not something that features in my own story, which resembles Sally's.

Some of the women reflected on how difficult they thought things were for their parents, and these accounts give us insight into the stresses and strains that a child's impairment and disability bring into families in a disabling society. They referred to the guilt they thought their parents carried for bringing an impaired child into the world, for having a child with a chronic illness, or for agreeing to medical procedures that caused or exacerbated impairments. It was stated a number of times that parents had no previous experience of disability and often found it difficult 'to cope'. Even in very supportive home environments, some women had been aware as children that their impairment and disability was a cause of friction or difficulty in the household:

> 'My dad's very angry about the whole thing and a lot of the time I feel the anger is directed towards me, but it isn't. It's more the situation – that he can't help but be reminded about it every time he sees me 'cos I'm in a wheelchair, and my dad gets angry knowing that it all could have been avoided and it all shouldn't have happened...so that caused an awful lot of friction at home during, you know, during all that time and I think my mum felt stuck in the middle...It was her that took me along to the consultant to begin with...I think it's ridiculous that she does feel guilty – I don't for one minute blame her...We're quite a close family and don't tend to argue at all but the only times that we do argue is to do with my health...' (Eve, now in her early 20s, a wheelchair user with chronic pain resulting from negligent 'corrective surgery' on her feet at age 11)

There are stories of parents moving house and changing jobs in connection with their child's disability, of parents endlessly seeking cures or treatments from orthodox medicine and complementary therapies, and of parents who 'fought' representatives of 'the system' on their child's behalf – teachers, doctors, social workers and others.

The theme of parents 'fighting the system' is present in a number of narratives, relating to the construction of parents as 'allies fighting on my behalf' or as people who made the struggle more difficult. Schooling was often the focus. A number of the women who went to mainstream schools talked with a strong sense of gratitude about their parents' 'fight' against 'experts' who recommended special education. The educational experience of the women was very variable: five talked about attendance at special schools (some residential, others as day pupils), nineteen went to mainstream schools, and three had both special and mainstream schooling. Two women with visual impairment had no regrets about their attendance at special schools. Those who went to mainstream schools had usually experienced some taunting or bullying by peers, and unsympathetic treatment by some teachers.

There are other themes in the narratives which space prevents me from exploring here. One is the inclusion or exclusion of disabled children from decision making about their lives – for example, the kinds of independent living aids to use, the type of schooling, medical treatments, the use of services and other matters. Older women, in particular, spoke of being brought up at a time when the opinion of children was not sought and things were often done without explanation. Children were kept in ignorance – they never understood *why* they were in hospital, what medical treatments were going to be performed, what was 'wrong' with them, why they were being sent away to school, what might happen to them. Some had spent long periods in hospital in the days when parents were kept out of the wards except for brief visits. These experiences had left some women with lasting fears (for example, of separation) and a strong sense of insecurity. Another important issue is that of physical and sexual abuse within families – talked about by two women.

Finally, in both Fiona's and Janette's accounts we can observe the theme of 'dependency reversal' – their non-disabled mothers relied, in these cases in an abusive fashion, on their young daughters for emotional and practical support, and made it difficult for them to establish independent lives. This theme finds milder echoes in some other women's narratives. Jenny Morris (1995) has written about the damaging cultural mythology that presents disabled people as 'dependent', as 'the cared for', and there is certainly evidence in the women's childhood stories that relationships with other family members were either ones of a healthy reciprocity and interdependence, or of a problematic dependence of a parent on a disabled child.

## Conclusion

Disability is fundamentally about social exclusion. In this chapter, disabled women's narratives have been treated as rich sources of information about growing up with disability, focusing on parents and family experiences. As well as being 'buffers' against disablism, parents can be part of the problem. To put it very sharply, they can act as agents of social exclusion on a number of practical and emotional levels. This has important policy and practice implications for social workers and other professionals working with disabled children and their families. It reinforces the need for a 'whole family' orientation – working with the parent(s) as well as the child – and the need for a social model perspective so that both parents and children are helped to understand that disability is not an individual 'tragedy' that has to be lived with in isolation but a product of social inequity and cultural prejudice. It also highlights the need to understand the ways in which gender and disability intermesh (along with issues of class and ethnicity, not discussed here). If parents can be won over to a social model perspective, then this may help their disabled children to be given the best possible start.

## References

Goffman, E. (1963) *Stigma: Notes on the Management of a Spoiled Identity.* London: Penguin.

Morris, J. (1989) *Able Lives: Women's Experience of Paralysis.* London: The Women's Press.

Morris, J. (1991) *Pride Against Prejudice.* London: The Women's Press.

Morris, J. (1995) 'Creating a space for absent voices: Disabled women's experience of receiving assistance with daily living activities.' *Feminist Review 51,* (Autumn), 63–93.

Morris, J. (ed.) (1996) *Encounter with Strangers: Feminism and Disability.* London: The Women's Press.

Oliver, M. (1990) *The Politics of Disablement.* Basingstoke: Macmillan and St Martin's Press.

Oliver, M. (1996) *Understanding Disability: From Theory to Practice.* London: Macmillan.

Riessman, C.K. (1993) *Narrative Analysis.* London: Sage.

Swain, J., Finklestein, V., French, S. and Oliver, M. (eds) (1993) *Disabling Barriers, Enabling Environments.* London: Sage.

Thomas, C. (1997) 'The baby and the bathwater: disabled women and motherhood in social context.' *Sociology of Health and Illness 19,* 5, 622–643

Thomas, C. and Curtis, P. (1997) 'Having a baby: some disabled women's reproductive experiences.' *Midwifery 13,* 202–209.

Zola, I.K. (ed.) (1982a) *Ordinary Lives: Voices of Disability and Disease.* Cambridge/Watertown: Apple-wood Books.

Zola, I.K. (1982b) *Missing Pieces: A Chronicle of Living with a Disability.* Philadelphia: Temple University Press.

# CHAPTER 7

# Leisure and Friendship

*Judith Cavet*

## Introduction: the significance of leisure

Although leisure is a major industry and an important feature of everyday life, there is no consensus about its definition. Leisure is sometimes thought of as having connotations of self-improvement, constructive occupation and therapy. On the other hand, there is evidence that many of the leisure activities which people regularly indulge in are illegal (Dorn and South 1989). The general definition which is adopted here is that of free-time activity which is chosen in order to provide enjoyment. This encompasses four elements which are often included in discussions about what constitutes leisure: a notion of non-obligated time (Roberts 1970), activity or interest, choice and relaxation or pleasure.

The focus for this chapter is social leisure for children and young people from junior school age to early adulthood. As this transition to maturity is accomplished, the nature of leisure changes, with implications for those involved directly and indirectly. During this period there is a shift from 'organised leisure' to 'casual leisure' and thence to 'commercialised leisure' (Hendry *et al.* 1993). Organised leisure consists of clubs and activities developed and run by adults for children and young people. Participation in these organisations begins to reduce by the age of about 13, a phase perhaps typified (or possibly stereotyped) as boys hanging about in groups outside and girls' development of what has been called 'the culture of the bedroom' (Frith 1978). Eventually these meeting places are deserted by teenagers in favour of commercially provided centres, such as pubs, clubs and cinemas.

Leisure, like play, its precursor, offers opportunities for different types of learning and development, so that participation in each of these phases is important. As Hendry *et al.* (1993) argue:

'Leisure in its widest sense can be significant in creating opportunities for self-agency, identity development and the development of social competence. Forms of self-presentation and social styles can be tried out without too many dire consequences should they fail to impress.' (p.39)

In addition, inclusion in each phase offers social encounters and the chance to make friends. The need for disabled children and young people to take part in leisure activities is therefore irrefutable. Leisure participation can act as a means of empowerment by the reduction of isolation, the promotion of a positive self-image and the development of community contacts.

## Structural constraints to full participation

There is substantial evidence that disabled young people have more limited opportunities for leisure activities outside their own homes than non-disabled people of the same age. Hirst and Baldwin (1994), in a study of 400 disabled young people (aged 13–22), found they were significantly less likely than a non-disabled comparison group to go to discos and cinemas or to watch or take part in sports, games and physical activities. The more severely impaired young people's participation was the most adversely affected, although there was evidence of home- and family-based activities. Overall, opportunities for participation in social activities were lower than for their peers, and this tendency became more marked with age. These findings are to a great extent echoed in a further study of 79 young people with learning disabilities (aged 14–22) whose leisure and social life was also constrained, especially for the young women (Flynn and Hirst 1992). The samples for both studies were drawn from the surveys carried out by the Office of Population and Census Surveys in Great Britain in 1985 and 1986. The studies employed interviews with the young people themselves, as well as with proxies.

These findings are congruent with research into parents' experiences. These also indicate the pervasive nature of the lack of leisure opportunities. For example, parents of adults with profound and multiple disability saw leisure as an area requiring further attention (Hogg and Lambe 1988). More recently a study of the experience of Scottish families of children with a visual impairment indicated a similar deficit. The Royal National Institute for the Blind (RNIB) and LOOK (The Scottish Foundation of Families with Visually Impaired Children) reported that 68 per cent of respondents felt there were not enough leisure opportunities available to their disabled children (LOOK and RNIB 1996). This experience of relative disadvantage as regards leisure opportunities is, of course, one aspect of more general disadvantage which affects disabled people of all ages in many areas of their lives. These origins are perhaps summarised most succintly by the journal article which begins 'What price theory if you cannot afford the bus fare?' (Brown 1994). The combined effects of the relative poverty of disabled people and their families, plus extra costs associated with disability, make leisure participation on an equal basis unlikely.

The significance of transport as an important consideration in social events is so well established that one hesitates to reiterate it, but there are few signs of major improvements in public transport. For example, bus companies in London will buy 500 new vehicles this year, but none will be wheelchair accessible (BOADICEA 1997). The autonomy of some young people is improved by the legal provision which permits a teenager receiving the higher rate of the mobility component of Disability Living Allowance to obtain a provisional driving licence at 16. However, many young disabled people will be dependent for transport on parental help or specialist services, both with inherent limitations. An unsuitable physical environment (for example, lack of vibrating signals for deaf-blind people at pedestrian crossings, or cramped shopping aisles) limits leisure activities for disabled people and reduces the opportunities of disabled young people to go out autonomously.

Public attitudes add an extra dimension to leisure outings and encounters. Some groups of disabled people have benefited from improved awareness, manifestations of this being theatre and opera performances interpreted into British Sign Language or tactile exhibitions in museums. However, lack of acceptance for people with learning difficulties is sufficiently strong for authors to recommend support and training for staff encountering it (McLean 1990) and discussion with service users about how to deal with such behaviour (Brown 1994). The implementation of the Disability Discrimination Act 1995 may improve matters, since entertainment and recreational facilities are specifically included within its remit. However, it is recognised as being a fairly toothless piece of legislation and its impact so far is very limited. Service providers are not yet required to make reasonable adjustments or change their practices to improve accessibility to disabled people (Letts 1997). Policy does not have to be changed if an additional service is required by a disabled person (e.g. lifting). Hence it was within the law for a wheelchair user to be turned away from rides at Blackpool Pleasure Beach because staff were too busy to lift him on and off rides (*Disability Now* 1997). This lack of civil rights for disabled people means they are left dependent on the goodwill and availability of others.

The structural barriers indicated above affect disabled people of all ages. However, it is likely that they have a particular impact on disabled adolescents, since adolescence has been described as the peak time of leisure need (Hendry *et al.* 1993). Later in the life span, home making and family commitments take up much time. By contrast, adolescents generally have considerable amounts of free time, but are restricted in their leisure access as compared with adults. This is because of lack of spending power and transport, plus restrictions as to permitted activities imposed by the law and by parents. Despite the emphasis in definitions of leisure on choice, freedom and preference, leisure options to all young people are heavily constrained. However, additional factors compound the limitations on disabled young people. One further major barrier to active leisure participation which requires recognition is that of unemployment. It is well established that unemployed people participate in fewer leisure activities outside the home than do those in employment (Glyptis 1989). Indeed, unemployment throws the whole concept of leisure into some confusion since definitions of leisure have often seen it as the converse of work. When all one's time is free, the value of so-called leisure may be lost, so that lethargy and depression set in. Again, unemployment is a risk which all young people face, but which affects disabled young people to a greater degree than their non-disabled peers (Thornton and Lunt 1995).

## Promoting choice and overcoming barriers

While full leisure participation by disabled people, including children and young people, is partly conditional on the dismantling of the barriers outlined above, individual participation can be promoted by many means. One of these is knowledge of welfare rights and other legal entitlements. The Chronically Sick and Disabled Persons Act 1970 makes provision for disabled people to take a holiday, although many are not receiving one (Mental Health Foundation 1996). The same law contains provision regarding recreational facilities. There are other avenues to the funding of holidays (see for example Mencap 1997): one possible source is the Family Fund Trust which offers means-tested assistance to families with a severely disabled child under 16 years. Information about accessibility of sports centres, arts centres and other leisure provision is also available (Cavet 1995a).

It is important to note that, despite the constraints, many successes have been reported, including greater participation by severely disabled children and young adults. This is true both regarding everyday activities (e.g. Leonard (1991), who writes about social opportunities in residental care) and with reference to more spectacular and adventurous ones (e.g. Rose and Massey (1993), who write of Alpine mountaineering).

A major recent debate about disabled people's leisure and recreation relates to the question of how far provision should be socially integrated, and how far provision which is designed specifically for disabled people is useful. The value of using mainstream services is now very well established (see, for example, Social Services Inspectorate 1994, or Mental Health Foundation 1996). It is now commonly accepted that disabled children and young people will join in mainstream leisure activities with their non-disabled friends and siblings. Hence, one parent respondent for the recent Scottish study into families of a child with visual impairment wrote:

> 'The activities in which my sighted son takes part are the same as the ones my blind daughter does. If the people involved are aware of her, they are always delighted to help. A positive attitude is paramount. It is infectious and costs nothing (Trite, but true).' (LOOK and RNIB 1996, p.18)

This use of community leisure settings has further potential. For example, a familiar leisure setting can prove a valuable venue in which to carry out mobility training for a young person who has recently become blind. Training in a location the young person already knows, and might wish to continue using, can help to develop their confidence and maintain local contacts. Opportunities exist also for the use of community leisure facilities for short breaks for carers, if service users are provided with individualised support. Innovative schemes providing short breaks exist for adults with learning disabilities which focus on the mutual leisure interests of a service user and a support worker. Use is made of ordinary settings, such as leisure centres, colleges, hotels and guest houses (Flynn *et al.* 1995).

The role of specialist leisure provision for disabled children and adults has been called into question because of fears about disabled people being segregated and excluded from the rest of society. Special leisure provision has tended to shift in the direction of greater social integration, a recent example being the Gateway clubs, which are associated with Mencap (Mental Health Foundation 1996).

It is increasingly recognised, however, that meeting other disabled people can provide opportunities for information sharing, consciousness raising and friendship making. Deaf clubs provide one positive example and play a key role in the development and maintenance of deaf culture. It is being increasingly recognised that disabled children need the opportunity to meet a wide group of their peers, both disabled and non disabled. The school of thought which saw socialising with disabled peers as potentially devaluing has been increasingly challenged as inherently disablist. Chappell (1994) explores the effects of this point as regards people with learning disabilities, highlighting the fact that ascribing a low value to friendship between disabled people is very damaging to their self-esteem, and to any potential for advocacy based on a sense of common experience.

A wide range of activities and companions is necessary if real choice (a necessary component of leisure, even recognising constraints on both disabled and non-disabled young people) is to exist. A key question to be asked in relation to the role of special provision is: how far is this provision extending and enhancing the possible choice as compared with that available in mainstream services, and how far is it serving to reduce the range of experience potentially available?

One area where special provision has played a major role is sport and physical activity. This has been partly related to the provision of adapted equipment and rules, and partly in order to provide an organisational framework within which competition can take place. The Para-Olympic and Special Olympic movements are well known examples. Holidays and weekend breaks are another area of leisure where disability organisations are often active. Examples are the holidays run for deaf-blind children by SENSE, which utilise a good deal of input from young volunteers and aim to contain an element of respite for parents (for reports by staff of typical activity holidays, see Howells 1996, or Smith, Nuttall and Jackson 1996).

Prior to participation in a holiday, sport or other leisure activity, the preference and needs of the person in question must be very carefully considered. One element in such an assessment must be an evaluation of the potential risks involved, although risk assessment is notoriously difficult. Although it may be true that 'Absailing under proper instruction is much safer than sloppy practice in the kitchen' (McLean 1990), there are specific risks attached to some physical activities carried out by people with some types of impairment and these risks require careful evaluation. Medical advice should be sought where necessary, and insurance checked by organisers.

Informal leisure arrangements may have a different sort of risk attached to them, as adolescence is often regarded as a time of particular risk-taking. Opportunities for risk taking by disabled adolescents may be reduced if their access to youth culture is limited by lack of support or by parental restriction. While the possibility of illegal or other dangerous activities is reduced, so also are opportunities for functional development, enjoyment and the making of relationships. The risk of loneliness is difficult to quantify, but there is evidence that young women with learning disabilities may be at particular risk, given particular restrictions found by Flynn and Hirst (1992) and the fact that loneliness is gendered (Amado (1993) suggests that this is because women assign a higher priority to relationships than men do). Lack of opportunities for gaining experience and confidence ultimately lead to vulnerability.

In any discussion of risk associated with leisure for disabled and non-disabled youth, there has also to be an acknowledgement of the risk of sexual abuse by leisure organisers. Fears have been expressed that recent moves to tighten regulation of those in paid employment in childcare services may result in paedophiles targeting sports and leisure organisations for young people. There is some evidence that disabled children may be at particular risk of sexual abuse (ABCD Consortium 1993), so that this has to be recognised as an issue that organisations must take seriously when recruiting and supervising volunteers, as well as in relation to paid staff.

A further consideration in the choice of a leisure activity is its cultural appropriateness for the person concerned. Baxter *et al.* (1990) have drawn attention to the danger of assuming that an activity which is highly valued in prevailing white culture is equally well regarded by other ethnic groups. Going to pubs and clubs falls into this category. In addition, staff involved need to be aware of relevant cultural norms, for example, as regards women exposing their bodies when swimming. Knowledge about the culture of minority groups has the potential to add to leisure opportunities, both from the point of view of gaining access to community support and settings, and by providing stimulation and diversity of experience. Wood (1996) describes how Jewish children with profound learning and multiple disability can be offered a culturally sensitive service in a non-Jewish setting. This includes the marking of festivals by food, music, cards and candle lighting. The potential for enjoyment of culturally appropriate leisure activities is also evident from a brief case study of 'Mr Cohen and Mr Joseph', described in Baxter *et al.* (1990).

## Assuming autonomy in adolescence

An issue that arises as disabled children grow older, and especially as they approach adolescence, is that of providing acceptable support as a parental presence becomes increasingly obtrusive. Maximising independence by teaching relevant skills is not always a complete answer. One parent in the survey carried out by LOOK and RNIB said:

> 'At present myself and friends will take her to anything but as she gets older I think she may resent being the only one with an adult along – she very much wants to be like other children but I don't have a solution to this.' (LOOK and RNIB 1996, p.17)

This question is also raised as a dilemma in staffed group homes for young people with learning disabilities. McLean (1990) asks at what age a teenage volunteer can assume responsibility on a leisure outing for providing support to a young disabled person with high dependency needs. The reason she poses the question is because she is aware that the young disabled people for whom she is providing a service are embarrassed by being accompanied to leisure activities by staff, in the same way as other teenagers might feel about their parents.

As an adult presence becomes less acceptable, older children may opt to manage without parental help and supervision but encounter difficulties in coping alone for extensive periods. An invisible disability may exacerbate this problem since help or allowances are unlikely to be made when a disability is unrecognisable. Effects on the leisure of children and young people with hidden disabilities are often overlooked, although special diets, routines and pseudo-nursing requirements may impose limitations. Diabetes is one example of a condition which may be experienced by affected young people as imposing irksome restrictions on their free time activity. Eiser (1993) describes how, as the peer group becomes more important, adolescents with diabetes may compromise about how far to adhere to treatments. Teenagers may be tempted to experiment with alcohol or drugs and this affects insulin requirements. While peer group pressure is not always negative, Eiser (1993) identifies a need for adolescents with diabetes to establish support groups beyond their family circle.

The desire not to lose face with one's peers is perhaps at its most extreme when an invisible impairment is also potentially highly stigmatising. Recent research carried out by the author (Cavet 1998) into the effects of bowel impairments on the lives of children and young people aged 8–22 years showed a marked restriction on overnight stays away from family support. Some of the children and young people in the sample had special techniques for managing the effects of their impairment, including colostomies and other less well-known procedures. It was partly the need for privacy (and sometimes the reassurance of a parental presence) that meant children were reluctant to stay away from home. They also feared discovery of their condition by peers from whom they usually hid any evidence of their impairment. Several children and teenagers reported that they had been on school holidays and run into difficulties. They found this very embarrassing and Jason (14 years) reported thinking on one such event: 'This is a disaster and I am supposed to be enjoying myself.'

Some parents put in extra support, going along on school or youth org-anisations' holidays to offer the assistance which might be needed at night as well as during the day. Parents went ostensibly as general volunteers, but in reality to offer discreet support to their son or daughter. This type of assistance was also often needed for school trips, swimming lessons and sometimes at sporting events. Samuel (13 years) was very active and played football for his school and for a local league, despite his colostomy. His team mates and the team manager were unaware of his impairment, and Samuel's parents were regular spectators so that he could be rushed home at half time for attention, if required. Where children had not had this sort of support for sports they often reported distressing incidents.

Spontaneity as regards leisure outings was reduced for these young people. Family holidays and other trips went ahead but with more forethought, planning and the taking of copious supplies. Accommodation needed more thought, as did privacy. The impact was probably greatest as adolescence approached. The younger children could be supported by paid assistants in school or by parents, although not all were. Verbal abuse from peers was very commonly reported. However, older children did not want assistance which drew attention to them and preferred to try to manage alone, although they were not totally in command of the situation.

There was evidence, however, that the restrictions experienced by many of the younger adolescents were overcome by the late teens or early twenties. Compare, for example, the experience of Robert, now 19 years old, when he went away for three days with school as a young adolescent and his description of a recent barge holiday with friends. Prior to Robert's going away with school, he and his parents went to inspect the accommodation. Nevertheless, although he enjoyed the holiday in many ways, he had been anxious and stressed, being in difficulties managing equipment which he had to use before his school mates got up:

> 'I were flapping and rushing around and what have you. It was a good trip obviously, because it were me first time away from home and all the excitement and this. But now I look back on it, it was difficult.'

But very recently, after further surgery and a new management technique: 'I went to Norfolk earlier this year with my friends for a week's holiday...No problems whatsoever. Absolutely brilliant'.

The success of Robert's recent holiday owed a lot to an improved means of management, but younger girls and boys who used the same technique were unwilling to do so outside the security of their own homes. Robert's increased maturity and resultant confidence were also important factors. This greater willingness to stay away from home was to be found in other older members of the sample, irrespective of what method they employed for management. The young people experienced a delay in gaining access to some leisure opportunities, as they paced themselves through a transition to adulthood which posed extra challenges.

## Leisure and people with multiple impairments

There is a danger, however, that the delay experienced by Robert and young people with similar impairments may become a permanent feature of the lives of more severely disabled young adults. Flynn and Hirst (1992) in their study of multiply disabled young people note the possibility of a truncation of the shift to adult levels of social participation, and this was despite the fact that their respondents' learning disabilities were not considered severe. For young people affected by profound learning and multiple disability their prospects might appear bleak. The constraints, however, are not in the range of activities which can be made available, but relate to problems in obtaining adequate resources and in maintaining the morale of formal and informal carers (Cavet 1995b). Services which offer individualised support in carrying out leisure activities (see Allen *et al.* 1989, for a report of an early example) offer potential for stimulation and community participation. However, this type of service will result in an unsatisfactory lifestyle if infrequent leisure expeditions are service users' only respite from a life spent almost entirely at home with carers. This sort of scenario demonstrates how endless free time is a problem, and highlights deficits in opportunities for meaningful daytime activity for some adults with profound learning and multiple disability.

Concerns about the paucity of friendships in the lives of people with severe and profound learning disability have led in recent years to the development of a variety of schemes and ideas which are intended to promote social relationships. These are particularly relevant to profoundly disabled young people as they become adults. Such initiatives involve encouraging volunteers to develop a friendly relationship with a severely or profoundly disabled person, with an eye to promoting greater social inclusion. One example is citizen advocacy. Although citizen advocacy schemes do not have friendship development as their overall aim, citizen advocates have been described as 'an unconditional ally for an individual who is vulnerable' (Simons 1993).

Circles of support are another example of an initiative which includes an element of friendship between a volunteer and a severely or profoundly disabled person. Members of a circle offer each other support to help meet the needs of the disabled person at their centre (see Gold 1994, for a description of how one circle operates). Strulley and Strulley (1993) describe how they employed a person to help form a circle of friends for their daughter who is described as having a developmental disability and complex needs. It is their view that putting their efforts into promoting the development of friendships for their daughter is the most effective way of giving her a good quality of life. The authors give this a higher priority than teaching skills: 'It is friendships that make life worth living' (Strulley and Strulley 1993).

## Conclusion

Taking part in leisure activities is a very important facet of growing up. Disability adds an extra component for adolescents and teenagers to manage as they move towards adulthood. Disabled young people are offered reduced opportunities for leisure as compared with their non-disabled peers. These limitations are linked to structural constraints facing all disabled people but these have a particularly powerful impact as young people reach an age when increased independence is generally expected. Current issues include how to gain ready access to community resources and how far specialist leisure provision is appropriate. Individual assessments are necessary which evaluate risk and recognise that young people's differing, cultural, religious and ethnic backgrounds offer opportunities for enriching free-time experiences. A first priority for all disabled children and young people should be 'a life of rich experiences, all the while having friends with whom to share them' (Strulley and Strulley 1993).

## References

ABCD Consortium (1993) *The ABCD Pack, Abuse and Children who are Disabled.* Leicester: NSPCC.

Allen, D., Gillard, N., Watkins, P. and Norman G., (1989) 'New directions in day activities for people with multiple handicaps and challenging behaviour.' *Mental Handicap 7,* 101–103.

Amado, R.S. (1993) 'Loneliness: effects and implications.' In A.N. Amado (ed.) *Friendships and Community Connections between People With and Without Developmental Disabilities.* Baltimore: Paul H. Brookes.

Baxter, C., Poonia, K., Ward, L. and Nadirshaw, Z. (1990) *Double Discrimination. Issues and Services for People With Learning Difficulties from Black and Ethnic Minority Communities.* London: King's Fund Centre.

BOADICEA (1997) 'Accessible, transport? No thanks.' BOADICEA, April/May, 2.

Brown, H. (1994) 'What price theory if you cannot afford the bus fare? Normalization and leisure services for people with learning disabilities.' *Health and Social Care in the Community 2,* 3, May, 153-159.

Cavet, J. (1995a) 'Sources of information about the leisure of people with profound and multiple disabilities.' In J. Hogg and J. Cavet (eds) *Making Leisure Provision for People With Profound Learning and Multiple Disabilities.* London: Chapman and Hall.

Cavet, J. (1995b) 'Leisure provision in Europe.' In J. Hogg and J. Cavet (eds) *Making Leisure Provision for People with Profound Learning and Multiple Disabilities.* London: Chapman and Hall.

Cavet, J. (1998) *People Don't Understand: Children, Young People and their Families Living With a Hidden Disability.* London: The National Childrens Bureau.

Chappell, A.L. (1994) 'A question of friendship: Community care and the relationships of people with learning difficulties.' *Disability and Society 9,* 4, 419–434.

Chronically Sick and Disabled Persons Act (1970). London: HMSO.

Disability Discrimination Act (1995). London: HMSO.

Disability Now (1997) 'Taken for a ride.' *Disability Now,* (April), 7.

Dorn, N. and South, N. (1989) 'Drugs and leisure, prohibition and pleasure: from subculture to the drugalogue.' In C. Rojek (ed.) *Leisure for Leisure.* Basingstoke: Macmillan.

Eiser, C. (1993) *Growing Up With a Chronic Disease. The Impact on Children and Their Families.* London: Jessica Kingsley Publishers.

Flynn, M., Cotterill, L., Hayes, L. and Sloper, T. (1995) *A Break With Tradition. The Findings of a Survey of Respite Services for Adult Citizens With Learning Disabilities in England.* Manchester: National Development Team.

Flynn, M. and Hirst, M. (1992) *This Year, Next Year, Sometime...? Learning Disability and Adulthood.* London: National Development Team.

Frith, S. (1978) *The Sociology of Rock.* London: Constable.

Glyptis, S. (1989) *Leisure and Unemployment.* Milton Keynes: Open University Press.

Gold, D. (1994) 'We don't call it a "circle": The ethos of a support group.' *Disability and Society 9,* 4, 435–452.

Hendry, L.B., Shucksmith J., Love, J.G. and Glendinning, A. (1993) *Young People's Leisure and Lifestyles.* London: Routledge.

Hirst, M. and Baldwin, S. (1994) *Unequal Opportunities. Growing Up Disabled.* London: HMSO.

Hogg, J. and Lambe, L. (1988) *Sons and Daughters With Profound Retardation and Multiple Handicaps Attending Schools and Social Education Centres: Final Report.* London: Mencap.

Howells, S. (1996) 'A day in the life of a...Dukes Barn.' *Talking Sense,* (Winter), 11.

Leonard, A. (1991) *Homes of Their Own. A Community Care Initiative for Children With Learning Difficulties.* Aldershot: Avebury.

Letts, P. (1997) 'Discrimination. Will the Act help?' *Community Living,* Jan, 6–7.

LOOK and RNIB (1996) *What Families Need Now. A Report of the Needs of Families With Visually Impaired Children in Scotland.* Edinburgh: LOOK.

McLean, E. (1990) 'Things to do–people to see...leisure, young people with mental handicaps and the community.' *Mental Handicap 18,* Dec, 169–171.

Mencap (1997) *Mencap Holidays. March 97–March 98.* Rochdale: Mencap's Holiday Service, 12–13.

Mental Health Foundation (1996) *Building Expectations. Opportunities and Services for People With a Learning Disability.* London: Mental Health Foundation.

Roberts, K. (1970) *Leisure.* Harlow: Longman.

Rose, S. and Massey, P. (1993) 'Adventurous outdoor activities: an investigation into the benefits of adventure for seven people with severe learning difficulties.' *Mental Handicap Research 6,* 4, 287–302.

Simons, K. (1993) *Citizen Advocacy: The Inside View.* Bristol: Norah Fry Research Centre.

Smith, S.J., Nuttall, B. and Jackson, S. (1996) 'Bodmin brings out the best.' *Talking Sense,* Winter, 12.

Social Services Inspectorate (1994) *Opportunities or Knocks, National Inspection of Recreation and Leisure in Day Services for People With Learning Disabilities.* London: Social Services Inspectorate and Department of Health.

Strulley, J.L. and Strulley, C. (1993) 'That which binds us: Friendship as a safe harbour in a storm.' In A.N. Amado (ed.) *Friendships and Community Connections Between People With and Without Developmental Disabilities.* Baltimore: Paul H. Brookes.

Thornton, P. and Lunt, N. (1995) *Employment for Disabled People: Social Obligations or Individual Responsibility?* York: Social Policy Research Unit.

Wood, J. (1996) 'The needs of Jewish service users in PMLD settings.' *PMLD Link,* Winter, 26, 4–6.

# CHAPTER 8

# Quality of Life of Children and Young People With Serious Medical Conditions

*Alison Closs*

## Introduction

This chapter's focus is on children whose conditions are life-threatening or life-shortening. The terminology used to describe these children regularly changes. Collective terminology and approaches, whereby 'disability' subsumes 'chronic illness', and 'in need' then subsumes 'disability', benefit the relatively small numbers of children affected by specific conditions but who together often face similar hurdles and restrictions in their lives (Eiser 1993; Hornby 1995; Kazak 1989; Pless and Perrin 1985). Condition-by-condition approaches, if their use is extended beyond the medical field, may risk pathologising and marginalising these children's lives.

Shorter lives must be optimised. Research emphasises the high value parents place on the lives of children with profound impairments but finds the response of most services to such children and their families is wanting (Beresford 1994; Closs and Norris 1997; While, Citrone and Cornish 1996a and 1996b). Consumer criticism has highlighted difficulties in achieving a 'normal' or merely acceptable life. There is general evidence of inequity in services to ethnic minority communities (Commission for Racial Equality 1996; Donovan 1986), and While *et al.* (1996a) found that children with life-threatening conditions from ethnic minorities, of lower socio-economic status, and from rural areas may all be disadvantaged.

The British Paediatric Association (1995) reports that approximately 10 per cent of children under 15 have illnesses which chronically reduce their functional capacity. Currently about 1100 children die every year from life-limiting incurable disorders in England and Wales, with more than one-third of these being under the age of five (OPCS 1991), but While *et al.* (1996a) note that reliable statistics are not available on those who continue to live with such conditions.

## The views of the child or young person

While parents' views are of enormous importance, it cannot be assumed that they represent their children's perspectives. In Closs and Norris (1997) a mother noted that her chronically ill son had few close peer friendships, unlike his brother. She attributed this to his illness and said that he spent his time, 'ninety per cent in the house. I feel he's super-glued to my hip'. In contrast, the boy reported himself as being:

> '...quite sociable. I have the friends I want. I see them at school and sometimes here. I don't want to be with them all the time. I need some peace.' (Annex 2.1)

Parents' frustrations and sense of loss, comparing their own and their child's experience with that of others or to their idealised conceptions of parenthood and childhood, may prevent recognition of the child's perspective. The same research found that parental pleasure in children's access to technology, from computers to electronic wheelchairs, was in marked contrast to their children's view that their apparently supportive technology was stigmatising them.

Six young people have contributed to this chapter by reflecting on their childhoods, responding to questions on key issues identified in the literature and supplemented by them, and criticising drafts. While time and changing circumstances, as well as the projection of their current preferred selves, will have 'cast some veils' over their reminiscences, they do nonetheless have their own validity (Cohen and Manion 1985). They were also asked about coping strategies and positive aspects of their lives. Eiser (1993) notes that:

> 'The traditional assumption that psychopathology is the common response to chronic disease in children is not substantiated. There is an anomaly in that much research has focused on the negative consequences of chronic disease, and individuals are often given little opportunity to describe their strengths and coping resources. In contrast, recent theoretical models stress the likelihood of normal growth and development, even in the face of serious and life-threatening disease.' (p.8)

The personalities, interests, socio-economic backgrounds, educational experiences and attainments, occupations and medical conditions of the young people are immensely varied. Their views are, however, illustrative rather than representative. They are profiled briefly below under assumed names.

Amy Bruce is 16 and has just sat six Standard Grade subjects, missing another because of illness. She would like to study medicine. Her interests are socialising, reading and going to the cinema. She has asthma, with acute attacks frequently requiring hospitalisation, and needed resuscitative ventilation twice in the last year. She must carry inhalers and a nebulizer constantly.

Laura Ritchie, 20, is a part-time youth newsletter editor for a voluntary organisation associated with her condition. She works voluntarily as an adviser for families and children. She enjoys her family, friends and dogs, shopping, writing, including personal correspondence, reading and watching television. She has acute juvenile chronic arthritis, resulting in blindness in one eye, widespread damage to her joints, and extensive surgery. She also has asthma and digestive difficulties. She has limited mobility but is able to drive. She needs help in everyday living and attended a special school.

John and Ronald Bayliss are 30 and 26 respectively. John is interested in photography, active in disability rights movements and organises the social group of the resource centre for people with physical impairments which he attends. He is a sports fan, following cricket world-wide and belonging to the local club. Ronald graduated in classical art, is completing his M Litt and tutors undergraduates occasionally. He enjoys cinema, theatre, music and reading, the company of friends and colleagues and foreign travel. John and Ronald have ataxia telangiectasia, a rare genetic progressive and life-threatening condition which affects balance and the immune system. They attended local schools. John is not independently mobile but has better health than Ronald whose immune system has malfunctioned since birth. Ronald is still independently, if erratically, mobile. Both tire quickly, their speech is affected and they need substantial help in everyday living.

Eleanor Fawcett is 18 and recently left school. She will soon be a university undergraduate in health studies, flat-sharing with a close friend and former classmate. Her interests are largely social and centre around her friends, although she enjoys reading, swimming and aerobics when she is well enough. She has cystic fibrosis and is being assessed for a heart-lung transplant.

Martin McColl is 16 and attends the same high school that his four older siblings attended. His interests are computer games, television, traditional Irish music and the company of family and friends. He has no clear post-school aims and has missed much schooling. He has a major congenital heart condition. He is on the waiting list for a heart transplant and a recent interim operation was unsuccessful. He uses a wheelchair.

All the young people live at home with their parents who are their main carers, supported in some cases by much-appreciated home helps, funded by social work, or other independent helpers.

## Key issues

The following were considered critical to the quality of children's and young people's lives:

- the individual's understanding of their condition
- feelings of sameness/difference
- educational experiences and attainments
- peer and other friendships
- family: upbringing, relationships and degree of independence
- experience of medical/paramedical services and hospital life
- practical and emotional coping strategies
- future plans and positive outcomes.

### *Understanding of condition*

Even young children may understand much about their condition, although this may be less in very young or less able children. They may visit hospital as day or in-patients. Other activities and interests may be curtailed. Modern medical policy is to involve children progressively and appropriately in their own treatment (Wysocki *et al.* 1990). Some parents inform their children about their condition/ diagnosis even if it is mutually painful. Children talk to fellow patients, overhear medical discussions and parental conversations, pick up leaflets or correspondence intended for professionals or other adults or read their own clinical records. The young people consulted remembered such early learning and 'wanting and not wanting to know' simultaneously.

One mother described how her daughter was only seven when the child referred to having 'only a short life' (Closs and Norris 1997). Children's 'secret lives' may hold extensive information, much of it potentially confused, deeply troubling and not shared. Voluntary organisations and health services have tried to address children's and young people's needs by developing peer support groups, telephone helplines and building in psychological support to treatment.

Becoming informed is not a once-and-for-all event, more a gradual or spasmodic progression. While the general pattern of a condition may be known, the particular path it follows is often individualistic and unpredictable. Laura describes this:

> 'I know as much as most doctors about juvenile arthritis in general and more than some, but this doesn't mean that you know how it is going to be for you. I know that many cases "burn out" after some years or there may be longer periods between flares and that a small number just go on and on getting worse. You hope...you think, you'll be one of the ones that burn out but I didn't know I wouldn't until I didn't, so then I had to face it and learn to live with it.'

For five of the young people, painful learning and emotional adjustment followed acute anxiety and depression after a crisis. For Martin and Eleanor it was the prospect of a heart and heart-lung transplant respectively, Laura was told by her consultant that further pain relief was not possible and that she would have to have neck surgery which might leave her paralysed, and Amy had to be resuscitated twice after asthma attacks. John's nurse training was terminated at the age of 18 because of both his clumsiness and the simultaneous diagnosis of his condition. 'It really seemed like the end of the world. I had no future. I was just devastated. It took me years to find my way again.' Even Eleanor, who hopes a transplant may be a new beginning, said, 'I was shocked. Had my illness really come to this? I cried. I cried a lot over the next while.'

All have faced their own mortality. Amy, Eleanor and John had easier early childhoods, but acute awareness came as their condition worsened later. For Laura, Ronald and Martin there was no 'time of freedom'. Ronald said, 'You could say I was born into it. I don't want to be self-dramatising but basically I was robbed of my childhood.' This feeling of ageing before their time, of being an adult while still a child, was common to the young people consulted.

Article 31 of the UN Convention on the Rights of the Child (1989) safeguards a child's right to play and recreation. Despite restrictions, treatment and crises, all six young people remembered happy aspects of childhood, playing with friends, going on holiday, staying with grandparents. Martin reflected:

> 'I don't think you can live for too long in the dumps, I've had lots of laughs, lots of highs, although in the end it's always there stopping you doing things.'

*Feelings of sameness / difference*

'We all had something so no one felt too different,' said Laura of her special school. Feeling different may arise from actual physical and experiential differences and is persistent, especially for older children for whom peer identification is the norm. The feeling can come from the excluding actions and attitudes of other children and adults rather than being self-generated. La Greca (1990) and Larcombe (1995) found that physical changes to appearance, for example, from steroid or irradiation treatment, and inability to share physical activities impact most on social adjustment and on resettling into school after absence. 'Whose social adjustment?' is a salient question. Feeling different is exacerbated by periods of isolation from peers and others beyond the family, sometimes unavoidable despite the best efforts of families and services.

The young people were particularly concerned about too frequently un-acknowledged commonalties: 'After all, I'm a person with arthritis, not an arthritic, it's only part of me,' said Laura. Ronald resented stereotypical assumptions, especially that any girlfriend should also be disabled. Fatigue was seen as the enemy of shared experience. Eleanor fumed, 'I either get tired and miss out on things, or go home to rest to avoid getting tired, in which case I still miss out.' Martin's wheelchair saved his energy but exposed him to the 'disbelief and disgust' of others if he walked away apparently able-bodied: 'People think you've been having them on.'

*Educational experiences and attainments*

Parents of children with life-threatening conditions hope that through education their children will fulfil their potential, make friends, develop interests, be distracted from their condition, leave behind a marker of their existence and experience 'normality' (Closs and Burnett 1995).

However, recent research in England and Wales (Bolton 1997) and in Scotland (Closs and Norris 1997) suggests that some children with medical conditions may experience partial or complete exclusion in relation to choice of school, to provision of adequate, efficient and empathic education in and out of school, and to peer acceptance. These children may not always be recognised as having 'special educational needs' nor receive appropriate support. Research in the US (Fowler, Johnson and Atkinson 1985) found greater educational losses through absence in such children from ethnic minority and disadvantaged backgrounds.

Reasons for such deficits include education personnel's lack of medical knowledge and insufficient experience and empathy with those affected by medical conditions (Eiser and Town 1987; Leamann 1995). Government policies have emphasised pupil progress, improved achievement, good attendance and application to work. Such policies, applied indiscriminately, plainly disadvantage these children. Recent legislation in England and Wales ensures an educational entitlement for children at home or in hospital, but this is not mandatory in Scotland, which is in default of Articles 23.3 and 28.1 of the UN Convention.

Educational under-achievement relative to ability or their peers is the norm. Those who do keep up are well supported by homework, have access to additional support when absent and on return to school, are self-motivated with supportive and resourceful parents, especially mothers who act as tutors, couriers and resource gatherers – a tall order. Absent and debilitated pupils put an onus on schools to be organised and empathic.

Amy's school has an alternative learning centre where any children not coping in their usual class may work in a quieter supportive atmosphere. This service is ideal for Amy when she is recovering from an asthma attack. Ronald found that teachers responded to his eagerness to learn despite frequent absence. Eleanor's school acknowledged her personal qualities by making her head of school despite her absences. Martin's headteacher asserted that 'problems are there to be overcome'. The importance of a positive school ethos was stressed by all the young people.

*Peers and other friendships*

Being bullied and excluded are common experiences for these children (Closs and Norris 1997; Eiser 1993). Laura reflected on her special school: 'Just because we were disabled didn't make us saints...There were some real thugs and they could say some horrible things.' Ronald's experience of bullying was acute and enduring. One tormentor was excluded: 'but after a bit it crept back, others took up where he had left off...There are no words really for the misery.' There is insufficient school recognition of these children's particular vulnerability even through new anti-bullying strategies (Scottish Council for Research in Education 1993).

Ronald had only one 'true friend' at school. At university he developed a small circle of friends through shared subject interests. John, whose condition was less apparent, was still the butt of school bullies but learned to deflect them through humour and a talent for drama. Several young people spoke of 'fair weather friends' who did not visit in hospital, chose other friends in their absence and 'backed off' when the reality of the condition became apparent. The young people all reported deploying strategies to avoid rejection; self-directed black humour, never asking too much of anyone, and hiding 'unappealing' aspects of their conditions.

Even when friendship is apparently strong there are doubts. 'I sometimes ask my friend if the others really like me or is it because they are sorry for me?' said Eleanor. Personal presentation is an enormous anxiety for these children. Eleanor had insisted that her intravenous 'portacath' for injection of antibiotics was inserted out of sight under her arm, and had opted to night-feed herself by naso-gastric tube rather than having an 'unsightly' stomach tube. Laura welcomed recent 'button access' advances in stomach tube technology.

Eleanor and Martin had fewer negative peer experiences. Their conditions were less noticeable than the others, and attending Catholic schools in smaller communities may also have helped. Martin also has an extensive family. Amy had joined her school in third year secondary when her family moved, further complicating friendship formation. Both she and Eleanor had supportive older brothers who facilitated their social life even when they were young children. 'He looks out for me, he isn't much good at expressing himself but I know he really cares,' said Eleanor.

Martin liked girls but found that 'some fuss over me too much'. Laura was now engaged to a former classmate from her special school, but had had several boyfriends whom she categorised as 'special needs or other'. The 'others' were further subdivided into those who 'smothered and fussed' and those who 'didn't want to know and just couldn't cope'. Ronald and Amy had both felt let down when possible romantic attachments, 'backed off', unable to accept their circumscribed lives. John and Ronald now thought that a lasting and reciprocated love was more dream than hope.

Many children develop close, if sometimes ambivalent, relationships with professionals. Learning to distinguish between professional care and personal attachment can be problematic. Most of the young people consulted did nonetheless identify some professionals with whom they had a lasting positive personal link. For John and Eleanor it was their careers officers, Ronald his physiotherapist, Amy the alternative education coordinator, Martin the psychologist at the heart transplant clinic and Laura her GP.

### Family: upbringing, relationships and degree of independence

'Quite simply, my family are my best friends. They have been through it all with me and I know that they always will.'

'I need them. The alternative would be some kind of residential care and I accept that one day that will be necessary, but I hope it's a long way off.'

'My family is always around. There's lots of them which is a help most of the time.'

Thus Amy, Ronald and Martin describe aspects of family life.

It would be naive to assume that these families are representative. Willis, Elliott and Jay (1982) list four key sources of stress on parents: first, the need to make complex judgements about conditions, second, physical and emotional demands and sharing of care-taking, third, maintenance of family life, including recreation, for other children and each other and fourth, staying afloat financially. Reviewing the research, Eiser (1993, p.139) notes that with very few exceptions studies indicate that parents of children with serious medical conditions, especially mothers, report marital distress and dissatisfaction greater than that of matched samples of healthy children. This inevitably impacts on children's quality of life.

Laura's parents divorced when she was an infant, and although her relationship with her stepfather is good, her life was periodically upset by the reappearance and intervention of her own father. She was also conscious through her voluntary work as an adviser for families affected by arthritis that the condition imposed strains.

Relationships with siblings may be positive as Eleanor's and Amy's relationships with their older brothers and Ronald and John's positive feelings for each other indicate. However children can also feel negative about their less healthy sibling. Martin's mother ascribes his nearest sister's dislike of him to:

'...a kind of jealousy, she was only a toddler when he was born and I had to be away with him when he had an operation. She didn't have a proper childhood because he really got all the attention.'

Amongst the families of the young people interviewed, single income status, sometimes supplemented by small part-time earnings, was the norm. Mother–child relationships tended to be closer than father–child relationships, though these were also basically good. The closeness of mother and child or young person, related to care giving, concurs with detailed case study research (Beresford 1994; Closs and Norris 1997).

Given such stresses, exacerbated by professional admonitions to lead a 'normal life', it would be surprising if parents and children did not sometimes feel pushed to their limits. Eiser (1993) suggests that life can never be truly 'normal' for a family with a child with a life-threatening condition. Nonetheless many aspire to 'normality' and achieve it to a remarkable degree. One mother described the process:

'The way I see it, we have two lives, the one that's like everyone else's where we eat and sleep and communicate and see friends and go on holiday, and the other that's tied to this condition with hospital and hospice visits, and lifting, and phoning and waiting for the special this, that and the next thing and waiting for all the professionals...and so on, a real struggle. I suppose what I try to do is to ensure that the second world doesn't take over the first. Sometimes, amazingly, I succeed.' (Closs and Norris 1997, p.107)

The growth of children's autonomy from parents in caring for themselves has occupied researchers (Seagull and Somers 1991; Wysocki *et al.* 1990) without producing significant findings of difference from 'well' children. The young people consulted differentiated between physical, mental and emotional de-pendence, recognising the inevitability of the first but feeling that they had achieved independence of the second and third kind, having the right to make important decisions even while continuing to live at home. Parents had often encouraged this from early childhood, although they were also described as over-protective physically. This led to family arguments but the young people did not perceive this as different from their peers and indeed felt that, because of their conditions, they actually made more decisions.

Eleanor's health suffered when she had briefly neglected self-care for her social life, but that experience had made her more responsible now. Laura's and Amy's parents actively encouraged them to learn to drive at 16. Martin's mother described how she and her husband opened the door for him at age 12 to storm out of the house in his wheelchair after an argument, even knowing that he might collapse: 'He had to be able to do it. It's part of growing up.' Reciprocated care was illustrated by Amy as she described how her mother needed to have time off work after Amy was resuscitated: 'It was worse for her watching and wondering if I'd make it.'

Laura's parents had extended their house to give her greater autonomy and privacy. There was a dilemma between wanting a closed door and needing someone near 'just in case'. Protection of privacy and indeed of the child as a whole when living away from the family is enshrined in Articles 16.1 and 19.1 of the UN Convention. This is relevant to hospital life.

## Experience of medical and paramedical services and of hospital life

'If they didn't call it treatment you could call it torture.'

'When I was very young, I remember hating being away from home, but then I got to like it...I got special treatment, like I always got the same bed.'

'I could write a book about doctors, good, bad and unspeakable.'

'I realised I had nothing on under the sheet. Maybe it was easier for them to put in tubes...but I felt really embarrassed.'

'My GP is great. He's quite clued up and he listens to me.'

'Some doctors and nurses can't stand that you really do understand your illness. They would rather you were ignorant and thought them superior.'

'Going to the adult ward was awful. They were really ill and dying and there was nothing to do.'

'You want the truth but you don't always get it because they [staff] can't always face it.'

Such comments from the young people consulted can illustrate only some of their responses to medical services and hospital life. Some experiences were distressing, some enjoyable and all were interesting. Given the extent of their experience in the world of medicine, to the partial exclusion of other experience, it is perhaps not surprising that all six young people want to work, full- or part-time at some level, professionally or voluntarily, in health and/or disability services. They do not perceive this as a default choice, but rather a positive use of their experience for the benefit of others.

Some symptoms, treatments and interventions can seem interminable and be painful and distressing. Reassurance and relief is needed along with honest information. Children of any age can feel betrayed when the promise of pain-free treatment is not fulfilled. Medical advances have reduced some suffering but each of the six young people has distant and recent experiences of pain and fear which came near to being, or actually were, out of control. Laura and Eleanor described their accumulative fear of giving blood, generated by – in Eleanor's case – 'running out of veins' and in Laura's, having her rheumatic elbow straightened to find a vein. Martin's recent unsuccessful surgery and infection were so traumatic that he thinks he cannot face surgery again.

Children and young people's knowledge about their condition can be threatening to doctors who may either not have in-depth, specialist knowledge themselves or realise that no further treatment is available. Brusque and apparently rejecting behaviour is felt deeply by children and young people. Laura described an 'end of the road' experience:

> 'It felt awful when he said there was nothing more to be done, that I'd have to have the operation and it could paralyse or kill me...I went into panic because there had to be a way out, but there wasn't. It was probably awful for him too.'

Trends towards more day-patient and home treatment for children are generally welcomed although the resulting need for professional support at home is not always met or may in itself impose strains on the family. Respite care and children's hospices are vital elements of the support network.

### Practical and emotional coping strategies

John describes 'coping' as, 'getting yourself through more or less okay in the end'. Compass, Worsham and Ey (1992) distinguish between problem-focused and emotion-focused strategies. Spirito, Stark and Tyc (1989) developed the KIDCOPE assessment scale for identifying the frequency and efficacy of commonly used strategies, such as distraction, cognitive restructuring, problem solving, withdrawal, social support and emotion regulation. They found that girls used more strategies generally and in particular more emotion-focused strategies.

As well as these, some of the young people had practised black humour and detachment. John had found peace within himself as an adult which he described as 'acceptance'. Confiding in 'true friends' was invaluable and Laura found extensive letter writing cathartic. None of the young people were strongly religious although they hoped for an after-life and had recourse to prayer throughout their childhoods. Laura thought that hoping for a cure was 'just fantasy. You need hope but after all it [the condition] is part of you, but you do wish it could just be a bit less.'

Information and support can be found through condition-related voluntary organisations, but these can also bring grim reality as peers deteriorate or die. Eleanor found this distressing both for their families and for herself, but was still in favour of participation. Laura is very committed to the organisation for which she works and feels she has both gained and given back.

Professional counselling may be suggested to help children cope with fears, sadness, frustration and anger. The young people consulted saw this as a fall-back position if closest friends and mothers, their first choices of confidante, could not cope. Parents and children may sometimes elect not to talk to each other about known negative prognoses. One mother described how her child rejected counselling in the final stages of terminal illness, when mother and daughter avoided talking about death, despite their closeness: 'They [psychologists] saw that as her bottling things up, but I think she just coped with it' (Closs and Norris 1997, Annex 2.2).

### Future plans and positive outcomes

The young people spoke of their sadness and anger about lessened capacities and threats to life, but loss of control of their lives caused greatest distress. Pragmatic future-planning may enable control. Ronald chose a subject where his grades were acceptable in his local university rather than go elsewhere. Eleanor would have liked to have been a doctor or teacher but chose health studies as equally interesting but less physically demanding. John wanted to be an active sportsman but still enjoyed being a fan. He had ambitions for publication of his writing and is fighting for his resource centre's survival. Ronald would like to complete a PhD and travel to India. All the young people wanted occupational and personal relationship satisfaction. For some there may be hopes of new treatments, but they have learned caution. They recalled more optimism and energy in their child-hoods, but also greater feelings of helplessness.

Most felt that they were wiser and better people than they might otherwise have been, their families had responded positively, they had much to give others and they appreciated each day they lived. They had had interesting experiences through their condition. They did not feel they could totally reject it, although they wished they could control and subdue it. Laura concluded, 'It's part of me and I quite like me'.

## Conclusions

Eiser (1993) suggests that:

> 'The way in which children think about the condition and its consequences, as well as the length of time they are required to spend in adult company, may result in different processes of development and relationships with both children and adults.' (p.65)

Looking at these children's lives within a social ecology model of inter-reacting concentric circles of social contacts (Bronfenbrenner 1979; Hornby 1995), the innermost core, the microsystem of the nuclear family, seems to be particularly influential and close even if stressed, while the next ring, the mesosystem of more distant friends, colleagues and neighbours may be depleted. Beyond that, how-ever, the exosystem of social, education and especially health services and voluntary organisations is undoubtedly more extensively developed in comp-arison with those of 'healthy' children.

The impact of such different structures may be considerable and result in patterns of childhood, adolescence and transitions to adulthood which are significantly different from their peers. We should not rush to judge them as inferior or defective. Archard (1993) writes: 'The modern conception of childhood is neither a simple nor a straightforwardly coherent one since it is constituted by different theoretical understandings and cultural representations' (p.40). For instance, the closeness between parents and children or young adults with serious medical conditions could be negatively construed as 'dependency' within the culture of autonomous youth in the UK and North America, although less so in southern Europe, or it could be perceived positively as the outcome of sharing, surviving and often triumphing over adverse circumstances. 'We've been through so much together. When I've really needed them, they've been there and never let me down,' said Amy. Ronald pointed out that such close relationships need not imply an unhealthy symbiosis: 'I can disagree with them and criticise them and have my views accepted, but at a deep level Mum in particular really understands.'

Rather than pathologising such differences, society's deficits in service provision and in attitudes must be addressed so that these children and their families may have, collectively and individually, real choices and a greater sense of inclusion and freedom in their lives. The young people interviewed experienced physical and emotional pain linked directly to the nature of their conditions, but they also sometimes felt hurt by the society in which they live. A medical cure may not yet be possible, but enhancement of life undoubtedly is (Baum, Dominica and Woodward 1990).

## Acknowledgements

The author would like to thank Amy, Laura, John, Ronald, Eleanor and Martin for their good humour and excellent advice.

## References

Archard, D. (1993) *Children: Rights and Childhood.* London: Routledge.

Beresford, B. (1994) *Positively Parents: Caring for a Severely Disabled Child.* Social Policy Research Unit, University of York. London: HMSO.

Baum, J., Dominica, F. and Woodward, R. (eds) (1990) *Listen, My Child has a Lot of Living to Do: The Partnership Between Parents and Professionals in Caring for Children With Life-Threatening Conditions.* Oxford: Oxford University Press.

Bolton, A. (1997) *Losing the Thread: Pupils' and Parents' Voices about Education for Sick Children.* London: National Association for the Education of Sick Children.

British Paediatric Association (1995) *Health Needs of School Age Children.* London: British Paediatric Association.

Bronfenbrenner, W. (1979) *The Ecology of Human Development.* Cambridge, USA: Harvard University Press.

Closs, A, and Burnett, A. (1995) 'Education for children with a poor prognosis: reflections on parental wishes and on an appropriate curriculum.' *Child: Care, Health and Development 21,* 6, 387–394.

Closs, A. and Norris, C. (1997) *Outlook Uncertain: Enabling the Education of Children With Chronic and/or Deteriorating Conditions.* Edinburgh: Moray House Institute of Education.

Cohen, L. and Manion, L. (1985) *Research Methods in Education*. London: Croom Helm.

Commission for Racial Equality (1996) *Special Educational Needs Asessment in Strathclyde: Report of a Formal Investigation*. London: CRE.

Compass, B., Worsham, N. and Ey, S. (1992) 'Conceptual and developmental issues in children's coping with stress.' In A.M. La Greca, L.J. Siegel, J.L. Wallender and C.E. Walker (eds) *Stress and Coping in Child Health*. New York: The Guilford Press.

Donovan, J. (1986) 'Black people's health – a different perspective.' In T. Rathwell and D. Philips (eds) *Health, Race and Ethnicity*. London: Croom Helm.

Eiser, C. (1993) *Growing Up With a Chronic Disease: The Impact on Children and their Families*. London: Jessica Kingsley Publications.

Eiser, C. and Town, C. (1987) 'Teachers' concerns about chronically sick children: implications for paediatricians.' *Developmental Medicine and Child Neurology 29*, 56–63.

Fowler, M., Johnson, M. and Atkinson, S. (1985) 'School achievement and absence in children with chronic health conditions.' *Journal of Paediatrics 106*, 4, 683–687.

Hornby, G. (1995) *Working With Parents of Children With Special Needs*. London: Cassell.

Kazak, A. (1989) 'Families of chronically ill children: a systems and social-ecological model of adaption and challenge.' *Journal of Consulting and Clinical Psychology 57*, 1, 25–30.

La Greca, A. (1990) 'Social consequences of paediatric conditions: a fertile area for future investigation and intervention?' *Journal of Paediatric Psychology 15*, 285–307.

Larcombe, I. (1995) *Reintegration to School after Hospital Treatment*. Aldershot: Avebury.

Leamann, O. (1995) *Death and Loss: Compassionate Approaches in the Classroom*. London: Cassell.

OPCS Monitor (1991) *Death by Cause: 1990 Registrations*. London: HMSO.

Pless, I. and Perrin, J. (1985) 'Issues common to a variety of illnesses.' In N. Hobbs and J. Perrin (eds) *Issues in the Case of Children With Chronic Illnesses*. San Francisco: Josey-Bass.

Scottish Council for Research in Education (1993) *Supporting Schools Against Bullying: The Second SCRE Anti-Bullying Pack*. Edinburgh: SCRE.

Seagull, E. and Somers, S. (1991) 'Autonomy expectations in families with chronically ill and healthy adolescents.' Paper presented at the Third Florida Conference on Child Health Psychology, Gainesville, Florida, April.

Spirito, A., Stark, L.J. and Tyc, V. (1989) 'Common coping strategies employed by children with chronic illness.' *Newsletter of the Society of Paediatric Psychology 13*, 3–8.

United Nations (1989) *The Convention on the Rights of the Child*. Geneva: United Nations Children Fund.

While, A., Citrone, C. and Cornish, J. (1996a) *A Study of the Needs and Provisions for Families Caring for Children With Life-Limiting Incurable Disorders*. London: Department of Nursing Studies, Kings College.

While, A., Citrone, C. and Cornish, J. (1996b) *Bereaved Parents' Views of Caring for a Child With a Life-Limiting Incurable Disorder.* London: Department of Nursing Studies, Kings College.

Willis, D., Elliott, C. and Jay, S. (1982) 'Psychological effects of physical illness and its concomitants.' In J. Tuma (ed.) *Handbook for the Practice of Paediatric Psychology.* New York: Wiley.

Wysocki, T., Meinhold, P., Cos, D. and Clarke, W. (1990) 'Survey of diabetes professionals regarding development changes in diabetes self-care.' *Diabetes Care 13,* 65–68.

# CHAPTER 9

# Disabled Children and Child Protection

*Helen L. Westcott*

Contrary to what we may wish to believe, growing up with an impairment does not protect children from abuse. Indeed, there is now considerable research and practice evidence that being disabled in fact increases the risk of victimisation (see Sobsey 1994 and Westcott and Cross 1996 for reviews). Despite a rush of professional and public awareness of child protection and disability issues in recent years, it is noticeable that disabled children's accounts of abuse are still missing from the literature. In the field of child protection, as in many others, disabled children are still waiting to be heard.

This chapter explores some of the issues which arise when we consider the protection of disabled children from abuse. First, it outlines the ecological model of child abuse which provides a framework for understanding the abuse of children who are disabled. Second, the chapter introduces some major areas of concern, such as the quality of service provision and communication issues. Third, the role of the child protection and criminal justice systems are evaluated before, finally, some key requirements for change are suggested.

## The vulnerability of disabled children

'My mum hit me, because I was deaf she took all anger out on me.'(Westcott 1993, p.30)

'He started telling me that he had a sister about the same age as me and was telling me about how her body was developing and stuff...and then he used to ask me to look at mine and he'd just undo my nightdress and look and then touch me...'(p.16)

'It would be the silliest things or the things that don't mean nothing, she'd pull my hair or kicked me around while I was on the floor or punched...I had to pull my clothes over my head and lay over a chair while she hit me over the back...'(p.16)

An important American study recently indicated that the overall incidence of abuse amongst disabled children was 1.7 times higher than the incidence for non-disabled children (Crosse, Kaye and Ratnofsky 1993). We can state quite clearly that disabled children are more likely to experience child abuse – be it physical, sexual, emotional or neglect – but we can also be quite clear at the outset about the source of their vulnerability. This is an important point, since many authors in the past have come dangerously close to labelling disabled children as 'abuse provoking' (e.g. Ammerman, Van Hasselt and Hersen 1988), locating the problem of their abuse in the child's impairment. If we listen to disabled people themselves, however, then it becomes clear that it is the way other individuals and society itself react to disabled people that creates a context in which disabled children are vulnerable. The following quotes are from disabled adults abused as children (in Westcott 1993, pp.17–19):

'The medical experiences I had made me very vulnerable to being abused, it just seemed the same as everything else that had been done to me, so I wasn't able to discriminate.'

'I'm not saying it would be 100% positive but maybe if they're white they get more support, more knowledge.'

'I don't think it occurred to people that it would happen to a disabled child, and I think that was very marked in the fact that my sister's abuse was investigated but it just didn't occur to anybody to ask me.'

'She chose me...probably because I had no one else, probably she knew I wouldn't tell anybody.'

The social model of disability helps to reinforce this message, since a society which takes no account of the requirements of disabled children – for example, creating artificial communication systems which do not have the vocabulary to describe intimate and abusive sexual acts – and which excludes disabled children from mainstream social amenities – such as child protection services – is obviously a society in which it is dangerous for disabled children to live.

The ecological model of child abuse embraces the social model of disability, and has been developed as an aid for understanding the reasons why disabled children are abused (e.g. Sobsey 1994; Westcott and Cross 1996). In brief, the ecological model makes us consider all the systems and power/ideological structures within which any disabled child exists. For example, at a *microlevel* we may consider the interaction between a disabled child and an adult providing intimate care; at a *mesolevel* we may review the communication networks between the child's parents, link family, school and hospital; the *exolevel* may focus on policies and procedures in relation to service provision for disabled people within social services; whilst finally the *macrolevel* highlights the oppression of disabled and black children, women and others. Only when we address the issues at all these levels do we begin to tackle the reasons why disabled children are vulnerable, and start to develop policy and practice that will protect children from abuse. This requires us to take responsibility for the safety of disabled children at personal, professional and organisational levels (Westcott and Cross 1996).

### Why are disabled children vulnerable? Some signposts for change

Growing up as a disabled child inevitably results in different experiences to those encountered by non-disabled children. In themselves, some of these experiences are potentially risky, such as the use of specialised services and provision of intimate care, the use of institutional and residential facilities. These are very complex areas and it is important to recognise the diversity both of requirements among disabled children, and of standards of services or facilities offered. It is also important to recognise that not all carers deliberately harm disabled children, and that working in partnership with carers will often itself offer protection to disabled children. The following discussion is not intended to scapegoat those living and working with disabled children, often in difficult circumstances; rather, it is hoped individuals will pause to consider their own behaviour or practice and its impact on disabled children. In highlighting some issues below, factors which have previously acted to facilitate the abuse of disabled children will hopefully instead act as signposts for change and protection.

*Service provision*

Disabled children have been described as 'ideal victims' for perpetrators of abuse, especially paedophiles, since their impairments often involve communication or mobility constraints and may increase dependency on others for physical needs. One man with cerebral palsy commented, when recalling his own childhood abuse:

> 'My disability probably did have some bearing on the situation because of the simple reasons I was already vulnerable, I already had problems and it's easiest to take the weakest one in the litter because they need more care and attention anyway and...there's more opportunity a) for the abuse and b) to cover it up.' (Westcott 1993, p.19)

It is the unpalatable truth that the greater the number of carers or adults in contact with the child then the greater the opportunity for abuse. Sobsey and Doe (1991) from their research estimated an additional risk of 78 per cent for disabled children and adults based on their contact with the 'disabilities service system' alone. Feeding, bathing and dressing may all require intimate touching of a child, offering opportunities both for secrecy (for example, private rooms such as bathrooms or toilets) and for confusing the child (for example, what is appropriate or inappropriate touch). Clearly some paedophiles seek out jobs where such situations will be available to them, other perpetrators may act opportunistically or may hurt the child unintentionally through insensitive or poor practice. It is essential to have guidelines for those who work with children which cover the practicalities of providing personal care, whether it be feeding, washing or using medical equipment. Guidelines need to make clear what action to undertake in the event of suspicions of abuse, and also that anyone can be a perpetrator. Earlier research has reported, for example, a hospital porter, nurses, physiotherapists and residential carers as abusers (Westcott 1993). Stereotypes of parents or carers of disabled children as 'saints' do little to encourage open awareness of child protection issues (Westcott and Cross 1996).

*Medical practice*

Disabled people have reported their contacts with the medical profession to be among the worst (e.g. Sutherland 1981). Not only do repeated experiences of being photographed, handled and 'probed' have deleterious effects on their sense of self, but they can also have implications for child protection. One disabled woman interviewed by Westcott (1993) made this link clearly:

'There's no way you can say "no" to what a doctor does to you: they just damn well do it. When you're a kid you don't have any choice about it...what the doctors did, they lifted up my nightdress, they poked here and they pushed there without asking me, without doing anything, but in front of a load of other people it was absolutely no different. I didn't say "no" to any doctor, the porter actually was to me doing absolutely nothing different at all than any doctor or nurse had ever done.' (p.17)

Fortunately, there has been some recognition that doctors – as many others – need to re-evaluate their responsibilities towards disabled people (Harrison 1993). Cross (1992) has spelt out a number of specific recommendations to prevent the disempowerment of disabled children through insensitive practice.

### Institutional abuse

Many disabled children spend long periods of time in institutions of all kinds during their lives, with often profound effects (Morris 1995). Institutional care is itself a risk factor for child abuse, with high profile cases of abuse featuring in the media with alarming regularity. Westcott (1991) has highlighted some of the major causes of institutional abuse, and again the ecological model is helpful to our understanding of the issues.

At the microlevel, individuals will sometimes abuse children within in-stitutional settings. This may, for example, be a physical assault, such as in cases where disabled children have been inappropriately restrained. Alternatively, it may be a planned sexual assault, as in the case of Ralph Morris at Castle Hill School (Brannan, Jones and Murch 1992). At a broader macrolevel, disabled children may be subjected to system abuse, where the whole institutional setting or programme is abusive, such as the over-use of sedatives to control 'disruptive' behaviour (Hubert 1991). Such abusive systems may also implicitly condone individual acts of violence towards disabled people. As inquiries into some of the recent high profile cases of system abuse have shown, it is incredibly difficult for children to resist abuse on such a scale, and for their disclosures to be taken seriously (Levy and Kahan 1991; Kirkwood 1993). How much more difficult it is for children whose impairments restrict mobility or communication, compounding their isolation:

'All that day at school I cried all day, the time I tried to tell somebody at school they must have rung her...When I got home, she got hold of me, bashed me about again and said that what she does in that home and how she runs it is her business and nobody else's, it's her house and no one can tell her what to do and if she hears me telling any one of the things she is doing she will kill me, she said "I'll even come and find you and kill you". One of the girls in the home did tell her mum and dad what the house mother had done to me and they phoned the council and told them...but nobody did anything, checked it out or did anything.' (Disabled woman speaking in Westcott 1993, p.22)

There are many other complex issues relating to institutional care which create dynamics likely to foster an atmosphere within which abuse is tolerated, for example, issues relating to the pay, conditions and training of staff. So long as society regards institutional care as a 'last resort' for children who cannot be placed elsewhere, then both adults and children who work or reside in it are likely to feel stigmatised and powerless. Within such a context, child abuse is much more likely to occur (Wardaugh and Wilding 1993; Westcott 1991, Westcott and Cross 1996).

*Communication*

When communicating with a child in the context of child protection, all the child's needs and requirements must be considered, including disability, race, culture, language, religion, gender and sexuality, all of which form the child's identity. Westcott and Cross (1996) argue that communication methods, styles and content can all be abusive, and that we need to consider broad macrolevel communication issues to understand the implications for disabled children who have been abused. For example, child abuse can have serious effects upon a child's self-esteem and self identity (e.g. Finkelhor 1988), yet disabled children will also have grown up in a society which strongly influences their identity as disabled. They may have been subjected to derogatory or offensive language, racist or disablist remarks. It is also likely that disabled children will have experienced a lack of positive role models, with stereotypical presentations of disabled people as either 'superhuman' or evil (Hevey 1992; Morris 1991). For some disabled children, their identity will be further influenced by the knowledge that their impairments were caused by abuse. In the Crosse *et al.* (1993) study, for example, the incidence of impairments that were caused or were likely to have been caused by abuse was 147 per 1000 abused children. If we are then to work with a disabled child who has been abused, these additional aspects of identity will need to be considered (Kennedy 1993a). In themselves, offensive language and negative stereotypes of disability may be viewed as abusive.

Another dimension to the communication issue, in practice, is the provision of so-called 'prevention programmes', most notably in the UK the 'Kidscape' materials (e.g. Elliott 1990, 1991). These programmes convey implicit messages for all children, that children have some responsibility for their own personal safety. However, there are additional considerations for children who are disabled. 'No, go, tell' messages are inappropriate for children who use non-verbal communication, who are physically immobile or who are visually impaired, for example. Concepts such as 'safe', 'private', 'uncomfortable' and 'touch' may be problematic for children with learning difficulties or children whose impairments result in frequent intimate body contact which may be painful. Although some attempts have been made to develop or adapt prevention programmes for disabled children (see Westcott and Cross 1996 for a review) many conceptual and practical difficulties can be anticipated. It is also important that any programmes should be developed as part of a wider educational package for disabled children which emphasises choice, control and positive self-image. From her interviews with disabled adults abused as children, Westcott (1993) comments regarding sex education:

> 'The problems were particularly acute for those interviewees with disabilities; more than once the stereotype of disabled people as "asexual" was referred to. The lack of appropriate education was felt to leave them even less prepared for interpersonal relationships, especially abusive ones.' (Westcott 1993, p.18)

## Child protection investigations and disabled children

Bernard (1995) examined black mothers' experiences of sexual abuse investigations, highlighting a number of cultural and racial factors which affected their experience, such as feeling torn about going outside their families and communities to report the abuse. In addition, some children had learning impairments and the mothers' 'overriding impressions were that their daughters' status as disabled deemed them not worthy of serious consideration' (p.12). This is a pervasive theme in the field of child protection and disability; that here, even more than elsewhere, disabled children are second-class citizens with services ill-suited to their needs and requirements. Sayers (1994), on the basis of her small study of disabled children in child protection investigations, called them 'objects without voices', commenting that:

'the children were dehumanised and became objects of the investigative process, who complied unquestioningly with the instructions of powerful professionals and were inadequately protected by their parents. In general, the adults viewed the children's statements as unreliable products of "a vivid imagination".' (p.76)

Marchant and Page (1992, 1993, 1997) have frequently argued that child protection and disability are 'two different worlds' with an urgent need for joint working relationships to develop between the two. In an investigation into suspected child abuse, an additional 'world' needs to be considered – that of criminal investigation – especially if video-recorded interviews are undertaken, as set out in the *Memorandum of Good Practice* (Home Office 1992). Despite the intentions of the Children Act 1989 that disabled children should be integrated into mainstream children's services, there remains considerable confusion about how this should be achieved. Indeed, disabled children are typically faring very poorly, with many Area Child Protection Committees (ACPCs) still failing to have developed any specific guidance. Black disabled children and disabled children from other minority communities are even more disadvantaged. Governmental guidance in the *Working Together* document (Department of Health 1991) is limited to two brief paragraphs on disabled children. The recent Department of Health review of its major child protection research programme states simply:

'It is also the case that important groups, such as children with disabilities, those placed for adoption or those living in residential or specialist foster care are not specifically dealt with. Similarly, issues of race, gender and rights may not be as salient in the studies as some readers might wish...' (1995, p.8)

The continuing debate about sections 17 and 47 of the Children Act 1989 fuelled by this review is particularly relevant to disabled children, since they are included in the definition of 'children in need'. The debate concerns the degree to which social work as a profession is concentrating on investigations into suspected child abuse at the expense of more general support services for children in need. Obviously, disabled children and their families would greatly benefit from the provision of properly resourced social support services. However, having only recently managed to place the abuse of disabled children onto the child protection agenda, it is of particular concern that an emphasis on family support does not distract us from the real risks facing many disabled children.

Despite these problems, it is important to acknowledge the developing resources for practitioners (for example, Sullivan and Scanlan 1987, 1990). Marchant and Page (1992, 1993, 1997) and Kennedy (1992, 1993 a and b) are particularly helpful in outlining their own experiences of working with disabled children caught up in child protection investigations. These authors show, for example, how interpreters or facilitators can work within investigative interviews, and which particular issues need to be considered in identifying the abused disabled child.

## The criminal justice system and disabled children

If disabled children fare badly in terms of child protection services, then they are totally failed by the criminal justice system. The Home Office's own evaluation of the special provisions of the Criminal Justice Act 1991 for child witnesses commented:

> 'Few cases are heard in court and this remains a major source of concern among the professionals involved...children with special needs are particularly vulnerable and it is of great concern that they should be afforded adequate protection by the courts.' (Davies *et al.* 1995, p.43)

Citing the example of a 15-year-old boy with learning difficulties who made detailed allegations against the defendant in a videotaped interview, they criticise the system for its failure to respond appropriately. The Crown Prosecution Service took the case to court where it was dismissed as the defence maintained they were unable to cross-examine the child. Davies *et al.* argue that:

> 'there would appear to be little point in providing extensive training for personnel to create videotape interviews with [disabled] children if the courts do not provide the expertise to allow cross-examination.' (p.43).

Although the recent legislative and procedural changes contained within the Criminal Justice Acts of 1988 and 1991 do offer more opportunities for disabled children (see Marchant and Page 1993, 1997; Westcott and Cross 1996), the Home Office and Department of Health reviews of their implementation, and especially the *Memorandum of Good Practice* (Home Office 1992), reveal serious shortcomings (Davies *et al.* 1995; Holton and Bonnerjea 1994). General concerns have been raised about the number of videotaped interviews being undertaken, the criteria for making a videotaped interview and the roles and relationship of police officers and social workers conducting the interviews, for example, the fact that police officers almost always act as the lead interviewer (Westcott and Jones 1997).

Among real fears for the welfare of children involved in *Memorandum* interviews, and frustration at the small numbers of interviews reaching courts, there are documented concerns about specific groups of children, including those who are disabled. Holton and Bonnerjea (1994) report that one-third of the local authorities in their survey had provided general awareness training to workers specialising with disabled children, while one-quarter reported some specialists having been trained as evidential interviewers. This reflects the dilemma noted by Holton and Bonnerjea as to:

> 'whether those working with [disabled] children should themselves be trained in video interviewing skills, or whether trained child protection workers should co-interview with them.' (p.60)

Strong feelings were reported such that disabled children were 'disadvantaged doubly during video interviewing' (p.18) with, for example, police interviewers not always interviewing at an appropriate pace.

Debates about the *Memorandum* and associated reforms are set to continue (Westcott and Jones 1997). However, until the primacy of oral evidence within the criminal justice system is truly challenged, then disabled children are unlikely to be heard (Spencer 1992).

## Protecting disabled children

> 'The thing I remember about it was the pain of course which was absolutely...and I remember the light was off and there was a clock in the room and I can remember the ticking of this clock and I can remember my screams...and I remember afterwards because the toilet was downstairs and I went down to the toilet and I can just remember the blood everywhere.' (Disabled man, in Westcott 1993, inside front cover)

The absolute pain experienced by this child must be matched by an absolute commitment to protecting disabled children and, for disabled children to be protected, change is required at a number of levels (Westcott and Cross 1996). Underlying change must be a commitment to regard the child's welfare as paramount, and to working in partnership with disabled children and adults. At the microlevel, personal change requires that we start tackling our own attitudes and prejudices towards disability and disabled people. Professionally, we must challenge discrimination in the development and delivery of services. At the macrolevel, we must challenge oppression within society – we must empower disabled children and adults through the provision of appropriate and accessible services and facilities which are adequately resourced. Rickell (1993) has linked empowerment to three basic rights – the right to choose, the right to participation as an equal, and the right to equality of opportunity. In the same way that society disables children who have impairments, it creates their increased vulnerability to abuse by subjugating these rights. Challenging society does not absolve us of the responsibility to challenge ourselves: we are all responsible for the welfare of disabled children with whom we live and work.

# References

Ammerman, R.T., Van Hasselt, V.B. and Hersen, M. (1988) 'Maltreatment of handicapped children: a critical review.' *Journal of Family Violence 3,* 1, 53–72.

Bernard, C. (1995) 'A study of black mothers' emotional and behavioural responses to the sexual abuse of their children.' Paper presented to the 4th International Family Violence Research Conference, 21–24 July, University of New Hampshire, Durham.

Brannan, C., Jones, J.R. and Murch, J.D. (1992) *Castle Hill Report: Practice Guide.* Shrewsbury: Shropshire County Council.

Children Act (1989). London: HMSO.

Criminal Justice Act (1988). London: HMSO.

Criminal Justice Act (1991). London: HMSO.

Cross, M. (1992) 'Abusive practices and disempowerment of children with physical impairments.' *Child Abuse Review 1,* 3, 194-197.

Crosse, S.B., Kaye, E. and Ratnofsky, A.C. *A Report on the Maltreatment of Children With Disabilities.* Washington D.C.: National Center on Child Abuse and Neglect.

Davies, G.M., Wilson, J.C., Mitchell, R. and Milsom, J. (1995) *Videotaping Children's Evidence: An Evaluation.* London: Home Office.

Department of Health (1991) *Working Together Under the Children Act 1989: A Guide for Inter-Agency Co-operation for the Protection of Children from Abuse.* London: HMSO.

Department of Health (1995) *Child Protection: Messages from Research.* London: HMSO.

Elliott, M. (1990) *Teenscape: A Personal Safety Programme for Teenagers.* London: Health Education Authority.

Elliott, M. (1991) *Feeling Happy Feeling Safe: A Safety Guide for Young Children.* Sevenoaks, Kent: Hodder and Stoughton.

Finkelhor, D. (1988) 'The trauma of child sexual abuse: two models.' In G. Wyatt and G. Powell (eds) *Lasting Effects of Child Sexual Abuse.* Newbury Park, CA: Sage Publications.

Harrison, J. (1993) 'Medical responsibilities to disabled people.' In J. Swain, V. Finkelstein, S. French and M. Oliver (eds) *Disabling Barriers – Enabling Environments*. London: Sage Publications in association with The Open University.

Hevey, D. (1992) *The Creatures Time Forgot: Photography and Disability Imagery*. London: Routledge.

Holton, J. and Bonnerjea, L. (1994) *The Child ,the Court and the Video: A Study of the Implementation of the Memorandum of Good Practice on Video Interviewing of Child Witnesses*. Manchester: Department of Health Publications Unit.

Home Office in conjunction with Department of Health (1992) *Memorandum of Good Practice on Video Recorded Interviews With Child Witnesses for Criminal Proceedings*. London: HMSO.

Hubert, J. (1991) *Home-bound: Crisis in the Care of Young People with Severe Learning Difficulties. A Study of 20 Families*. London: King's Fund Centre.

Kennedy, M. (1992) 'Not the only way to communicate: A challenge to voice in child protection work.' *Child Abuse Review 1*, 3, 169–178.

Kennedy, M. (1993a) 'Signs and indicators.' In the ABCD training and resource pack: *Abuse and Children who are Disabled (ABCD)*. Leicester: The ABCD Consortium.

Kennedy, M. (1993b) 'Human aids to communication.' In the ABCD training and resource pack: *Abuse and Children who are Disabled (ABCD)*. Leicester: The ABCD Consortium.

Kirkwood, A. (1993) *The Leicestershire Inquiry 1992*. Leicester: Leicestershire County Council.

Levy, A. and Kahan, B. (1991) *The Pindown Experience and the Protection of Children: The Report of the Staffordshire Child Care Inquiry*. Stafford: Staffordshire County Council.

Marchant, R. and Page, M. (1992) 'Bridging the gap: investigating the abuse of children with multiple disabilities.' *Child Abuse Review 1*, 3, 179–183.

Marchant, R. and Page, M. (1993) *Bridging the Gap: Child Protection Work with Children With Multiple Disabilities*. London: NSPCC.

Marchant, R. and Page, M. (1997) 'The Memorandum and disabled children.' In H. Westcott and J. Jones (eds) *Perspectives on the Memorandum. Policy, Practice and Research in Investigative Interviewing*. Aldershot: Arena.

Morris, J. (1991) *Pride Against Prejudice: Transforming Attitudes to Disability*. London: The Women's Press.

Morris, J. (1995) *Gone Missing? A Research and Policy Review of Disabled Children Living Away From Their Families*. London: The Who Cares? Trust.

Rickell, S. (1993) 'The process of empowerment and service user involvement.' In the ABCD training and resource pack: *Abuse and Children who are Disabled (ABCD)*. Leicester: The ABCD Consortium.

Sayers, L. (1994) 'Objects without Voices: An Exploration of the Experiences of Parents and Professionals who have been Involved in an Investigation of the Abuse of a Child With Disabilities.' Unpublished MA Dissertation, University of Leicester.

Sobsey, D. (1994) *Violence and Abuse in the Lives of People With Disabilities: The End of Silent Acceptance?* Baltimore, Maryland: Paul H. Brookes Publishing Company.

Sobsey, D. and Doe, T. (1991) 'Patterns of sexual abuse and assault.' *Sexuality and Disability 9,* 3, 243–259.

Spencer, J.R. (1992) 'The complexities of the legal process for children with disabilities.' *Child Abuse Review 1,* 3, 200–203.

Sullivan, P.M. and Scanlan, J.M. (1987) 'Therapeutic issues.' In J. Garbarino, P.E. Brookhauser and K.J. Authier (eds) *Special Children – Special Risks: The Maltreatment of Children With Disabilities.* New York: De Gruyter.

Sullivan, P.M. and Scanlan, J.M. (1990) 'Psychotherapy with handicapped sexually abused children.' *Developmental Disabilities Bulletin 18,* 2, 21–34.

Sutherland, A.T. (1981) *Disabled We Stand.* London: Souvenir Press.

Wardhaugh, J. and Wilding, P. (1993) 'Towards an explanation of the corruption of care.' *Critical Social Policy 13,* 4–31.

Westcott, H.L. (1991) *Institutional Abuse of Children – From Research to Policy: A Review.* London: National Society for the Protection and Care of Children.

Westcott, H.L. (1993) *Abuse of Children and Adults With Disabilities.* London: National Society for the Protection and Care of Children.

Westcott, H.L. and Cross, M. (1996) *This Far and No Further: Towards Ending the Abuse of Disabled Children.* Birmingham: Venture Press.

Westcott, H.L. and Jones, J. (1997) *Perspectives on the Memorandum. Policy, Practice and Research in Investigative Interviewing.* Aldershot: Arena.

# CHAPTER 10

# Group Advocacy in a Residential Setting

*Chailey Young People's Group with Sue Virgo*

In this chapter I wish to convey the experiences of young people at Chailey Heritage in setting up and using their group, Chailey Young People's Group (CYPG). Chailey Heritage provides assessment, medical, therapy and educational services for children and young people with severe, complex and multiple physical impairments. Approximately 120 children and young people attend the school and about half of those are resident at Chailey or live in the community supported by Chailey staff.

The material that I shall use is, where possible, the group's. As many of the group members have difficulty with communication, and use communication systems which rely on an indication of 'yes' and 'no' from them, in some of the discussions the views are brief and, to a degree, open to interpretation by those assisting with the communication.

### Getting the group 'off the ground'

CYPG originated from a group of four young people, ranging in age from 12 to 20 years. The following letter, composed and circulated by these young people after nine months of considering existing groups and questioning invited people, explains how the group evolved:

> *We are four people who enjoy meeting weekly to discuss our feelings about Rights and Responsibilities and how young people are treated at Chailey. We were asked by the Child Protection Working Group to think about ways for young people who come to*

*Chailey Heritage to be able to complain, express their worries or to communicate their opinions.*

*We feel a good way to start is to form a 'Chailey Young People's Group' (CYPG) who will be able to listen if you have a problem, help if you need to complain and put you in touch with someone who can advise you on what to do. When necesary we will find someone who can help us to communicate and we can pass on ideas and concerns to Chailey Heritage on your behalf. This term we shall be inviting others to join us in setting up this first Chailey Young People's Group. We plan to get the help of an 'advocate' who will be independent of Chailey Heritage, to help us all by being able to listen and make it possible to be heard. A leaflet will be sent to everyone and posters will be put up around Chailey, explaining how to contact the group when we are able to start...*

*Thank you for listening to us.*

*Yours sincerely,*

*The Student Rights Group*

Following the go-ahead for the group, The Children's Society was approached to employ an independent advocacy worker to manage and supervise the scheme. I was appointed as advocate and was then 'vetted' by the group before proceeding. I was asked questions such as: Are you a determined person? Can you be persistent? Will you be loyal to the young people? Are you a good listener? Are you patient? You will treat the children and young people as equals, won't you? Does that present a problem for you? Are you willing to give physical and emotional comfort to the young people if necessary? I answered and was accepted.

The advocacy scheme started at Chailey in November 1994 and was initially funded for four hours per week (increased to seven per week in November 1995). From January to March 1995 the group of four young people designed a poster and leaflet to publicise and promote the group. The young people were active and democratic in expressing exactly how the poster and leaflet should be worded and illustrated. One of the group members contributed her own art work. The leaflet reads:

*'Chailey Young People's Group (CYPG) enables every young person to meet together and speak out. It is run by Chailey young people, for all who use Chailey services. We provide a safe place to have fun and communicate with each other, share points of view, express ideas and help solve problems. You can attend regularly, or just come*

*along when you have a problem or a view you want to share. The Chailey Young People's Advocate, who is independent of the organisations providing the services at Chailey, will be at the meeting to help and pass on your ideas and concerns on your behalf.*

The leaflet was circulated to every child at Chailey and displayed in areas used by out-patients.

CYPG began officially on 27 April 1995, meeting weekly in the evening, and was immediately successful in attracting members. There are no age restrictions but the age range of group members has generally been from 12 to 18 years. The group has varied in attendance with between four and fourteen members, settling to a core group of eleven, with an average attendance of eight or nine. A total of twenty-four young people have used the group. Almost all of the members are resident at Chailey, either full-time, term-time, weekdays or for one or two nights a week. The increasing support from Chailey staff has had an enormous benefit for group members, both in getting members to the group and in assisting with communication with the young people. Lack of adequate assistance with communication denies members access to using the group.

## CYPG

In essence, CYPG is a 'talking' group. Holly, one of the original group members, has written her views on what the group is for:

> *'Last night I turned on the TV to see that all too familiar advert for BT. At the end the actor turned to the camera and said that famous phrase "It's good to talk". This made me think.*
>
> *What if you can't talk because of your disability and you use a book or board? What if you have a speech defect and people don't listen to what you have to say? What if you are too frightened or embarrassed to talk? What if you talk but don't feel as if you have anyone to talk to?*
>
> *The fact is that you can talk until you are blue in the face but if you have no one to listen it's not going to do you much good. Many disabled children and teenagers find it hard to make a close circle of friends in which normal problems and worries can be shared. Speaking to teachers and care staff can be embarrassing and awkward especially if it's about another member of staff. That is where CYPG comes in. We offer a*

*place where problems can be discussed openly. A forum in which ideas can be put forward and worries talked over. Because CYPG is run by young people for young people we understand what you are going through. We have the power to help you solve your problems either on your own or with our help. Just talking helps sometimes.'*

Two of the early group sessions involved an outside speaker, but the remaining groups have been solely for discussions between group members. Rules were drawn up by the original Student Rights Group, emphasising confidentiality, and were revised and extended by the larger group after the group had been meeting for a year. The group rules as they stand now state:

1.  The group is a safe place to talk where things won't be talked about outside, either by group members or staff.

2.  The group is a place to bring problems where someone will help you.

3.  No one will laugh at your problems.

4.  Young people should be able to speak for themselves unless they want someone to speak for them.

5.  Members of the group should be able to communicate with everyone.

6.  Members should be able to bring a helper with them to the group.

7.  If a member of the group is not happy with the adults they can ask them to leave.

8.  When decisions are made, everybody has their say.

9.  Members of the group should listen when someone is trying to talk to the group.

10. Group members should be able to have transport to the group every week.

The advocate's role is to organise and facilitate the group and be available for advocacy issues either in the group context or on an individual basis. A member of Chailey staff, Mike Martyn, acts as co-facilitator, when necessary, freeing me to withdraw from the group to deal privately with individual advocacy issues. Mike's role is a practical one, making sure that group members can get to the group and keeping conversation going in my absence. Since Mike is employed at Chailey, he does not play an advocacy role. Originally, it was hoped that group members would facilitate the group themselves, but practice has shown that the group is more confident with someone else taking on that responsibility. Group members choose what issues or ideas they wish to bring to the group for sharing or discussion. If discussion dries up, I offer a topic such as 'what makes you happy or sad?', or 'what makes you angry?'.

## Advocacy through CYPG

Within CYPG, group members both advise each other and decide which issues need pursuing. Issues raised within the group which require action are taken up by either the young person concerned with support from the group, by another group member if they are willing, by a member of staff, or by the advocate. The young person always makes the choice of action. Themes that recur in discussions are passed on to management so that they have an awareness of current concerns for the young people.

The following are examples of issues brought to CYPG where action was wanted or needed.

Relationship issues are a key concern of group members. These involve relationships with care staff, family, keyworkers and teachers. Areas of concern have been misunderstandings, personality differences, wanting changes, finding it difficult to 'voice' praise of staff, wanting more or better communication, wanting choices. Group material and individual advocacy within the group highlight how difficult it can be for young people who are dependent on carers, and not wanting to risk their relationships, to ask for something to be changed.

It is often the case that the closer the young person is to the carer, the more difficult it is to ask for changes. However, some of the young people have, with the support of the group, felt able to tackle concerns themselves, while others have been able to let the advocate speak to the appropriate person for them.

It is primarily because the young people are so dependent on carers, families, teachers and other professionals that an independent advocate is valued by them. The concern for hurting someone's feelings or of reprisals is reduced. Also, some young people have found it easier to talk about personal problems to a relative 'stranger' rather than to someone they are close to.

Group members have raised practical issues, such as wanting to try different equipment, or wanting repairs or changes to existing equipment. They have asked to have their preferences regarding basic things such as drinks or flavour of crisps conveyed to the appropriate person. It has sometimes felt difficult to communicate what may appear to be minor requests. It is important that personal preferences are conveyed because they contribute to the quality of life.

Young people have wanted advice on finding friends. Having an impairment often means young people socialise with their parents rather than with their peers. Volunteers have been found to accompany young people to concerts and other places of interest.

CYPG wrote to British Rail complaining about the service for disabled people, using their personal experiences to illustrate their argument. They wanted British Rail to acknowledge its responsibility for accommodating disabled passengers. They wrote about having to be lifted on to the train because there are no ramps, of sitting in the guard's van 'like a bit of luggage – not a human, just a suitcase shoved in the guard's van'.

Members have discussed boredom and tried to find ways to alleviate it. The group is in the process of trying to organise the use of school computers within the residential homes at weekends and holidays.

There have been discussions about the 'sibling rivalry' which sometimes takes place in residential settings when residents compete for attention and group members have developed responses to it.

## Empowerment: group/peer support

CYPG is also used as a forum for discussion of shared personal experiences. Sharing experiences in the group context enables peer support and facilitates strategies for change. One example is the group discussion about the experience of disability. There was much anger from group members about the 'outside' world disabling them. From this discussion came the idea to write personal accounts, in prose and poetry, for publication and circulation to groups, agencies and schools to educate others. This project is likely to take some time, but the following piece of writing by Laura Carter is an example of the material to be included:

## The Polar Bear

*The Polar bear lays on its side bleeding, a fox runs past quickly. The Polar bear sees the fox and tries to call out to him but no sound escapes him. The bear knew he had to get away before the men with guns came back. Slowly, the bear tries to get to his feet but he can't. Pain shoots through his leg so he falls back on to the now very crimson snow. Once more the great animal tries to struggle to stand, using his front paws. He thinks of nothing except the pain. His claws are making gashes in the show. The ice is too slippery and the Polar bear is too weak and so he drops back on to the snow and dies.*

Provoked by the expression of the fears of a young person who was about to have a major operation, group members were able to share their experiences of being in hospital and of operations. All the members present in the group that evening had experienced spells in hospitals and most had negative experiences and feelings to relate. However, summing up at the end of the discussion, seven of the eight young people felt they had benefited from hospital treatment.

One session focused on the birth experiences of group members and the implications for their impairment. Some group members were well informed and very graphic, while others were less informed and wanted to find out more about their birth from their parents.

Another session centred on being able to make choices and decisions. This was prompted by a young person sharing her difficulty in asking her mother if she could have a particular hairstyle. Discussion led to mothers and how they appear to want to stop their children from growing up. The young people felt this was a particular issue for disabled children whose parents seemed to be overprotective.

Group members have regularly brought up the subject of being 'heard'. For some, the experience is that people who are not known to them assume they cannot talk or communicate. For others, the problem lies in letting people know that they want to communicate something. In practical terms, many of the young people have to rely on others to be pro-active to enable communication to take place. One of the group members, who has speech which takes time to understand, states:

> 'People don't listen to me and talk to me, but T (member of staff) does. He listens to people more...At home, Mum and Dad are often rowing – I don't like it – it means they haven't time for me. In the group people listen to me and talk to me. I like coming to the group so that I can help others communicate with their books – I like to help them – it's fun.'

The group discussed ways to make people listen and talk to them.

## Group discussions

The following examples of group members' responses to set topics illustrate some of the experiences of the young people who attend CYPG.

**Question:** *What makes you angry?*

'When people stare at me. I feel upset, cross and angry. It makes me want to get away.'
'Having my swimming costume put on – it's uncomfortable.'
'When night staff don't come.'
'My mum makes my squash too strong.'
'I want more help to feed myself.'
'I want to use my walker more – my legs get stiff.'
'Going out – there are always problems.'
'Being pushed around by...'
'I don't like having to get up early at home to get to school.'
'I want the drinks I like.'
'I miss my family.'

**Question:** *Is it different being at Chailey rather than being at home? What is different?* (Topic chosen for this particular research.)

'I like being at Chailey – I get bossed around at home – Mum and Dad chase me up to get ready – there are loads and loads of games here and I can go to bed when I want to.'
'It is different – more people of my age at Chailey – I like school but miss my family – I like it at home because my sisters boss me around a bit and spoil me – some of the kids at Chailey get on my nerves.'
'Mum decides my bedtime at home – I do here.'
'It is better at Chailey – I like the people – especially my keyworker.'
'I find it hard to ask for my favourite foods here.'
'I don't choose what clothes I want to wear at home – I do at Chailey.'
'I like it better at home because I miss my Mum and Dad and sister.'
'Having lots of people around is better at Chailey – I don't see so many people at home – I like school and my friends.'
'I like school best – my unit is better than at home because of friends – but I miss my brother – people do more with me at Chailey although it is sometimes boring at weekends – home is better then.'

'I like it better at home – I miss my family.'
'I like the staff on my unit – I like the garden at home – I like going shopping at Chailey.'

**Question:** *Is it difficult to ask for things?*

'Yes – sometimes difficult at school not at home or on my unit–I can't ask for drinks or to go in my "stander".'
'Yes – sometimes if something is important.'
'I can ask the care staff but not my keyworker.'
'It is difficult to ask night staff for things.'
'It is difficult to ask for activities in school.'
'It is difficult to do the asking.'
'It is difficult to let people know I want to talk to them – when people do listen they don't take any notice – they don't do anything about what I ask for.'
'I get embarrassed sometimes.'

## Difficulties and dilemmas

A very important aspect of the success of CYPG has been the commitment of its members. CYPG is an open group and young people attend when they wish to, not being pressured to attend or to contribute to discussion. Inevitably, membership of the group changes for a variety of reasons. Young people leave Chailey for college, some 'outgrow' the group and want a change of activity, some find the group boring. One of the original group members left after a year and gave the following reasons:

'The main reasons I don't come any more are because I find it boring and there are people closer to me that it is easier for me to discuss things with. Sometimes I felt that the discussions had moved on without me finishing what I wanted to say. From time to time I found the group helpful but for the most part I don't think the issues raised were resolved.'

The reasons given here are valid in a group such as CYPG. As mentioned above, communication is a crucial issue for many of the young people who use CYPG. Although Chailey Heritage has developed a comprehensive communication system designed to meet the child's physical ability and developmental language level, communication of ideas, views and concerns can take a great deal of time. Many of the group members have no speech or very limited speech and rely on indicating 'yes' or 'no' to words offered to them from their communication system. This indication may consist of a particular type of glance, a blink or facial expression. In some instances, when a young person has very restricted facial control, the distinction between the indicating sign for 'yes' or 'no' is barely perceivable to those not familiar with communicating with the young person. Lack of time may mean that issues are therefore not always completely resolved at that particular moment.

Sometimes it is not possible to get to the crux of an issue because the young person's understanding and use of vocabulary is limited. This can cause immense frustration for the communicating person and a sense of failure for the advocate who is trying to determine the details of a concern.

In addition, some young people have attended the group expecting immediate solutions to concerns they present and often this has not been possible to achieve.

However, some regularity of members and staff is necessary to enable young people to trust the group and feel safe in expressing their views and feelings. This has been achieved and is due to the commitment of members and to the practical support of staff who have ensured that the young people are able to meet and communicate with each other.

A significant dilemma for the group is ensuring that young people are 'heard'. It is important that the group is felt to be empowering, rather than perpetuating the young people's experience in the 'outside' world. Group members who rely on another person to facilitate their communication depend on that person to interpret their views accurately without 'putting words into their mouths' for expediency.

A further dilemma for a few group members has been the response by carers to their new found 'voice'. It is crucial that the young person's communication is taken seriously and that the assumption is not made that 'ideas' are put into the young person's head by discussion topics.

Confidentiality is an issue that the group has attempted to tackle within its rules. The group is considered to be a safe place to talk, where things will not be discussed outside by group members, staff or advocates without the young person's permission. The young people are able to exclude any staff member from the group and choose with whom they talk. They also choose how, or if, concerns are progressed. However, if an issue arises, either within the group or individually, which indicates that any child or young person might be at risk, I explain to the young person that I have to pass on the information but that they will be informed of that process.

## Positive outcomes and learning from CYPG

The group context of CYPG has clearly demonstrated that a 'safe', committed group creates both the pre-conditions and a site for advocacy. In particular, as many of the young people at Chailey do not have speech, or they have difficulty or lack confidence in communicating, their reliance on communication systems and the pro-activity of other people increases their vulnerability and dependence. The creation of a specified environment where young people feel able, and are enabled, to express themselves offers the potential for improving the quality of life and for empowerment.

Issues raised and taken up within the group, and individually, indicate that the quality of life for young disabled people may be significantly improved if they are facilitated and encouraged to 'voice' their preferences and feelings.

The members of the CYPG have become increasingly eager to be 'heard', particularly outside of Chailey. The letter to British Rail and the planned book of experiences are only part of the intention both to educate non-disabled people into changing their views and behaviour and to change the 'disabling' environment within which they find themselves. Members participated in an advocacy workshop for South Downs Health NHS Trust in March 1996; they featured as an example of good practice in a BBC TV Esther Rantzen programme about advocacy in August 1996. They have also recently contributed to research being undertaken to determine disabled young people's understanding of 'independent living' and what happens when disabled young people become adults.

Crucial to CYPG has been the independence of the advocate. For many of the young people who have spoken to me personally, or who have used the group, the fact that the advocate is not employed by Chailey has been significant in freeing them to raise concerns and ideas.

CHAPTER 11

# Disabled Children in Permanent Substitute Families

*Rena Phillips*

*A permanent family placement refers to adoption and permanent foster care.*
*The term 'black' refers to children with at least one parent from the following ethnic groups:*
*African, African-Caribbean, Asian, Chinese or Arab origin.*

'Was I given away because there was something wrong with my hand?': the charged question of a disabled adopted man, in a TV documentary, on meeting his birth mother many years after his adoption. She reassures him that there were other reasons for his adoption. Whatever her answer might have been, this scenario vividly illustrates the themes explored in this chapter of identity, difference and stigma that may affect disabled children living in permanent substitute families.

It is important to highlight in the introduction two facts about disabled children in permanent substitute families. First, the literature on adoption and permanent foster care contains very little directly in terms of research on, and services for, disabled children. The authors of a recently published practice guide about substitute care for disabled children comment that they were motivated to write because of the lack of material in this field (Argent and Kerrane 1997). Readers will notice that their work comes up frequently in this chapter. Second, as with other disabled children, we have a limited knowledge of their experiences and views. In a review of the literature on social support for disabled children and their families, Baldwin and Carlisle (1994) highlight the striking fact that very little of it is based on direct communication with the child about her/his experience of living with disability. Historically studies of children have mainly been 'on' them rather than 'with' them. Increasingly, researchers have recognised the importance of engaging with children by directly recording their views and perspectives. However, this is still relatively new and raises many important ethical and methodological questions (Alderson 1995; Beresford 1997; Morrow and Richards 1996). As Middleton (1996) has commented:

> 'disabled children have yet to be consulted about their views in any meaningful or systematic fashion. As a potential area of research it is fraught with difficulty, not least in effectively separating the views of the child from those of their parents.' (Middleton 1996, p.3)

Recent years have seen an encouraging growth in the number of disabled children adopted and fostered, but they still face barriers to securing permanent family placements. This chapter starts by identifying difficulties such as shortage of appropriate placements, the lack of specialist skills in this area of work and prejudicial attitudes. It moves on to examine identity issues for disabled children in relation to long-term separation from birth parents, the importance of life-story work to help them make sense of the past and move into the future, and the challenges posed by the placement needs of black disabled children. The final section deals with post-placement support and services.

## Barriers to placements

Disabled children, like other children, enter the care system for a variety of inter-related and complex reasons. There can be failure by their families to look after them due to chronic disadvantage through long-term poverty and unemployment, abuse and neglect, alcoholism, domestic violence and mental illness (Bebbington and Miles 1989). The Children Act 1989 and the Children (Scotland) Act 1995 require local authorities to provide a range and level of services which safeguard and promote the welfare of children who are 'in need'. This concept for the first time specifically and significantly includes disabled children. Whilst the majority of disabled children live at home with their families, there has been little improvement in their circumstances: current levels of service provision as well as the types of services being offered do not adequately meet their needs (Beresford 1995; NCH Action For Children 1994; Social Services Inspectorate 1994). For some families it may prove too difficult to go on coping. Adoption is usually the preferred choice for children who permanently cannot live with their birth parents, as permanent foster care does not provide the legality and full security of adoption (Hill, Lambert and Triseliotis 1989; Triseliotis 1983). There is also evidence from children in permanent foster care that the traditional perception of foster care as low status in comparison with adoption seems to lead to feelings of low self-esteem (Triseliotis and Hill 1990). However, children may be placed either for adoption or permanent fostering, as in some situations the latter option may be the right choice for children, their foster carers and birth parents, for example, when the latter continue to be involved although they are not able directly to care for their disabled child.

Until about 25 years ago, the idea that disabled children could be placed for adoption was totally inconceivable and unheard of, and rarely considered in relation to foster care. They were labelled as 'unfit' medically, and if their parents could not cope with them they spent most or all of their childhood away from their families and in some form of residential provision. A combination of demographic and social changes and some influential studies and projects since then (referred to below) have enabled 'special needs' children, as they became known, to live in substitute families. This category encompasses older children, those from backgrounds of neglect and abuse, children who display serious emotional and behavioural disturbance, disabled children, groups of siblings and those from minority ethnic groups. On the other hand these developments have been patchy and uneven, denying many such children the opportunity of family life.

## Adoption

The change in adoption practice was quite dramatic. The early 1970s saw a drastic drop in the number of white babies available for adoption due to more effective contraception, legalisation of abortion, increasing acceptance of single parents and the smaller number of women of childbearing age. The seminal study by Rowe and Lambert, *Children Who Wait* (1973), revealed thousands of children drifting in residential or unsuitable foster care without any prospects of returning to their birth families. There was increasing recognition that it was essential for all children's development that they experience a sense of permanence, which provided them with a foundation from which to develop relationships not only throughout their childhood but into their adult lives. As a result, concerted efforts were made to move them to long-term family placements (Barker 1996). In the United States and Britain innovative specialist projects demonstrated that children with very severe impairments could be placed in substitute families (Argent 1984; Sawbridge 1975). This shift was encouraged by research such as Catherine

Macaskill's influential study, *Against The Odds* (1985), on the adoption of children with learning difficulties, which demonstrated the remarkable progress the children achieved with their new families.

The changes described did not come without difficulties and criticisms. Macaskill, in the study referred to above, concluded that negative professional attitudes towards children with learning difficulties were major barriers to their placement in substitute families:

> 'Professionals labelled the handicapped children as different to normal children and tended to set them apart from others by emphasising their weaknesses, difficulties and abnormalities.' (Macaskill 1985, p.95)

Families who make a deliberate choice to care for disabled children can evoke a variety of responses from the community as well as from professionals. These range from being seen as 'heroic' and 'wonderful' to being viewed with suspicion as to why and how such a commitment is undertaken, thus reinforcing the view of disabled children as departing from the norm. As an adoption worker in the mid-1980s, I witnessed the discrimination towards disabled children, when a family was denied the opportunity, by a senior manager in a local authority social work department, to make an application to adopt a second Down's syndrome child, on the grounds that this was an impossible and foolish task for any family!

Owing to the absence of detail in the published adoption statistics, it is not clear how many special needs children, including disabled children, are adopted. A British study of 1165 adoptive and permanent foster placements undertaken by voluntary agencies between 1980 and the end of 1984 provides some useful indications about disabled children (Fratter *et al.* 1991). Most of the children placed were adopted with only 12 per cent in permanent foster care. Out of the total, 1136 were special needs children showing emotional and behavioural problems, having experienced multiple moves and the effects of neglect and abuse. Eight per cent of the sample had Down's syndrome and 9 per cent were defined as having other 'mental disabilities'. As regards outcomes, 8 per cent of the former and 21 per cent of the latter experienced a disruption, i.e. their placements could not continue. In contrast, two studies in Scotland provided evidence of high levels of placement stability for children with severe learning difficulties (Borland, O'Hara and Triseliotis 1991). In a review of placement outcomes for children with special needs, Triseliotis, Shireman and Hundleby (1997), whilst acknowledging that outcome studies present many methodological problems, conclude that special needs adoption works well for most children. They report however increasingly higher breakdown rates and a decline of such placements. The enthusiastic view of the 1970s and 1980s, that a permanent family placement could be found for every and any child, has given way to a more cautious approach. It is easier to find adoptive homes for younger children, even for many who are disabled, than for older children. Increasingly tougher demands are being placed on permanent substitute families as they care for the most damaged children and young people in society. These include the challenge of coping with children with high emotional and developmental needs, the fight for their educational rights and opportunities, helping the development of racial and cultural identities and the complexities involved in maintaining contact with birth families. Today the hardest to place children are adolescents with serious behaviour or emotional problems, sibling groups of three or four, boys over 10 years of age and children with multiple impairments.

Finding homes for special needs children requires professional expertise and commitment. A recent Social Services Inspectorate Report (SSI) (SSI 1996a) on adoption services heavily criticises the low priority given to this area of work by local authorities. It found that one in four children had to wait more than three years for adoption, and this situation is particularly acute for children with special needs. More than one in three prospective parents wait longer than two years after their application before being matched with a child because there are still too few couples prepared to adopt special needs children. The furore created by the previous Tory government's view that politically correct social workers deny families a chance to adopt, missed the basic point that most local authorities face a serious mismatch between the aspirations of would-be adopters and the needs of children, with the danger that the emphasis will shift from the needs of children to the desire of the adults to adopt (Hirst 1997).

## Foster care

The number of children fostered has remained constant since the mid-1960s, with some 34,000 children in foster care at present. About a quarter have been defined as having an impairment, but this includes emotional and behavioural impairments (Berridge 1996). Foster care is seen as very successful in providing children with positive family experiences. However, there are increasingly serious concerns regarding the growing demands placed on foster carers, the gradual decline in the quality of the service in terms of the ability to recruit more carers and provide them with adequate support, training and remuneration (Association of Directors of Social Services 1997). Since the mid-1970s, there has been a proliferation of specialist fostering schemes in the UK. These were initially used to divert adolescents who were in trouble with the courts away from residential care, and were time-limited. The ideas underlying professional fostering were normalisation, community care, treatment, and better pay, training and support to foster carers (Hill *et al.* 1993; Triseliotis, Sellick and Short 1995). Subsequently, such schemes acquired a wider remit both in terms of type and age of children placed and length of stay, including special needs children on a long-term basis. However, most children with impairments are placed through the mainstream fostering services and not through special schemes (Mountney 1991). A report published by the National Foster Care Association, on the crisis facing foster care, is calling for the professionalisation of all foster carers (Valios 1997).

There are some accounts of voluntary agencies providing imaginative foster care to disabled children (Reed 1993), but such projects are thin on the ground. The picture in the statutory sector is less positive. In a survey by the National Foster Care Association of the provision by 69 local authorities and 9 voluntary agencies of long-term foster placements for disabled children, one of the most important findings was that children with impairments can lose out in the care system. Many who could benefit from foster care are left in residential homes or hospitals with insufficient efforts being put into finding carers who are willing to look after them. Also many of these children are not legally 'in care', and are therefore unlikely to be known to social work departments. The majority of agencies do not have specialist staff in the area of foster care for disabled children (Mountney 1991).

Berridge (1996), reviewing research on foster care over the past 20 years, draws attention to the significant shortage of foster carers. The latest Social Services Inspectorate report of local authority fostering (SSI 1996b) found no choice of placement in the majority of cases. Local authorities referred to recruitment difficulties for disabled children and needing to buy specialist placements as their in-house provision was insufficient. In a survey of foster care by the Association of Directors of Social Services (1997) 69 per cent believed they had insufficient foster carers to meet placement needs and a further 11 per cent had difficulties for specific groups of children with special needs.

Further barriers to the placements of disabled children in substitute permanent families may result from the attitudes of their birth parents, many of whom feel depressed and guilty about not being able to care for their own child. In a report by Morris (1995), which includes the life stories of adults who have experience of living away from their families for large parts of their childhood, Suba recalls wanting to be fostered rather than be in a residential school:

> 'I remember when I was about 14 they had a case conference and there was some discussion about me being fostered, about me going to live with a family. I really wanted it but my dad wouldn't agree.' (Morris 1995, p.4)

Lyon (1990), in a study on the legal status of children with significant learning difficulties in hospital and residential settings, found their parents preferred to see them placed there to avoid the stigma associated with formal care arrangements. She concluded that the children's legal status to a large extent determined where they ended up, with those in formal care having a much greater chance of being placed in substitute family care. She anticipated that the requirements under the Children Act 1989 to work in partnership with parents might stand in the way of substitute family placements if parents were reluctant to consider such an option. Equally important were the attitudes of social workers, who rarely raised the issue of family placements in child care reviews, even though they were aware of the benefits. Some of the reasons were intensity of family feeling against substitute family placement, not wishing to rock the boat and difficulties in finding a placement for children within the area where their parents lived:

> 'Nevertheless the abiding impression was of everyone accepting that such was to be the fate of the children to remain in residential projects and saying that "well, they were well cared for and everything was okay".' (Lyon 1990, p.111)

Lyon argues that as clear a differentiation in the case of children with severe learning difficulties must be made as between the needs of any children and their parents.

## Identity issues

The development of a clear sense of personal identity, or sense of self, is a consistent theme in the literature about human development (Erikson 1968; Marcia 1980; Gilligan 1982). Knowledge about background, family history and race and ethnic group are essential parts of this identity. This depends also to some extent on how other people see us and behave towards us. Goffman (1963) coined the term 'spoiled identity' to indicate the negative community attitudes to minority groups. Children who are disabled, black, adopted or fostered can be stigmatised and labelled because they are different.

There is ample evidence from adoption practice and research that the achievement of a healthy sense of identity is more difficult for children who are adopted. The lack of likeness between adoptees and adopters can lead to a sense of difference and of not belonging (Raynor 1980). Jenny Morris (1991) has written powerfully about the importance of physical difference in relation to disabled people and the generally negative reactions to that difference. This can assume particular significance for disabled children placed in permanent substitute families who may feel that they have been rejected by their birth parents because of it. It may also raise concerns about their new family such as their motivation to care for a disabled child and what they themselves look like. In relation to the placement needs of black children, the arguments for same race placements (as opposed to transracial placements) are that they need to grow up in black families who can provide them with positive black role models and the knowledge, experience and coping strategies for dealing with racism (BAAF 1995). It could be argued that the same reasons applied for placing disabled children with disabled substitute parents. Most people I have discussed this with, whether professionals or substitute families, respond with the counter arguments that the majority of disabled children have birth parents who are not disabled and that such a policy would create a greater shortage of placements as disabled applicants for adoption or foster care would have difficulties in getting approved.

Whilst difference can lead to stigma, an adoptive parent of a disabled child, writing in relation to special needs at school, reminds us of the importance of acknowledging differences and difficulties:

> 'Of course we should assert that all children are the same, but only in the sense they are of equal worth and, for example, deserve to be treated with respect, loved and given the opportunity to learn. We would be fooling ourselves if we did not recognise that in other important ways children are all different and that some are "more different" than others...Of course we need positive attitudes and actions and the best teaching and equipment but, for my daughter, it is still hard to see, to learn and to make relationships. A sense of pain of living with those differences often seems missing from the current, positive professional perspective, which seems keen to recognise her similarities to most children but reluctant to acknowledge her difficulties.' (Dumbleton 1996, p.28)

*Life-story work*

A vital aspect of children's identity is the means to understand and accept their history. Children separated from their families will experience loss and guilt. Life-story work, with a sympathetic adult, aims to help children in permanent substitute families to understand and come to terms with their past and to move forward into the present and future. For some, however, full background information may not be readily available: 'they may have changed families, social workers, homes and neighbourhoods. This past may be lost, much of it even forgotten' (Ryan and Walker 1993, p.5).

The term 'genealogical bewilderment' was coined by Sants (1964) to describe the predicament of people growing up in substitute care without access to information about their origins. Retrospective research on adopted people who have sought access to their birth records highlights their frustrations and criticisms about the stage at which their adoptive status was revealed to them by their adoptive parents, the kind of information they were given and the shock and pain when they accidentally discovered that they were adopted (Haimes and Timms 1985; Lambert *et al.* 1991; Triseliotis 1973; Walby and Symons 1990). Not being told about being adopted until late in childhood or even into adulthood is a thing of the past. The major issues now are when and what to tell adopted children. Adoption is a very difficult concept for children to understand and needs to be matched to their changing intellectual and emotional development and not done on a once and for all basis. For quite large number of families, 'telling' children of their background is problematical (Brodzinsky 1984). There is the danger that children with learning difficulties will be seen as unable to understand the facts of their adoption, thus denying them the opportunity to make sense of their experience.

There has been no substantive research on current practice in relation to both the quantity and quality of background information available for children in substitute family care and the kind of information that they request. What evidence there is, and practice experience, suggest the lack of social, psychological and medical information on children's backgrounds (Phillips 1988; Phillips and McWilliam 1995; Wassel 1993). A recent study on compulsory adoptions examined the information requests of adopted children as reported by their adoptive parents. Whilst the range of information sought was vast, the author reports that 'it is a matter of appreciable concern that more than half of the responses indicated the lack of sufficient information to respond adequately to children's questions.' (Ryburn 1995, p.58)

This has particular implications for disabled children. They can have complicated medical histories, for example, a genetically determined condition which requires good quality medical information. In the case of infant adoption, the difficulties in acquiring satisfactory family medical history from the birth parents has long been recognised and social workers are not trained for this task (Turnpenny 1994). Other issues which arise are whether information about a child's genetic profile be disclosed to a child, and if so at what stage and to what extent (Plumtree 1995). As discussed previously, an increasing number of children who have been abused are now being placed with substitute families. Often their past history is painful and distressing. For some disabled children a sensitive issue is the fact that their impairment was caused by their birth parents which can generate distressed and angry feelings and requires skilled help. In some cases, birth parents are a securely married couple with other non-disabled children which is equally difficult to bear for children placed away from home.

Since the 1980s, a rich variety of methods and techniques has been devised in effectively working and communicating with children separated from their birth families, such as life-story books, videos, cassettes, diaries, exercises, games, projects and the use of computers (Jewett 1984; Triseliotis, Sellick and Short 1995; Triseliotis, Shireman and Hundleby 1997). *Life Story Work* by Tony Ryan and Rodger Walker (1993) has become a classic for invaluable suggestions in working with children. They emphasise the commitment, time and skill this work requires and that it is the process rather than the product which will yield the most benefits.

Children with communication or learning difficulties present particular challenges, whether it is in involving them in research (Beresford 1997) or direct work (Marchant and Page 1992). Reid (1991), in a study on the use of life-story books with children with severe learning difficulties, points out that they can be seen to be exempt from otherwise accepted theories of human development about attachment, separation and loss on the grounds that they cannot understand what is happening to them. She reports a social worker as saying that people undertaking direct work with children with severe learning difficulties were 'just kidding themselves on if they thought they could achieve anything'. Other barriers identified by Atwell (1993) are social workers not being comfortable with children with learning difficulties, a wish to overprotect, and lack of communication skills. She advocates using different methods for children who may have speech problems or may lack the use of one or more of the senses:

> 'For example, for David who was blind, much of his life story work was interspersed with tactile stimuli, for example, buttons from a favourite person's jacket, a shell from a seaside outing with the family, dried flowers from the garden. It also included a handkerchief perfumed with the mother's favourite perfume.' (Atwell 1993, p.58)

Argent and Kerrane (1997) have produced a timely and useful practice guide for working with disabled children separated from their birth parents. The central concept, that no child is too impaired to be informed about what is going to happen in some way she or he can understand, is applied by them to several other important aspects of direct work with disabled children who are moving to permanent substitute families. They need information about the process of adoption and foster care. They require to be reassured that their substitute family both understands and will be able to manage their condition, especially if their birth family could not:

> 'Will my wheelchair go in? Will they understand me when I speak funny? Will they stay with me in hospital? What happens if they can't manage?' (p.72)

In planning introductions to the new family, the nature of the impairment has to be taken into account in relation to distance, escorts and stamina, and the authors ask: 'what does this child see, hear, comprehend, retain and anticipate?' They also raise issues of contact with birth families after the placement, which will be discussed later on.

## Ethnicity and childcare placements

The needs of disabled black children in substitute family care have to be viewed against the evidence of the social and economic disadvantages confronting all black children in Britain and the unsatisfactory level of social work provision for them (Caesar, Parchment and Berridge 1994). Black children are under-represented as regards preventive services and over-represented in the care system and tend to stay there longer (Barn 1993).

The Children Act 1989 and the Children (Scotland) Act 1995 both emphasise that issues of race, culture, language and religion have to be considered in providing services for children in need, and suggest that this usually requires careful matching in childcare placements. At the same time, social workers have been criticised for an over-reliance on political correctness on this issue. The subject of transracial versus same-race placements has generated a lot of passion and controversy and the evidence in many ways is still inconclusive (Smith and Berridge 1993). In a review of empirical studies which have assessed transracial placements, Triseliotis *et al.* (1997) report that most children and adolescents are doing well in their families and school. There is little research yet on transracially placed young adults but practice and anecdotal evidence suggest identity difficulties in this age group (Hayes 1996). Whilst the emphasis these days is on finding same-race placements, such a policy requires strategies and ideas for recruiting black families (BAAF 1991, 1995). However, apart from a few successful demonstration projects not enough effort is put into such recruitment (Kaniuk 1991). What little evidence there is points to the fact that the majority of black children in this country have been placed transracially (Association of Directors of Social Services 1997; SSI 1996b; Thoburn, Rashid and Charles 1992). There is equally a lack of information about black disabled children placed with black substitute families. However, what we know about disabled black children and their birth families points to the paucity of accessible, supportive and sensitive services (Shah 1992). Such racism in social service practices can create extra problems for disabled children which they may be less able to cope with than other children. As argued by Middleton (1996) disabled black children are in great jeopardy since they are likely to be in the hands of non-disabled white professionals, who are focusing not on race but on disability. Additionally they are more vulnerable to being isolated from other disabled black children.

Linked to the issue of transracial placements is the debate, again inconclusive, about whether black children in this country have a tendency to view black people negatively and to prefer white to their own colour. Maxime, a clinical psychologist, is quoted as saying:

> 'There are children who are burning their skins off, slashing their wrists, hating themselves, because they are black. I wish I could reassure you that this is something from the past, but it is not.' (Lee 1994, p.22)

Others claim that such examples are used to perpetuate the myth of a negative black self-concept with the danger of black children being viewed as having behavioural, psychological, educational and other problems due to their identity confusion, which in turn can lead to inappropriate and sometimes potentially damaging services (Owusu-Bempah 1994). Steering a middle path, Banks (1992) offers techniques for direct identity work with black children, arguing that:

> 'To deny the importance of cultural diversity, skin colour and its significance for the Black child is to deny the Black child confirmation of his or her likely experience.' (Banks 1992, p.24)

There is the risk, however, that children with learning difficulties will be seen as not aware of their own and other people's skin colour. Yet research in a number of countries has demonstrated that children develop racial awareness as young as three years of age (Furnham and Stacey 1991). Some of the issues identified by Ryan and Walker (1993) in direct work with black children in substitute permanent families are the correct terminology to use when referring to black people, that every effort should be made to involve a black worker, learning about black family life in the context of British society and helping children value their cultural heritage. By implication, much extra care and sensitivity is required when disability is also a factor.

## Post-placement support

Until the 1980s the legalising of an adoption was seen as the logical cut-off point between agencies and adoptive families in order to 'normalise' the latter. Increasingly, research has indicated that children with special needs in substitute family care may require medical, counselling and practical services from a range of professionals long after the adoption order has been granted (Hill, Hutton and Easton 1988; Howe 1990; Macaskill 1985; Phillips and McWilliam 1996; Rushton, Quinton and Treseder 1993). The Adoption Act 1976 and the Children (Scotland) Act 1995 place a duty on local authorities to provide continuing post-placement support. In the late 1990s, post-adoption services are at a critical point. On the one hand, recognition of their importance is gathering momentum and, on the other, they continue to suffer from a lack of funding, with good practice expected on a nil cost basis. The result is a patchy development of services. For a large number of children there is little ongoing support offered. Yet in some areas, imaginative specialist services, particularly in the voluntary sector, have been established. Whilst there are concerns about the level of support provided to

disabled children in long-term foster care, the contractual nature of the relationship of foster carers with placing agencies means that they gain access to resources in a more routine way. However, the post-placement needs of disabled children in adoption and permanent foster care are similar.

Post-placement support for disabled children may have extra elements in terms of the following: hospital visits, contact with a variety of professionals and the requirement for effective interagency collaboration, practical matters such as appliances and allowances, sitting and short-break services, special needs at school and therapeutic help. There will be periods of particular vulnerability to stress:

> 'Disability will remain a factor to be reckoned with throughout the family's life cycle: births, marriages and deaths; going to school, leaving school and leaving home (if able to pursue independent living) will be crucial times for the disabled child, for the carers and any other children in the family. Moves towards independence can be particularly traumatic if the young person with disabilities appears to be totally dependent on the carers.' (Argent 1996, p.5)

Research on children in the care system has shown the benefits for them of maintaining contact with their families but also that such links are seldom given enough consideration (Millham *et al.* 1989). Contact with children's families is often seen as the most difficult part of fostering (Verity 1995). A study of children with learning difficulties in a fostering project run by a voluntary agency showed that maintaining and developing family networks had not been fully addressed by the social workers themselves or with the foster carers (Lyon 1990). A central issue in post-placement work with adopted children is their continuing contact, including face-to-face contact, with birth relatives after placement. Until the mid1980s, this was viewed as incompatible with achieving a permanent family placement. Research on face-to-face contact points out that on the whole it is beneficial in meeting the identity needs of children, lessening their powerlessness and helping them feel more secure in their adoptive families (Triseliotis 1993; Ryburn1994). There is evidence on the other hand of ambivalence and cautiousness from practitioners and users of adoption services. Some of the reservations are that it could lead to divided loyalties in the children and that some adoptees do not wish to make contact (Kanuik 1994; McWhinnie 1994; Rushton *et al.* 1993). There have been no large-scale longitudinal studies on the impact of contact on adopted children. Recent research on contact by Fratter (1996) is the first of its kind to focus exclusively on the adoption of children with special needs. Of the sample of 25 children and young people, there were 12 whose views could not be discovered, including four with severe learning difficulties. Positive feelings about contact in some form were expressed by all but one of the adopted children interviewed. Fratter is careful to stress that children's participation in decision making can be obstructed by agency policies and individual attitudes rather than what will promote children's welfare. However, she suggests that her findings of positive views about contact, linked to the Children Act 1989 presumption that contact will usually be beneficial, should guide policy makers and practitioners when contact is being considered for children whose wishes cannot easily be ascertained.

Contact between disabled children in permanent substitute families and their birth families presents extra challenges. These include the guilt of birth families at not being able to care for their children, the feelings of substitute families towards parents who might have caused the impairment, communications hampered by problems with reading, writing and speech and even problems associated with using the telephone (Russell 1995). As Argent (1996) reminds us:

> 'It is never good enough to presume that a child does not comprehend the meaning of relationships and that therefore contact has no significance. On the contrary, it could be argued that only by maintaining continuity can a child with learning difficulties make sense of her world or a child with physical disabilities accept himself as he is.' (Argent 1996, p.2)

Children in permanent substitute families have so far had little say in the future of post-placement services. This is a reflection of the fact that whilst there has been some progress in the development of post-placement services for birth and adoptive parents, there is a gap in the provision of services to adopted children in their own right. For example, would they want a key worker outside their substitute family or a support group they could attend? Whilst sharing many common needs, the wishes and feelings of adopted children will be affected by their impairment, gender, race and culture. In the move towards more openness and contact in adoption, we need particularly to hear their views on how they can achieve both a sense of permanence and a clear sense of personal identity. They have a right to expect that their opinions will be taken into account in deciding the way that scarce resources are distributed.

## Conclusions

Writing about the 'powerlessness' of adoption, Hartman and Laird (1990) describe adopted children as the most disempowered of all, 'having generally had no opportunity to participate in the decisions that have so powerfully shaped their lives and their identities' (p.228). Add to this the ingredients of race and disability and children will experience a powerful combination of discriminatory attitudes and practices. Disabled children in permanent substitute families have unique circumstances, capacities and needs and will experience such discrimination differently. For example, adopted children with learning difficulties might have at times more in common with other children with learning difficulties than with those who are adopted. What is applicable to all of them however, as highlighted in this chapter, are some serious shortcomings: the lack of adequate research and information, the shortage and inappropriateness of placements, pressure to ration time and expertise, the dearth of post-placement services and, most importantly, not knowing what disabled children in substitute permanent families think and feel about their lives.

Working in partnership with service users has become one of the key phrases of the 1990s. As some commentators have pointed out, 'working in partnership with families is one leap forward, but working in partnership with children is another gigantic leap' (Wheal and Walder 1994). Whilst much has been achieved and learned about placing disabled children in permanent substitute families, we need to offer them an increasingly responsive and skilled service by listening to their voices, acting upon what they ask for and working alongside them.

## References

Adoption Act (1976). London: HMSO.

Alderson, P. (1995) *Listening to Children – Children, Ethics and Social Research.* Essex: Barnardos.

Argent, H. (1996) *The Placement of Children With Disabilities. Practice Note 34.* London: British Agencies for Adoption and Fostering.

Argent, H. (1984) *Find Me a Family.* London: Souvenir Press.

Argent, H. and Kerrane, A. (1997) *Taking Extra Care – Respite, Shared and Permanent Care for Children With Disabilities.* London: British Agencies for Adoption and Fostering.

Association of Directors of Social Services Children and Families Committee Report (1997) *The Foster Carer Market: A National Perspective.* Ipswich: Suffolk Social Services.

Atwell, A. (1993) 'Working with children with a learning disability.' In T. Ryan and R. Walker (eds) *Life Story Work.* London: British Agencies for Adoption and Fostering.

BAAF (1991) *Recruiting Black Families. Practice Note 18.* London: British Agencies for Adoption and Fostering.

BAAF (1995) *The Placement Needs of Black Children.* Practice Note 13. London: British Agencies for Adoption and Fostering.

Baldwin, S. and Carlisle, J. (1994) *Social Support for Disabled Children and Their Families – a Review of the Literature.* Edinburgh: HMSO.

Banks, N. (1992) 'Techniques for direct identity work with black children.' *Adoption and Fostering 16,* 3, 19–25.

Barker, S. (1996) *Planning for Permanence.* Practice Note 33. London: British Agencies for Adoption and Fostering.

Barn, R. (1993) *Black Children in the Public Care System.* London: Batsford/British Agencies for Adoption and Fostering.

Bebbington, A. and Miles, J. (1989) 'The background of children who enter local authority care.' *British Journal of Social Work 19,* 5, 349–368.

Beresford, B. (1995) *Experts' Opinions: A National Survey of Parents Caring for a Severely Disabled Child.* Joseph Rowntree Foundation/Community Care. Bristol: Bristol Policy Press.

Beresford, B. (1997) *Personal Accounts – Involving Disabled Children in Research.* Social Policy Research Unit. Norwich: The Stationery Office.

Berridge, D. (1996) *Foster Care: Part 1 Children and Families. Highlight No.141.* London: National Children's Bureau.

Borland, M., O'Hara, G. and Triseliotis, J. (1991) 'Placement outcomes for children with special needs.' *Adoption and Fostering 15,* 2, 18–28.

Brodzinsky, D. (1984) 'New perspectives on adoption revelation.' *Adoption and Fostering 8,* 2, 27–32.

Caesar, G., Parchment, M. and Berridge, D. (1994) *Black Perspectives on Services for Children in Need.* London: National Children's Bureau.

Children Act (1989). London: HMSO.

Children (Scotland) Act (1995). Edinburgh: HMSO.

Dumbleton, P. (1996) 'Special needs at school.' In R. Phillips and E. McWilliam (eds) *After Adoption – Working With Adoptive Families.* London: British Agencies for Adoption and Fostering.

Erikson, E. (1968) *Identity: Youth and Crisis.* New York: Norton.

Fratter, J. (1996) *Adoption with Contact –* Implication for Policy and Practice. London: British Agencies for Adoption and Fostering.

Fratter, J., Rowe, J., Sapsford, D. and Thorburn, J. (1991) *Permanent Family Placement – A Decade of Experience.* London: British Agencies for Adoption and Fostering.

Furnham, A. and Stacey, B. (1991) *Young People's Understanding of Society.* London: Routledge.

Gilligan, C. (1982) *In a Different Voice.* Cambridge, Mass: Harvard University Press.

Goffman, E. (1963) *Stigma: Notes on the Management of Spoiled Identity.* London: Prentice-Hall.

Haimes, E. and Timms, N. (1985) *Adoption, Identity and Social Policy.* Aldershot: Gower.

Hartman, A. and Laird, J. (1990) 'Family treatment after adoption: common themes.' In D. Brodzinsky and M. Schechter (eds) *The Psychology of Adoption.* New York/Oxford: Oxford University Press.

Hayes, M. (1996) 'Post-adoption issues in transracial adoption and same race placements.' In R. Phillips and E. McWilliam (eds) *After Adoption – Working With Adoptive Families.* London: British Agencies for Adoption and Fostering.

Hill, M., Lambert, L. and Triseliotis, J. (1989) *Achieving Adoption With Love and Money.* London: National Children's Bureau.

Hill, M., Hutton, S. and Easton, E. (1988) 'Adoptive parenting – plus and minus.' *Adoption and Fostering 12,* 2, 17–23.

Hill, M., Nutter, R., Giltinian, D., Hudson, J. and Galaway, B. (1993) 'A compartative survey of specialist fostering in the UK and North America.' *Adoption and Fostering 17,* 2, 17–22.

Hirst, J. (1997) 'Adopting a stance.' *Community Care,* 23–29 January, 11–12.

Howe, D. (1990) 'The post-adoption centre: the first three years.' *Adoption and Fostering 14,* 1, 27–31.

Jewett, C. (1984) *Helping Children Cope With Separation and Loss.* London: BAAF/Batsford.

Kanuik, J. (1991) 'Strategies in recruiting black adopters.' *Adoption and Fostering 15,* 1, 38–41.

Lambert, L, Borland, M., Hill, M. and Triseliotis, J. (1991) 'Adopted people and counselling.' In J. Triseliotis (ed) *Adoption Services in Scotland: Recent Research Findings.* Edinburgh: Scottish Office Central Research Unit.

Lee, F. (1994) 'Teach your children.' *Community Care,* 21 April, 22–23.

Lyon, C. (1990) *Living Away from Home: The Legal Impact on Young People With Severe Learning Difficulties.* Staffordshire: University of Keele/Barnardos North West.

Macaskill, C. (1985) *Against the Odds.* London: British Agencies for Adoption and Fostering.

Marchant, R. and Page, M. (1992) *Bridging the Gap: Child Protection Work With Children With Multiple Disabilities.* London: NSPCC.

Marcia, J. (1980) 'Identity in adolescence.' In J. Adelson (ed.) *Handbook of Adolescence Psychology*. New York: Wiley.

McWhinnie, A. (1994) 'The concept of "open adoption" – how valid is it.' In A. McWhinnie and J. Smith (eds) *Current Human Dilemmas in Adoption*. Dundee: University of Dundee.

Middleton, L. (1996) *Making a Difference – Social Work With Disabled Children*. Birmingham: Venture Press.

Millham, S., Bullock, R., Hosie, K. and Haak, M. (1989) *Lost in Care: The Problems of Maintaining Links Between Children in Care and Their Families*. Aldershot: Gower.

Morris, J. (1991) *Pride Against Prejudice: Transforming Attitudes to Disability*. London: The Women's Press.

Morris, J. (1995) *Gone Missing – A Research and Policy Review of Disabled Children Living Away From Home*. London: WHO Cares? Trust.

Morrow, V. and Richards, M. (1996) 'The ethics of social research with children: an overview.' *Children and Society 10*, 2, 90–105.

Mountney, J. (1991) *Children With Disabilities in Foster Care: A Survey by the National Foster Care Association*. London: National Foster Care Association.

NCH Action For Children (1994) *Unequal Opportunities – Children With Disabilities and Their Families Speak Out*. London: NCH Action for Children.

Owusu-Bempah, J. (1994) 'Race, self-identity and social work.' *British Journal of Social Work 24*, 126–136.

Phillips, R. (1988) 'Post-adoption services: the views of adopters.' *Adoption and Fostering 12*, 4, 24–29.

Phillips, R. and McWilliam, E. (1995) 'Developing a post-adoption service for adoptive families.' *Practice 7*, 3, 45–58.

Phillips, R. and McWilliam, E. (1996) *After Adoption – Working With Adoptive Families*. London: British Agencies for Adoption and Fostering.

Plumtree, A. (1995) 'Confidentiality, disclosure and non-disclosure of genetic information: legal perspectives.' In P. Turnpenny (ed.) *Secrets in the Genes*. London: British Agencies for Adoption and Fostering.

Raynor, L. (1980) *The Adopted Child Comes of Age*. London: George Allen and Unwin.

Reed, J. (1993) *We Have Learned a Lot from Them: Foster Care for Young People With Learning Disabilities*. London: National Children's Bureau.

Reid, L. (1991) 'The Use of Life Story Books With People With Severe Mental Handicap.' University of Stirling. Unpublished Social Work Report.

Rowe, J. and Lambert, L. (1973) *Children Who Wait*. London: The Association of British Adoption Agencies.

Rushton, A., Quinton, D. and Treseder, J. (1993) 'New parents for older children: support services during eight years of placement.' *Adoption and Fostering 17,* 4, 39–45.

Russell, P. (1995) 'The importance of contact for children with disabilities–issues for policy and practice.' In H. Argent (ed.) *See You Soon – Contact With Children Looked After by Local Authorities.* London: British Agencies for Adoption and Fostering.

Ryan, T. and Walker, R. (1993) *Life Story Work.* London: British Agencies for Adoption and Fostering.

Ryburn, M. (1995) 'Adopted children's identity and information needs.' *Children and Society 9,* 3, 41–64.

Sants, H. (1964) 'Genealogical bewilderment in children with substitute parents.' *British Journal of Medical Psychology 37,* 133–141.

Sawbridge, P. (1975) *Opening New Doors.* London: British Agencies for Adoption and Fostering.

Shah, R. (1992) *The Silent Majority: Children with Disabilities in Asian Families.* London: National Children's Bureau.

Social Services Inspectorate (1994) *Services to Disabled Children and Their Families.* London: HMSO.

Social Services Inspectorate (1996a) *For Children's Sake: An SSI Inspection of Local Authority Adoption Services.* London: Department of Health.

Social Services Inspectorate (1996b) *Inspection of Local Authority Fostering 1995–96 National Summary Report.* London: Department of Health.

Smith, P. and Berridge, D. (1993) *Ethnicity and Childcare Placements.* London: National Children's Bureau.

Thoburn, J., Rashid, S. and Charles, M. (1992) 'The placement of black children with permanent new families.' *Adoption and Fostering 16,* 3, 13–18.

Triseliotis, J. (1973) *In Search of Origins.* London: Routledge and Kegan Paul.

Triseliotis, J. (1983) 'Identity and security in long-term fostering and adoption.' *Adoption and Fostering 7,* 1, 22–31.

Triseliotis, J. (1993) 'Open adoption – the evidence examined.' In M. Adcock, M. Kaniuk and J. White (eds) *Exploring Openness in Adoption.* London: Batsford/BAAF.

Triseliotis, J. and Hill, M. (1990) 'Contrasting adoption, foster care, and residential rearing.' In D. Brodzinsky and M. Schechter (eds) *The Psychology of Adoption.* New York/Oxford: Oxford University Press.

Triseliotis, J., Sellick, C.. and Short, R. (1995) *Foster Care: Theory and Practice.* London: Batsford/BAAF.

Triseliotis, J., Shireman, J. and Hundleby, M. (1997) *Adoption – Theory, Policy and Practice.* London: Cassell.

Turnpenny, P. (1994) 'The dilemmas of sharing genetic information.' In A. McWhinnie and J. Smith (eds) *Current Human Dilemmas in Adoption.* Dundee: University of Dundee.

Valios, N. (1997) 'Foster carers bid for professional standing.' *Community Care,* 22–28 May, 18–20.

Verity, P. (1995) 'Contact and foster carers.' In H. Argent (ed.) *See You Soon – Contact With Children Looked After by Local Authorities.* London: British Agencies for Adoption and Fostering.

Walby, C. and Symons, B. (1990) *Who Am I: Identity, Adoption and Human Fertilisation.* London: British Agencies for Adoption and Fostering.

Wassel, S. (1993) *Survey of Post-Placement Services, Part III, Carers.* London: British Agencies for Adoption and Fostering.

Wheal, A. and Walder, D. (1994) 'The voice of the child.' In A. Buchanan (ed.) *Partnership in Practice.* Aldershot: Avebury.

# CHAPTER 12

# Young People's Aspirations

*The Leighton Project with Simon Grant and Daisy Cole*

## Introduction

This chapter was compiled following group discussions with members of the Leighton Project based in Kentish Town, London. This project, run by Elfrida Rathbone Camden, is a Further Education College accommodating 18 students. The young people with learning difficulties featured in this chapter were aged 17–23. All members were asked to think about their aspirations for the future in relation to work, leisure, relationships and housing.

In order to facilitate discussion, individuals were invited to talk about their current situation or past experiences before thinking about what they would ideally like. Some group members attended all the meetings at which these issues were discussed; others attended only one or two meetings. Consequently, the case studies which are presented are of variable length and detail. Some of the young people were also more vocal or imaginative than others about possibilities for the future.

Efforts have been made to present the verbatim words of the group members wherever possible. At other times, comments or questions posed by the interviewers, Simon and Daisy, who are the group's usual facilitators, were simply confirmed or denied and the opinions expressed were often limited to 'yes' or 'no' statements. These responses are nonetheless reported, although there is some risk that the statements reflect the interpretations of the interviewers as much as the views of the interviewees. However, in producing this chapter, everyone had an opportunity to give their own opinions. The names of some individuals were changed; others opted to use their real names.

## John

John is 19 years old. He lives with his aunt and attends the Leighton Project four days a week. Three days a week he does woodwork with his foster brother and helps him by holding wood.

John attended a large special school between the ages of 5 and 16. He enjoyed his school years and got on well with the teachers and other pupils. He particularly liked PE and computers, but found English and maths 'a bit hard'.

John went from school to college and has had work experience on a farm, where he helped with milking the cows and cleaning out the stables. He would like to work in an office because he likes writing letters on the computer, but he enjoys woodwork too and of the two kinds of work, woodwork is what he would prefer.

With four days spent in college and three days in his foster brother's workshop, John has very little free time. In the evenings, he stays home and watches TV – his favourite programmes are *The Bill, Coronation Street* and *EastEnders*. They have satellite TV at home so John has plenty of choice of television programmes. At the moment he does not go out socially, although he would like to go to the pictures with friends.

John has had several camping holidays with school and college. He enjoyed the college holiday because he went with friends. Some years ago he went to Malta with his aunt. He has an ambition to travel to America one day.

John does not attend church, but he was christened as a baby and he does believe in God. For John, God is 'something for all different people' and he takes care of people. Religion too is about caring for other people.

In ten years time, John does not want to be in a personal relationship, but he would like to live in a house in central London. He would like to be earning his living through woodwork and be able to go out more than he does now.

## Damien

Damien is aged 23. He currently goes to college, where he attends a men's group and studies computers, currents affairs, employment and mobility issues. Damien lives in a residential home, but goes to stay with his cousin sometimes. He has one younger brother and no sisters.

Damien's earlier years were not entirely happy. He has been to four different schools. The first one, which he attended between the ages of 5 and 14, provided a happy experience, largely because of one particular woman teacher. After this, he went to live with foster parents in Devon for about a year and attended a strict day school. On returning home, he went to a new school where he was very unhappy. He explained why:

> 'That was the school where I got picked on every day and I got kicked out of there as well. There was one teacher called Mr H. and he used to pick on me and made you put your hands behind your back.'

And later:

> 'The other students used to ask me for money every day, used to beat me up in the corners and chase me after school.'

When asked if he had told the teachers about it, Damien was clear that he had, but to no avail:

> 'Yeah, but they weren't listening to no stupid stories.'

After being 'thrown out' of this school, Damien was sent to a boarding school, but by this time he was not interested in school and it is only his first school that he remembers with any fondness.

Damien has had a lot of work experience. His first placement was with Safeway where he pushed trolleys, put bags into people's trolleys and helped them load their cars. He has also worked in a garden centre watering the plants, in a garage fixing cars and in a warehouse where he packed hospital products. On the whole, these placements have gone quite well, although Damien did not enjoy people being bossy or rushing him, because this makes him feel agitated. Equally, he is not happy if the environment is very crowded with people.

Damien has very clear ideas about jobs he would like to try in the future, including working in a timber shop and more particularly becoming an actor. The latter ambition partly derives from Damien's current interest in, and attendance at, a drama group where he has the opportunity to act regularly.

In fact, Damien has a fairly full social life. Although he stays at home on a Monday and watches videos, he visits his foster parents in London every Tuesday and attends a drama group on a Wednesday. On Thursday evening he stays home to read the Bible and pray. He is not at college on Friday and he goes out during the day, usually to the cinema. In the evening he goes to Church Club and sees his girlfriend. On Sunday Damien sees his Dad and attends church twice during the day.

Damien has had several holidays with family, school and his residential home, and is going to Spain for a holiday soon. Damien says:

'I'm a nice person and I like to joke about.'

### Dean

Dean is 16 and lives in a 'care unit' at present, but was previously living with his mum and dad. His current life is restricted by a three-year supervision order which requires him 'to be in' by 7.30 pm, so although Dean says he has plenty of girlfriends, he cannot go out with them in the evenings.

His girlfriend of two years (Zoe) lives in the same area as Dean's family. Dean does not like Zoe's dad and it seems that the feeling is mutual. Dean handles this by keeping out of his way. However, Dean sees a future with Zoe, because 'her mum likes me, her sister likes me and her brother likes me'. Dean wants to live in a normal house with a garage and two bedrooms, have two children and take his wife 'out clubbing, out driving, to restaurants, to see my mum and on holiday to Spain and Italy'. He also wants to 'take the kids out, get them bikes and that'.

Dean has career ambitions too. He would like to be a professional footballer and, if that were not possible, he would like to be a window cleaner like his dad. Dean thinks window cleaning brings in good money and he has experience of helping his dad. He would like a convertible BMW car and enough money for holidays abroad.

### Abbie

Abbie is 20 years old and lives in a residential home in Hackney. She was born in London and is the youngest of six girls and three boys. She attended two special schools, including one in Liverpool. She learnt some computing, cookery and woodwork, as well as maths and English, but says that school 'didn't help me'. Abbie still keeps in touch with some friends from school, but she did not enjoy her time there. She thinks that it would have been helpful for her to have learnt about looking after children, because she now has a little boy of her own.

## Khai-lee

Khai-lee is 21 years old and lives at home with his family. He is particularly close to his brother with whom he goes out socially. He currently attends college four days per week. He attended a special school where his favourite lesson was sports. He particularly enjoyed basketball and tennis, but he also says that he found maths and writing 'good'. He left school with a record of achievement and finds that he likes college even better than school.

Khai-lee also has had experience of bullying at school. He says he was picked on by two boys outside the school. Although this was a long time ago, he now finds that people's reactions can be 'good and bad'. Sometimes, he says, people try to push him around; they get angry and he gets upset.

Khai-lee says he has lots of friends and when he goes out, two or three times a week, he often visits friends. Most of Khai-lee's friends are at college, but some are not. When he is at home, he watches TV or listens to music. He enjoys the weekends when he will either visit friends or cook a meal for them. He does this with his brother. In the past he has been on holiday to America with family friends.

Khai-lee's family is Chinese and they are religious. The family prays together in the morning. Khai-lee prays to God and says that talking to him about his problems makes him feel better.

In the future, Khai-lee would like to live with friends and his mum 'in a big house' in a noisy place. He would like to model clothes and have a wife and children. He would like to be able to go out to clubs and for meals.

## Ian

Ian is 19 and lives in north-west London. He comes from a large family and lives with his mum and dad whom he 'loves so much'. His brothers and sisters are no longer at home. Ian attended two special schools. He enjoyed his time at school, but would like to have taken exams. In fact, he left with a record of achievement. Ian has had several work experience placements, including working in a cafe, on a farm and at the Abbey National. Ian preferred the cafe work 'because I've got one of my friends [there], they always help me out.'

He has experience of cooking and serving in the cafe and one of the jobs he would like to do is running his own hotel business. Ian understands that he would need money and a licence before he could open a hotel. 'Yes [I need money], but the first thing I need is a licence, but I don't know how I'll get it.'

However, Ian has other ideas about jobs he would like to do. When asked if he had thought of any other jobs he might be interested in, he replied: 'Yes, actually, carpentry. I'd like to do that on my work experience if I can.' Later again he expressed an interest in a third type of work: 'Yes, now that you mention it, I do actually. Yes, fun fair.'

In addition, Ian was interested in a job to do with clothes and fashion. Overall, he was clear that he would prefer to work with his hands rather than sit in an office and concluded: 'I'm looking forward to woodwork most.'

At present Ian has three male friends who live close by. Ian explains that 'some of them come to my house, sometimes we go out to the pictures'. However on closer questioning, Ian seems to spend a lot of time going to snooker and drama clubs and spending time with his mum and dad. Some of Ian's friendships are not as he would like: 'One of them, yeah, is in college, he doesn't play fair with me because I do all for him and he do nothing for me.'

Ian also has a girlfriend called Fiona, whom he has known for about two years, from college. He says: 'She's lovely and she was in college and now she's not and she is about 19, same age as me.'

Ian foresees this relationship leading to marriage and he wants to have 'a real big wedding where they throw money.' He would like to have a baby and ideally, lots of children, but either he or his wife would need to work and earn money. 'Well if I got a job, she must stay at home or else she can work and I look after it.'

Ian imagines that in ten years' time he will be living with his wife, but that he might go into the airforce, so he would only come back from time to time. He also says: 'I can see myself rich. My girlfriend seeing me saying: "Hello Ian, I missed you badly".'

### Susie

Susie is 23 years old and lives with her mum, a lodger, two cats and a dog. She currently attends the Leighton Project and previously attended a community college. Susie attended both a day school and boarding school and preferred the latter. Working on the computers was Susie's favourite lesson. Since the school closed down, Susie does not see anyone from there: 'Yeah, I miss one of my teachers but I miss my school more.'

However, Susie, like many of the other young people, could remember bullying from school: 'There was a big bully at school: T., he was a big boy, he hit me.'

Fortunately, in this case, telling the teacher what happened proved sufficient and T. 'got sent out.'

Susie has never had a boyfriend, but she has a friend whom she sees on a Friday at 'the club'. She also has a friend, Corrie, who visits her at home, whom she has known for a long time. She does not go out on other evenings.

Susie says that people stare at her and point. Sometimes, too, people 'push in front of me in a queue'. Susie is clear that if someone calls her names, she would 'tell them to stop it'. When asked about the future, Susie initially said she would like to stay with her mum but, when encouraged more, said she imagines herself living in the supported living arrangement where she sometimes stays for short breaks.

Susie wants to live in London with other people around. She does not want a husband or children or a paid job. She would prefer to spend her time playing videos and cassettes and watching TV. She does not want any pets, but she does want to keep supporting Spurs football club.

### Bridget

Aged 19, Bridget lives with her mum and her younger sister. She also has a brother. Her dad has recently started working in Newcastle and no longer lives at home. She currently attends college where she does pottery and goes to the women's group. Bridget made quite a few friends at her special school and describes her years at school as 'okay'. Bridget keeps in contact with her school friends though a social club that she attends three times a week. She has had some work experience in a bakery, but in her words she 'messed it up'. If she has a choice about the kind of work she does in the future she would choose to write and draw. Her ambition is to write a book about New Zealand, because that is where her grandparents live.

Bridget practises her writing and drawing skills each week at the club she attends. Thursday is Bridget's favourite night at the club, because it is a girls' only night. Bridget states very clearly that 'girls is better than boys' and that she prefers girls. It is not therefore very surprising that Bridget does not express much interest in having a boyfriend or husband.

At present, Bridget's social life revolves around the social club she attends on Mondays, Tuesdays and Thursdays and occasionally going to her friend Tara's house. She also meets many of her sister's friends who come to the house. Most nights Bridget stays at home and watches TV, but she does not have a favourite programme. At the weekends, Bridget helps cook and wash up. Sometimes on a Sunday she chooses to stay in bed until late afternoon and then gets up, has food and goes out. She generally goes on holiday with her sister and her mum and she has been to Spain, America and New Zealand. However, she once went to Ireland to stay with her dad and on another occasion went to the seaside with the social club she attends regularly.

Although Bridget is not religious, she likes buildings and says 'when I walk down the street I pop in the churches sometimes to see what they're like, because all churches are different'.

Bridget would rather live in the country or by the sea than in a city. She thinks she would rather live alone, although if she lived with another person she would prefer it to be a slightly older woman. She would like to work with computers and have four pet cats. She would like to keep learning and thinks she might one day be an artist or writer.

### Hoshmen

Hoshmen is 19 years old, and came to London from Iraq. He speaks Kurdish at home, but speaks good English too. Hoshmen is the eldest of three boys and he lives with his parents and two brothers.

Hoshmen is very family-oriented. He usually stays at home, playing music, watching television or playing or writing on his brother's computer. He is not interested in going to clubs or to other social places. He accompanies his family to the supermarket each week. His important friends are his cousins and his dad's cousins who visit regularly.

Hoshmen has had three work experience placements through school. One of these was in a day nursery, working with small children. The other placement was on a building site. Hoshmen found the building site hard work, dirty and cold. However he preferred this to working in the day nursery. His third placement was with a carpenter where he helped cut wood. Of the three placements, this was the one he liked best.

In the future, Hoshmen would still like to live in London. He would like to be married and have three children. He believes his family will arrange a marriage for him with another Iraqi family. This is something to which he looks forward. Hoshmen thinks he would like to work in a post office, but would not mind if his wife went out to work instead of him. He wouldn't mind staying at home with the children. He would like to have a big house, a car, a computer, a big stereo and if he had all these he would be 'a happy man'.

## Chantelle

Chantelle is 21 years old and lives with her mum and her eight brothers. She sometimes goes to stay with her dad who no longer lives at home. She was born in Jamaica. She attends college four days a week and goes to an extra pottery class on a Wednesday. Chantelle attended two special schools which she enjoyed. She especially liked going on outings and learning to cook and read, but maths was 'a bit hard'. Unlike most of the other young people, Chantelle had no experience of being bullied, nor of getting into trouble at school. She would have liked to do more sports such as hockey and trampolining whilst at school.

She has had work experience in a children's nursery, which she really enjoyed. She would like to do similar work in future, because 'the kids are good...all the time'. Alternatively, Chantelle would be interested in painting and decorating as a job and possibly, cafe work or Sainsbury, but her preferred option is to work in a day nursery.

Chantelle believes in God, but does not go to church. Her social life involves going to the same club as Susie two nights a week, where she plays snooker and games. She also attends a self-defence class on a Wednesday. She likes pubs and visiting people. She has been dog racing on one occasion. When she is at home she telephones her friends, watches cable television, does puzzles or listens to the radio.

However since leaving school, Chantelle has experienced people calling her names which makes her feel 'cross'. She says that when people point and say horrible things to her she sometimes does not want to go to places. She thinks these people are 'bad'.

In the future, Chantelle would like to live in her own flat, by herself. She realises that she will need to learn to cook, shop and handle money before this can happen.

### Muzzy

Muzzy is 17 years old; he lives with his family. Although he is a Moslem, he does not practice his faith. He has attended many different schools. Having begun his school life at his local primary, he says that he moved on 'because of my temper'. In total he has spent time in five schools, an education centre and a college. He preferred his local 'normal' schools to the special schools he attended. He studied cookery, computers, maths, English, science, information technology and PE and liked computers and cookery best of these subjects. He still sees some of the people he was at school with, mainly because they also attend college. Overall, Muzzy says he enjoyed school.

He has had work experience in both Safeway and Sainsbury and has stacked shelves, packed bags, moved trolleys and helped customers. He enjoyed this work, but would like to work in a sports centre in future.

Muzzy has also experienced problems with people calling him names: 'The names which people called me were bad or racist.' Muzzy says all the bad names he has been called are to do with the colour of his skin, rather than because he has a learning difficulty. Muzzy says he tries to ignore the comments. 'When I went to my friend's, he said to me just to ignore it because I try to ignore it, but I got into trouble instead because I beat him up.'

Muzzy usually copes by 'taking a deep breath and counting to ten'. He remembers that name-calling was worse at school than it is at college. He is clear that the things people say are wrong and they make him feel 'terrible.'

At present, Muzzy does not have a girlfriend although he hoped that, at the time of the interview, his imminent blind date would lead to a relationship. His previous girlfriends 'keep on cheating behind my back' so he 'dumped them, straight away.' Muzzy would very much like a girlfriend with whom he could go out to the cinema or to a restaurant. He would like to be married, but he is not sure whether he wants children.

He has a vision of his life in ten years' time. He would like to live in a big French city with his wife or girlfriend. He would like to teach football and work in a sports centre, but he would not want his partner to work. Instead, he says she would be: 'cooking my food and getting ready.' Ideally, in future he would be a smart dresser with two cars and he would go to the cinema, eat out and attend football matches. He would return to England from time to time to visit friends and family.

### Robert

Robert is 25 years old and lives at home with his mother. He has two brothers and two sisters but they have all now left home. He attends college four days a week where he enjoys learning skills to help him travel independently. In the past Robert attended three special schools, including one boarding school. His favourite subject was sports. Robert, like many of the other young people, had been verbally abused at school and says he did not enjoy going there. He still sees some of the people he knew at school through a social club he now attends.

Robert's social life comprises staying in two or three nights of the week and going to drama and social clubs on four nights. On Sunday, he goes to church, sometimes twice, because as Robert explained, he is a Catholic and 'Catholics, every Sunday they go to church and pray. I pray for my mum'.

He has had two work experience placements: one in a greengrocer's shop, the other helping with meals on wheels, but it is not clear whether he really enjoyed these. In the future, Robert would like to work for the post office. He wants to live in London with his mother and says he is not interested in relationships at the moment.

## Commentary

The most striking feature of these case studies, considered collectively, is the contrast between the unusual or atypical life experiences of these young people, compared with their non-disabled peers, and their very 'ordinary' or typical aspirations. When these 12 young people were interviewed for the purposes of this chapter, they were not responding to structured questionnaires and therefore we do not have the views of each of them on exactly the same topics – for example, two people did not talk about their school days. The rest did, however, and it is clear that all ten attended special and/or residential schools for some or all of their school careers. As children, several had been subjected to bullying at school, and, as young adults, were now facing prejudiced attitudes in the wider community. This prejudice was as likely to be expressed in racist terms as it was in disablist ones if the individual was both black and disabled.

Eight young people reported they had work experience placements but none of them said they had ever been in paid employment. Three had lived, or were still living, in residential care, one of whom had previously been fostered. The remaining nine were living with relatives, an unusually high number for young people of their age. Although several respondents had busy social lives, often going out with family members, in some cases social activities were dominated by attendance at 'social' or segregated clubs. None of the young people were married or living with a partner, again, an unusual finding in the 17–23 age group. Three men reported having a girlfriend and one woman was the mother of a young child. It should also be noted that religious belief was an important aspect of life for almost half the group; again, this may be unexpected in this age group, although the reason for the finding is unclear.

Turning to these young people's hopes and aspirations, a quite different picture emerges. Eight wanted to have paid jobs, in a range of occupations. A few were undecided about what area they would like to work in and were ready to consider a number of options. Five wished to 'settle down' and marry; four of these also wanted to have children. Several people mentioned the importance of living in an ordinary house, and had clear ideas about where this would be – in a city centre, in the country or by the sea. At least three did not appear to be interested in having a partner; a few preferred to live alone. Several young people were attracted by what might be called the 'consumer' lifestyle, and imagined themselves living in some affluence, having material possessions generally seen as indicative of relatively high status. An active social life was an ambition for some, as was the desire to travel.

In conclusion, there is a wide disparity between these young people's past and present life experiences and their future ambitions. Their accounts bring home to us, if we did not already know, that most young people with learning difficulties do not wish to lead segregated lives, diverging from their non-disabled peers in life experiences and everyday activities. Yet these young people and others like them are ill-prepared to achieve their aspirations because of their experiences of segregated schooling, widespread exclusion from the job market, and by the negative attitudes, and sometimes outright hostility, of others. It is only when these disabling barriers are overcome that they will have the same sort of chances as other young people to realise their ambitions.

# CHAPTER 13

# The Dynamic of Transition to Adulthood

*Sheila Riddell*

## Introduction

If the funding of research programmes may be regarded as an index of public concern, then it is evident that youth transition is an area which periodically reaches the top of the agenda. In the late 1980s, a number of programmes investigating the position of youth (Bynner 1991; Gallie 1988) were supported by the Economic and Social Research Council (ESRC). These were intended to investigate the impact on young people of the collapse of the youth labour market. The fear was that, deprived of any chance of employment, many young people would fail to develop a work-orientated ethos and would remain in a permanent state of limbo, unable to cross the boundary between youth and adulthood. In the late 1990s, the preoccupation with the condition of youth, reflected in the funding of research programmes, seems to have returned. Programmes supported by the ESRC, the Rowntree Foundation and the Carnegie Trust all require researchers to turn their attention to questions of youth, transition and the acquisition of adult status. Key questions to be addressed within these studies concern the nature of transition to adulthood and how this varies according to social class, gender, ethnicity, disability and so on. The purpose of this paper is to explore the nature of transition for young disabled people. To what extent is it possible for this group to fulfil the normally accepted criteria of adult status? In addition, how do young disabled people experience what Jones (1997) has described as 'the dynamic of transition', that is, the pressure exerted on young people to attain adult status, whether assisted or hindered in this process by their parents and the state? Drawing on case studies of young disabled people in transition undertaken during the early 1990s, it is argued that the dynamic of transition continues to operate relatively unimpeded in relation to those with physical and sensory impairments. For young people with learning difficulties, however, the forward momentum appears to be arrested or diverted, partly because of their own difficulties but also because of the expectations and fears of those around them. Before turning to the case studies, I would like to say something about changes at a wider structural level which have affected the nature of transition for all young people.

## The policy context of transition

In order to understand the nature of transition to adulthood, it is necessary to have a sense of the economic and policy conditions within which young people live their lives. The late 1970s saw a radical restructuring of the labour market, with growth in the service sector offset by a rapid shrinking of the manufacturing sector. Global recession, as well as a crisis within the UK economy, had a devastating effect on the youth labour market: whereas in 1975, 60 per cent of 16-year olds were in full-time employment, by 1983 only 18 per cent moved into full-time jobs on leaving school. For young people with learning difficulties, the situation was even more dire. Whereas in the mid-1970s, around 70 per cent of these young people gained employment on leaving school (May and Hughes 1985), by the mid-1990s this had shrunk to less than 10 per cent. An unprecedented number of schemes were initiated to occupy young people whose idleness was seen as a serious threat to the social order. Youth Opportunities Programmes, introduced in the late 1970s to create work for young people, were superseded by Youth Training Schemes (YTS) (later known simply as Youth Training) in the early 1980s. These initiatives were underpinned by the belief that the way to regenerate the national economy was to attend to the supply side and produce a generation of workers with highly marketable skills, infused with a spirit of enterprise. Accompanying the introduction of YTS was the abolition of the right to state support under the age of 18. Those who were not in education or employment were compelled to undertake some sort of training, for which they were paid an allowance. This was fixed at a level well below that of unemployment benefit and reflected an assumption that young people would continue to live at home until their mid-20s, subsidised by parents. This policy was, of course, not introduced with the consent of families, and indeed was likely to be at variance with the cultural expectations of many parents. Jones (1997), for example, maintained:

'...government policies have tended to assume that the longer-standing middle class patterns of extended family support can be applied to working class families where this has not in the past been common practice.' (p.9)

Even though working-class families were expected to adopt these essentially middle-class practices, there was of course no way of compelling them to do so and there is evidence that many families were neither willing nor able to support their children into their early 20s (Jones 1995a). During the late 1970s and early 1980s, it is clear that social welfare and training policies had a profound effect upon family structure and culture, although there is ample evidence of a mismatch between government expectation of an extended period of semi-dependence and the wishes of both young people and their parents.

The economic crisis of the late 1970s and the changes in welfare which it heralded also had ramifications for schools. These were judged to be failing in their mission to produce young people equipped with the qualities required by employers. The Manpower Services Commission, under the auspices of the Department of Employment, was therefore charged with the remit of addressing this failure by shaping a work-orientated curriculum, the Technical and Vocational Educational Initiative (TVEI), to be delivered to pupils across the ability range, from the most able to those in special schools. The Department of Education and Science White Papers *Employment for the 1990s* (Department of Employment 1988) and *Education and Training for the 21st Century* (Department of Education and Science 1991) signalled the desire for employers rather than the state to take a lead role in determining the nature of training in England. In Scotland, the situation was slightly different: educators were extremely hostile to the idea of the curriculum being controlled by the Department of Employment and were suspicious of interventions from Whitehall into the Scottish education system (Weir 1988). As a result, the introduction of TVEI was delayed in Scotland and did not finally make an appearance until the early 1990s; this time lag meant that TVEI was in full flight in Scotland after its counterpart initiative had been 'normalised' in England and Wales, and Scottish teachers were able to learn a great deal from their English counterparts about how to domesticate and neutralise a potentially radical intervention. (A major result of the TVEI both north and south of the border was a significant injection of cash into equal opportunities work, a far cry from the Conservative party's stated aim of waging war on 'egalitarianism' (Turner, Riddell and Brown 1995). Having launched a massive onslaught on the education system, it suddenly seemed as if a more traditional tendency within the Conservative party had triumphed and it was decided to redraw the boundaries between education, training and employment. Bynner (1991) has described this conflict within the Conservative party between those seeking to uphold traditional boundaries between education and training and those supporting a radical redrawing of the map in the following way:

> '...the apparently unresolvable conflict in Britain between the desire to modern-ise – "catch up with our competitors" – and allegiance to the structures which underpin social allocation, privilege and cultural division.' (p.648)

Thus, in the early 1990s, responsibility for training was ostensibly handed over to employers in the form of Training and Enterprise Councils in England and Wales and Local Enterprise Companies (LECs) in Scotland. This shift in locus of responsibility was accompanied by a renewed emphasis on training outcomes measured by the acquisition of vocational qualifications and the attainment of paid employment. Whereas TVEI had a strong equal opportunities ethos, and YT had special initiatives to encourage the training of young people with special educational needs, Skillseekers was driven by an economic rationale which allowed little scope for increased investment in the training of young people with learning difficulties. Although some LECs felt that their responsibility extended to a widely defined group of young people with additional training needs (including those with cognitive difficulties, social, emotional and behavioural difficulties and mental illness) others focused on the more easily employable.

Despite the shift in the locus of responsibility for training back from ed-ucationalists to employers, the assumption remained in place that young people between the ages of 16 and 18 should be in full-time education or training, apart from those who were employed. As Jones (1997) noted, this created the anomalous situation in which young people were deemed to be responsible for making social security contributions before they were eligible to claim from this source.

To summarise, triggered by global and national economic crises, the period from the late 1970s to the 1990s witnessed radical changes in the areas of social welfare, education, training and employment. As explored in greater detail in the following section, these changes had knock-on effects on young people's ex-perience of transition which ceased to be a predictable linear progression and became both more protracted, variable and provisional. The transition process for young disabled people, always precarious because of the nature of their difficulties, became perhaps even more tenuous and unpredictable as their position in the labour market declined.

## Markers of adult status

Development from childhood through adolescence to adulthood is at one level a process of biological change and as such is not merely a social construction. At the same time, it is evident that within different cultures and at different historical periods the social construction of childhood, adolescence and adulthood changes markedly (Aries 1973). This implies the existence of a state of interaction between biology and culture so that the physiological and emotional process of maturation is overlaid by a range of cultural expectations which will be subject to change over time and will be influenced by the wider economic context. Understanding the nature of the interaction between biological givens and social and cultural practices lies at the heart of the disability studies project. Commentators have differed in their emphasis on the central importance of impairment on the one hand and social, economic and political conditions on the other. Writers such as Abberley (1992) have maintained that the material reality of impairment should be understood as the basis on which oppressive and exploitative practices are based. He argues:

> 'it is crucial that a theory of disability as oppression comes to terms with the "real" inferiority, since it forms a bedrock upon which justificatory oppressive theories are based and, psychologically, is an immense impediment to the development of political consciousness amongst disabled people.' (Abberley 1992, p.234)

Pointing up the interaction between biology and culture, he argues that it is important not to deny the significance of 'germs, genes and trauma', but to recognise that:

> '...their effects are only ever apparent in a real social and historical context, whose nature is determined by a complex interaction of material and non-material factors.' (p.239)

One of the aims of this paper is to explore the way in which the dynamic of transition for young disabled people is influenced both by the nature of their impairment and by wider social and political factors which impinge upon their lives and have a profound impact on the way in which impairment is understood by themselves and others.

Adulthood within modern industrialised societies is construed as a central social status, part of which is ascribed and part of which is attained. The achieved status of adulthood depends on crossing various age-specified thresholds and involves both rights and obligations. These thresholds include criminal resp-onsibility, sexual consent, voting rights, conditional or unconditional marriage rights, the right to enter full-time paid or unpaid employment, the right to welfare benefits, to give or withhold medical consent and to donate blood or organs. Obligations include the requirement to pay income tax if in employment, to register for national insurance and to attend if summoned to jury service. Although these rights and obligations accrue automatically to most young people, for young people with learning difficulties or mental illness they may be much more tenuous.

Jenkins (1990) notes that common law defines 'idiots' and those of 'unsound mind' as incapable of voting. Various pieces of legislation such as the Road Traffic Act 1960 and the Matrimonial Causes Act 1973 have clauses which exclude people with learning difficulties and mental illnesses from the normal provision. The issue of medical consent is again an uncertain right and one which is susceptible to sudden change. For example, Riddell, Ward and Thomson (1993) give an account of a case involving 'Jeanette', a young woman with Down's Syndrome, and Sunderland Borough Council which applied for legal authority to carry out a sterilisation in the absence of the young woman's consent but with the support of her parents. The case went to the appeal court and to the House of Lords at the request of the Official Solicitor. Ultimately, the appeal went in favour of the Borough Council and the girl was sterilised before her eighteenth birthday, although it was stated that this case should not be seen as creating a precedent.

The legal markers of adulthood, then, may be withheld from young people with learning difficulties and mental illness. Even more difficult to attain, however, may be the benchmarks associated with achieved adult status, which include financial independence, paid employment, independent living and adult social relationships, including parenthood. Of these, gaining paid employment has been seen as the most important, since it provides not only a sense of identity, but also access to an independent home base outside the family home and the adult relationships which are thus made possible. Indeed, it has been maintained by some commentators that in the absence of paid employment, full adult status cannot be attained. Willis (1984), for example, argues:

> 'properly to understand unemployment, we need to understand what is missing – the wage. The wage is not simply an amount of money...It is the only connection with other social possibilities, processes and desirable things. As such it operates as the crucial pivot for several other processes, social and cultural transmissions quite unlike itself.' (p.34)

Other writers (e.g. Coffield, Borill and Marshall 1986; Hutson and Jenkins 1989; Jones 1997) have disagreed with this analysis, pointing to the alternative markers of adult status which can be brought into play in the absence of paid employment. Of particular significance in moving young people from childhood to adulthood is what has been termed the 'dynamic of transition' (Jones 1997). Mothers, according to Jenkins, play a particularly significant role here, 'cajoling, bullying, supporting, constructively neglecting, pushing, whatever it takes...' to ease children out of the family nest. Hutson and Jenkins (1989) identify a similar process:

> 'there is a considerable psychological and social head of steam which pushes and pulls young people into adulthood, unemployment notwithstanding.' (p.154)

Jones (1997) points out that it was precisely the existence of this dynamic which interfered with the logic of economic rationalism. By prolonging the period of children's financial dependence on parents, the government clearly believed that it would deter them from leaving home. Jones' research demonstrated that young people were leaving home earlier than ever before, particularly those who were living with step-parents or parents who were unemployed. The desire for independence, she concluded, was greater than the perceived risk of homelessness.

The literature on youth and transition, then, provides a general sense of the key indicators of adult status, but there is a lack of detailed ethnographic work providing insight into how the dynamic of transition operates for young disabled people. The pen portraits included in a later section of this chapter provide some insights into the operation of the dynamic of transition for this group, but a greater volume of more detailed ethnographic work is also required.

## The nature of the transition process

It is clear that the process and time scale of transition to adulthood has changed markedly over the past four decades. Leonard (1980), in her study of courtship and marriage in Swansea in the late 1960s, describes a traditional pattern, with working-class young people moving straight into employment on leaving school. During the early years of their working lives, they generally stayed at home, enjoying a relatively privileged existence as valued contributors to the household economy but without the full burden of responsibility carried by their parents.

Table 13.1 Extended transitions to adulthood

| Childhood | Youth | Adulthood |
|---|---|---|
| Dependence <16 years | Semi-dependence 16–18; 18–21; 21–25 years | Independence >25 years |
| School | College or training scheme | Labour market |
| Parental home | Intermediate household Transitional housing | Independent home |
| Child in family | Various statuses, inc. single parenthood | Partner, parent |
| Citizenship through parents | Semi-citizenship | Adult citizenship |

This period was also used to save up money to purchase or rent a future home and, in the case of young women, to collect items for a 'bottom drawer' to furnish a future home. Courtship and marriage generally preceded the move to an independent home, since cohabitation was frowned upon. The collapse of the youth labour market and the imposition of a protracted period of semi-dependence through the withdrawal of state support has led to an extension of the period of transition and the outcome (employment, independent living and family formation) less certain. Jones (1997) produced a figurative representation of the extended transition to adulthood and her research (Jones 1995a; 1995b) has put some flesh on the bones of this model. However, as noted above, we still lack a clear view of how the transition of young disabled people differs from those of their peers.

Reliable data are available, however, in the area of post-school destinations. Table 13.2 shows that in 1996 approximately a third of mainstream school leavers from the City of Edinburgh moved into employment. Twenty-seven per cent went into higher education, 19 per cent into further education and 18 per cent into a Skillseekers training scheme. By way of contrast, among special school leavers in the same area, only 9 per cent went into employment. Seventeen per cent were unemployed, 28 per cent entered a Skillseekers training scheme and 42 per cent embarked upon a full-time course of further education. Although these statistics clearly indicate the different routes followed by mainstream and special school leavers, if anything they underestimate the scale of the difference. This is because the type of Skillseekers and FE programmes followed by special school leavers are likely to be very different from those pursued by the mainstream population. The Skillseekers courses available to special school leavers will be those considered appropriate for people with special training needs and are likely to focus on confidence building, with little prospect of open market employment at the end. Further education provision for young people leaving special school is usually in the form of extension courses. These are one- or two-year programmes designed to foster independent living skills, delivered on a segregated basis and with little expectation that participants will secure employment at the end. With a very few exceptions, young people with severe and profound difficulties are not catered for in further education. As we noted earlier in relation to the work of May and Hughes (1985), the contrast with previous outcomes of special school leavers is very marked. Whereas employment for young people leaving mainstream school has become a less common option, a rump of employment possibilities remains. For young people leaving special school, the depletion of the youth labour market has been even more drastic, and, some have argued, the training which is available represents little more than a rather ineffective palliative measure. May and Hughes (1985) characterised the post-school possibilities for young Scottish people with moderate learning difficulties in the following way:

'where once they might have expected to find jobs of one sort or another eventually, and with them some measure of economic independence, now it would seem that the best they can expect in the short term at least, is a series of short-lived placements on a variety of government-sponsored schemes of dubious meaning and value, punctuated by successive and growing periods of unemployment as they move further beyond the range of emergency measures set up to assist the post-school transition.' (May and Hughes 1985, p.158)

Table 13.2 Known mainstream school leaver destinations 1996 – Edinburgh

| | |
|---|---|
| Employment | 984 |
| Skillseekers | 571 |
| Further education | 608 |
| Higher education | 833 |
| Unemployed | 142 |
| Unavailable | 48 |
| Unknown | 121 |
| **Total** | **3307** |

## Case studies of young people

In order to illustrate the transitional experiences of young disabled people, condensed case studies are drawn from a study funded by the Scottish Education Department and carried out by researchers at the Universities of Edinburgh and Stirling between 1989 and 1991 (Ward *et al.* 1991). The aim of the research was to investigate factors associated with the successful transition to adulthood for young people with recorded special educational needs, interrogating the notion of successful transition for this group. The first phase of the project involved an analysis of the school placements and post-school destinations of a cohort of recorded pupils due to leave school in the academic year 1986/87. The second phase of the study consisted of case studies of 11 young people selected on a range of criteria including the nature of their impairments, school placements and post-school destinations. The case studies were conducted by means of detailed interviews with the young people (where possible), interviews with parents and periods of observation. Here, I present data drawn from case studies of two young women, one with a physical impairment and one with learning difficulties, with a view to illustrating the way in which the dynamic of transition may operate. All the young people in the case studies were 19 or 20 at the time of the research and were therefore at a relatively early stage of their passage from adolescence to adulthood.

Table 13.3 Known special school leaver destinations 1996 – Edinburgh and Lothians

| | |
|---|---|
| Employment (entering a job directly) | 15 |
| Skillseekers (on skillseekers with trainee status or employee status) | 49 |
| Further eduction (following a full-time programme at a College of FE) | 72 |
| Higher education (following an advanced course at a University or College) | 3 |
| Adult training centre (placed at an ATC) | 3 |
| Day centre for adults with a physical disability (placed at a day centre) | 2 |
| Unemployment (continuously unemployed from leaving school until 1 December 1996) | 29 |
| Unavailable (due to severe disability, illness or pregnancy) | 5 |
| Unknown (no information available) | 30 |
| **Total** | **208** |

## Linda

Linda was a young woman with spiky blonde hair and a very muscular upper body, reflecting her commitment to participation in a range of sporting activities. Since childhood she had a form of ataxia which greatly affected her mobility. She was living at home in a small village about seven miles outside a large city, but expected to move into independent accommodation at some point in the future. Family relationships were good, although some tensions were evident. For example, Linda was irritated by the forgetfulness of her retired father, quarrelled with her older brother, whom she felt was the favoured child and argued with her mother over the allocation of household responsibilities. Mrs H. explained:

> '...we had a row about leaning on Mum and she said "I don't need you." So I said "Fine, we'll see how you get on with your ironing." I let her do it for a week. She didn't like it much but she can do it...I don't work because I really feel I'm needed here so the washing and ironing is done during the day when Linda's not here – as has been done for them all! There's none of them would be particularly self-sufficient in the house because they've never had it to do.'

A further complaint was that Linda was too independent over mealtimes. At the time of the research, Linda had just finished a physical and community studies course at a local further education college, the first disabled young person to be admitted. She received a full grant from the local authority and managed her money well. Transport was not a problem because she had access to the family car and used it to meet up with her college and former school friends in the evening.

A recurring theme in Linda's story was the resistance of herself and her parents to the acceptance of a disabled identity. Linda began her education in a mainstream primary school and transferred to mainstream secondary but shifted to a special school when her walking deteriorated and it became apparent that few efforts were being made to facilitate physical access. Her mother described her memories of this period thus:

> 'she needed help and OK a couple of kids did help her. I think the teachers sort of said: "You'll take Linda from class to class." But when these particular girls were off Linda panicked and became ill every morning. She said: "I don't feel well, I feel sick." But we didn't realise how great her problems were at that time.'

Because of the school's reluctance to take concerted action, Linda's parents decided to move her to a special school. Linda described her feelings about this move thus:

> 'My reaction was the same as what everybody else's reaction is out here – you're in a wheelchair and you're mental. That's exactly what I said. The first day that I went there, I came home and said I don't want to go back because they were all mental in there. I'd done the same work so long ago and they were on the same work and I just couldn't handle that. But I stuck it out and after a while it was

fine. I certainly blended in fine and there was no problem with that because everybody has got a disability.'

Linda was a strong advocate of integration and was irritated by the assumption that people with physical impairments also have learning difficulties·

> 'the public really annoys me because first of all they're ignorant of anybody with any disability. Somebody with sticks – they stare at you when you go past because they see there's something different. You're physically disabled and you're also mentally handicapped when you're in a wheelchair and that REALLY annoys me. One incident that sticks in my mind – she was an old lady and I must have been about 15 or 16 and I was sitting in a shop in my wheelchair. She comes up to me and says: "What are you getting from Santa Claus?" Now that is really so degrading!'

Contributing to a television programme about the school she attended, she commented:

> '...the disabled need to be integrated more with able-bodied because people just don't understand that there is a difference between mentally and physically handicapped and, just because you're in a wheelchair, there isn't something wrong with your brain.'

Her mother explained that for practical reasons her daughter would not consider a long-term relationship with a disabled person:

> '...she wouldn't entertain a disabled boyfriend because I think she realises that through time she'll need more help than she does now. That sounds very selfish but if she was living with a disabled person then they would obviously need someone to come in and care for them both.'

Linda was strongly resistant to the idea that her career choice might be constrained by other people's perceptions of what was possible and appropriate. She had always enjoyed physical activity, excelling at swimming, and decided that she wanted to be a PE teacher when she left school. Her careers adviser encouraged her to explore this option but warned that she might be disappointed due to the level of academic qualification required and the restrictions on entry to teacher training imposed by the General Teaching Council for Scotland (GTC). Linda interpreted these warnings as active discouragement and was determined to prove herself right and the careers service wrong:

'I think if I'd given in to her [the careers adviser] then I would either be doing a YTS or an office job – not doing what I wanted to do but what she wanted me to do...Then I was offered the [Physical Education and Community Studies] place at college and I think she was even more surprised than me because she'd been so negative all the way through.'

After completing the college course, Linda was bitterly disappointed that she was debarred from entering a teacher training course because of GTC regulations and felt this should have been spelt out to her more clearly. At the time we interviewed her, she had applied unsuccessfully for more than 40 clerical posts. However, shortly after the end of the research she succeeded in gaining employment in a travel agency and felt that this would be more fun than a traditional 9– 5 office job.

In many aspects of Linda's experience we can see the dynamic of transition at work. Although still in a state of semi-dependence on her parents, it is evident that she would be able to move into an independent home at some point. Indeed, the tensions and irritations attendant on living in the parental home which push young people into seeking out their own living space were very much in evidence. She had taken independent decisions about her future, defying professional advice when she felt this was too limiting. Her views of herself as a disabled person were somewhat ambivalent. 'Normality' was what she sought, and she was particularly distressed when her physical impairment was confused with an intellectual impairment. Above all, she was resisting the dependency which she associated with the adoption of a disabled identity. Her mother was clearly instrumental in encouraging this resistance, describing the following critical incident:

'I must, in all honesty, say that when she had the problems at secondary school – and we'd had it before then when the walking was getting worse and there were a lot of things she couldn't do that the other kids could do – I wouldn't say I was depressed then but Linda was driving me nuts. She was whining all the time "I can't do that". I got constant tears, tears and more tears. Well, we tried bribing her, coaxing her, a bit of persuasion and then I lost my temper and said "I don't care how you feel but don't stand there and say you can't or girn. Kick the floor, do something. But don't say 'I can't'". She doesn't remember me losing my temper. I have asked her since. But from then on Linda never looked back because it was just taboo. But I just got to the end of my tether. It was either I was going under with her or she pulled her socks up. So it was a case of wiping the floor with her. I'm not canny when I start!'

*Lorraine*

At the time of the research, Lorraine was participating in a market garden project as a trainee. She was described as a 'fashion-conscious' young lady, rather resistant to wearing the protective clothing required for working on the land. Although the researcher felt she was relatively knowledgeable about the plants and worked hard, she expressed a dislike of the cold and dirty working conditions. Lorraine lived in local authority housing in a new town about ten miles from a larger city, with her parents and her younger sister who worked locally as a nanny. She had moderate learning difficulties and a speech impairment resulting in unclear articulation, especially when she was nervous or excited. In many ways her experience illustrates the operation of a delayed or arrested dynamic of transition.

Lorraine began her education in a mainstream primary school but her teacher was concerned about her inability to speak in complete sentences and her attention-seeking behaviour. Her mother was warned that special education might be required to meet Lorraine's needs; according to Mrs F., Lorraine was victimised at the school and got the blame for anything that went wrong. When Mrs F. went to see the headteacher and 'kicked up holy murder' about what was happening to her daughter, Lorraine was finally placed in a special unit attached to a mainstream school.

The perception of the teacher within the special unit was that Lorraine was not being adequately cared for at home.

> 'She was treated in a very derogatory manner by her mother and her younger sister. If, for example, Mum came up to school to see about Lorraine, she would bring the younger sister with her, who seemed to have an attendance problem. And the sister would, very aggressively almost, take the part of the parent and say "How's she behaving?", and she always spoke in a very derogatory manner, but this was encouraged not perhaps actively by the mother but it was obvious that within the household this was the way Lorraine was spoken to. Lorraine was spoken to as if she was the "daftie", so she was treated as the "daftie" for want of a better term. It wasn't nice.'

According to the teacher, Lorraine's appearance was often unkempt and the house was also dirty. She would eat with her hands and wipe food over herself. In addition, she had inappropriate bird-like movements of the head and at one point a psychologist came to observe her, although there was never any follow up.

At Lorraine's Future Needs Assessment, it was decided that she should enrol in an extension course at a local further education college, but she decided to leave after one year on the programme. After a period of unemployment, a traineeship at the market garden was found for her by the careers service. The organiser of the project explained that in Lorraine's case:

> 'the work element is not the most significant factor and the reason for Lorraine going there was to enter a work-based environment which would enable her to develop personally. The vocational skills are secondary.'

This was despite the fact that Lorraine was judged to be 'more than capable of getting a job and keeping it.'

The development of friendships 'over the next few years and even over the rest of her life' was seen as one of the purposes of the YTS placement. However, the fact that the other trainees were all young men meant that long-term social support was unlikely to be forthcoming as a result of Lorraine's involvement. Indeed, the formation of meaningful social relationships seemed to be an area of particular difficulty for Lorraine, who described herself as having no friends. At the special unit, the teacher said that Lorraine often 'took punishment' from some of the more aggressive boys. Her mother and sister maintained that Lorraine had been raped the previous year and as a result she was not permitted to go out to the shopping centre by herself.

Lorraine also had difficulty managing money. The special school teacher described an incident when Lorraine had proudly displayed a pound note that had been given to her as pocket money and the following day had said that her sister had given her lots more money; on inspection this turned out to be a collection of small change in place of the pound note. Uncertainty about the value of money persisted. At the market garden, the mother of one of the male trainees had telephoned to express her concern about the fact that her son kept on coming home with money apparently given to him by Lorraine.

In terms of her future, professionals were concerned that Lorraine might find it difficult to move into a state of greater independence because of the lack of support from both the state and her family. Her mother expressed anxiety about the future and confided in the researcher:

> 'if only they'd come and tell me what her future's to be, then I'd be able to find out and make her understand.'

In the absence of any firmly mapped out course, the assumption seemed to be that after her sister's marriage, Lorraine would move in with her. Given the suggestion that this relationship might be exploitative and abusive, the possibility of Lorraine attaining a state of greater independence seemed bleak. At the end of the project, Lorraine had just gained a place on an urban-aid funded training scheme, with the aim of developing her social and employment skills further, but paid employment and an independent home base remained elusive.

## Conclusion

A concern with the nature of the transition from youth to adulthood appears to have its roots in the economic crises of the 1970s. World economic recession led to the rapid reduction in the size of the UK youth labour market and high levels of structural unemployment became accepted as permanent features of the landscape in the UK and other post-industrial countries. The response of the state to this economic crisis was to extend the period of transition from youth to adulthood. Young people were expected to remain in full-time education and training until their early 20s and youth wages became the norm for many young people. The move to an independent home and the establishment of adult relationships were made more difficult both by the shortage of available accommodation and the absence of a wage. Despite powerful state disincentives, young people continued to leave the family home and the problem of youth homelessness grew throughout the 1980s and 1990s. Young people's desire for independence and their parents' support of this enterprise, it appeared, were more powerful than the state's attempts to enforce a protracted period of semi-dependency.

The cases of Linda and Lorraine provide some insights into the nature of the support which may assist young people in the process of transition and the barriers they may encounter. Their experiences were affected by the nature of their impairments and the extent of support from the family and the state in the transition process. Linda's transition had not been unproblematic; her initial attempts to enter teaching were thwarted by her lack of academic qualifications and her impairment. However, the process of making difficult life choices (and living with the consequences) may have been important for her longer term development. She was well supported by her family during the period of transition both emotionally and practically (loan of the family car, domestic support). This enabled her to develop an independent social life which was likely to lead to a separate existence in an independent family unit. By the end of the research, Linda was about to take up her first post in paid employment. The dynamic of transition, involving both herself and her parents, was moving Linda towards adulthood in a relatively gentle fashion. Her impairment, which might have severely restricted her access to youth culture, training and employment opportunities, had been partially overcome by her physical prowess in certain areas, her personal motivation and her access to material resources.

For Lorraine, transition to adulthood appeared to be far more problematic. She found it difficult to form friendships and in the special unit attached to the mainstream school had been socially isolated. Her family lacked the social skills necessary to communicate effectively with professionals which might have brought educational benefits. Indeed, it was suggested by some professionals that Lorraine's impairments might have been exacerbated by her impoverished social environment. For example, her untidy eating was seen as evidence of lack of appropriate social training in the home. This of course might be an example of professionals employing a social deficit model but, on the other hand, the association between social disadvantage, educational failure and the identification of special educational needs is well established (Riddell 1994; Tomlinson 1982). The training programmes provided by the state were failing to assist Lorraine in gaining employment or indeed in developing effective social relationships. Her mother was fearful of the possibilities of sexual exploitation and therefore restricted Lorraine's freedom of movement. Professionals, on the other hand, felt that Lorraine was exploited and abused within her family. By the end of the research, Lorraine was to embark upon her third period of post-school training, but in the absence of effective support from either the state or her family, there appeared to be a breakdown in the dynamic of transition.

The cases of Linda and Lorraine illustrate an important division between the experiences of young disabled people. In our study, young people with physical and sensory impairments appeared to find the transition to adulthood less problematic and were better supported by the family and the state. For young people with learning difficulties, not only was there less certainty about the goal of transition (the possibility of the Warnock notion of 'significant living without work' remained unresolved), but there was also less effective state support. This, in part, reflected the dilemmas posed by human capital theory, in particular, the economic viability of investing heavily in the education and training of young people with learning difficulties in the light of the likely returns on the investment. Furthermore, the persistent association between the occurrence of learning difficulties and social disadvantage meant that these families might well lack the material and cultural resources needed to offer support. This clearly illustrates the iterative relationship between impairment and the social, economic and political context in which it is experienced, a point highlighted by Abberley (1992) and others. The dynamic of transition is clearly a powerful force pushing and pulling young people into a state of independence. Despite the elongated process of transition imposed by the state, perhaps exaggerated for young disabled people because of notions of intrinsic dependence, the dynamic is clearly evident in the lives of many young disabled people. However, particular types of impairment, coupled with social disadvantage and lack of appropriate training, may lead to an arrested dynamic of transition for particular groups; of these, young people with learning difficulties may be particularly vulnerable.

In terms of policy implications, this suggests a need for more support for certain groups of young people during the period of transition. However, what is certainly not needed is more ill-conceived and poorly articulated training programmes. Supported employment, on the other hand, may well have more to offer in terms of opening the door to financial independence. At a more fundamental level, it is clear that while Western industrial societies continue to operate highly stratified labour markets with significant levels of structural unemployment, there is a persistent danger that young people with learning difficulties will continue to be marginalised, regarded (perhaps mistakenly) as a bad return for investment in reductionist economic terms. Much work remains to be done in terms of gaining acceptance for the idea that the development and maintenance of human capital is ultimately dependent on the establishment of a cohesive society based on the principles of social inclusion.

# References

Abberley, P. (1992) 'The concept of oppression and the development of a social theory of disability.' In T. Booth, W. Swann, M. Masterton and P. Potts (eds) *Policies for Diversity in Education.* London: Routledge.

Aries, P. (1973) *Centuries of Childhood.* Harmondsworth: Penguin.

Bynner, J. (1991) 'Controlling transition.' *Work, Employment and Society 5,* 4, 645–658.

Coffield, F., Borill, C. and Marshall, S. (1986) *Growing up at the Margins.* Milton Keynes: Open University Press.

Department of Education and Science (1991) *Education and Training for the 21st Century.* Cmnd. 1536, Vol. 1. London: HMSO.

Department of Employment (1988) *Employment for the 1990s.* Cmnd. 540. London: HMSO.

Gallie, D. (1988) *The Social Change and Economic Life Initiative.* Working Paper No.1. Swindon: Economic and Social Research Council.

Hutson, S. and Jenkins, R. (1989) *Taking the Strain: Families, Unemployment and Transition to Adulthood.* Milton Keynes: Open University Press.

Jenkins, R. (1990) 'Dimensions of adulthood in Britain: long-term unemployment and mental handicap.' In P. Spencer (ed.) *Anthropology and the Riddle of the Sphinx: Youth, Maturation and Ageing.* London: Routledge.

Jones, G. (1995a) *Family Support for Young People.* London: Joseph Rowntree Foundation and Family Policy Studies Centre.

Jones, G. (1995b) *Leaving Home.* Buckingham: Open University Press.

Jones, G. (1997) 'Barriers to adulthood: dependency and resistance in youth.' Paper presented to the Third Annual Colloquium of the International Social Sciences Institute, *Families and the State: Conflicts and Contradictions.* University of Edinburgh, 23–24 May 1997.

Leonard, D. (1980) *Sex and Generation: A Study of Courtship and Weddings.* London: Tavistock.

Matrimonial Causes Act (1973). London: HMSO.

May, D. and Hughes, D. (1985) 'The prospects on leaving school for the mildly mentally handicapped.' *British Journal of Special Education 12,* 4, 151–158.

Riddell, S., Ward, K. and Thomson, G.O.B. (1993) 'Transition to adulthood for young people with special educational needs.' In A. Closs (ed.) *Special Educational Needs Beyond 16...* Edinburgh: Moray House Institute.

Riddell, S. (1994) 'Education.' In G. Fyfe (ed.) *Poor and Paying for It: The Price of Living on a Low Income.* Glasgow: Scottish Consumer Council.

Road Traffic Act (1960). London: HMSO.

Tomlinson, S. (1982) *A Sociology of Special Education.* London: Routledge and Kegan Paul.

Turner, E., Riddell, S. and Brown, S. (1995) *Gender Equality in Scottish Schools: The Impact of Recent Educational Reforms.* Manchester: Equal Opportunities Commission.

Ward, K., Riddell, S., Dyer, M. and Thomson, G.O.B. (1991) *Transition from School for Pupils with Special Educational Needs.* Final report to the Scottish Education Department from the project: Post-school Outcomes of Recorded Pupils. University of Edinburgh, University of Stirling.

Weir, A.D. (1988) *Education and Vocation 14–18.* Edinburgh: Scottish Academic Press.

Willis, P. (1984) 'Youth unemployment: Thinking the unthinkable.' *Youth and Policy 2*, 4, 17–24, 33–36.

# The Contributors

**Judith Cavet** is Principal Lecturer in Social Work and Applied Social Studies at Staffordshire University. She is an experienced social worker, with a special interest in disability. She has undertaken several research projects in this field, including a European study of leisure opportunities for people with profound and multiple impairment. She is currently engaged in research, funded by the Joseph Rowntree Foundation, regarding the effects on children of an invisible impairment.

**Chailey Young People's Group** The main contributors are the 24 young people who have planned and used the group since 1974. Aged between 12 and 20 they come from a variety of backgrounds. **Mike Martyn** is a member of staff at Chailey and was on a working group that supported and encouraged the group. **Sue Virgo,** the 'author' and the independent advocate, is based at St Gabriels, a Children's Society family centre in Brighton.

**Alison Closs** is Lecturer in Special Education at Moray House Institute of Education, Edinburgh. She has worked as a teacher in primary, secondary, further and community education services, in both mainstream and special provision, as an adult education tutor in a large 'mental handicap' institution and as a local authority research officer. Her particular research and publication interests in this country are the educational entitlement of minority groups, including children with serious medical conditions and refugee children, and post-sixteen education of young people and adults with special educational needs. She has also been involved intermittently over many years in former Yugoslavia and in the Czech Republic in the education and human rights of disabled adults and children and of Romany children.

**Caroline Jones** is 39 years old. She has taught in primary schools for 16 years. She is currently a part-time tutor in the BA (QTS) course at the University of Warwick, Institute of Education. As proprietor of Pathways Childcare Centres, in the West Midlands, Caroline has worked with children under five and their families for the past eight years. She is studying part time for a PhD researching the identification and assessment of special educational needs in the early years.

**The Leighton Project** is a further education college for young adults with a moderate learning difficulty and is part of the services provided by Elfrida Rathbone, Camden. The project has spaces for up to 18 students all aged between 17 and 25. Students spend two years at the project following a course of study broadly programmed around independent living skills. The group featured in the chapter consisted of both first- and second-year students who met for two hours per session over six weeks. **Simon Grant** and **Daisy Cole** are the facilitators for the group.

**Maureen Oswin** taught children with cerebral palsy at Queen Mary's Hospital, Carshalton, from 1960 to 1974. She was seconded to the Hospital Advisory Service in 1972 to advise on 'mental handicap' hospital care, and was a research officer at the Thomas Coram Research Unit, London, from 1975 to 1991. Her special concerns are quality of residential care and the effects of institutional care on the lives of disabled children. Between 1963 and 1983 Maureen visited most large 'mental handicap' hospitals in England, and a variety of other long-stay hospitals and small residential facilities for disabled children. She has written several books including *Children Living in Long-Stay Hospital* (1978), *They Keep Going Away* (1984) and *Am I Allowed to Cry?* (1991).

**Rena Phillips** is Lecturer and Course Coordinator on the Diploma in Social Work Programme in the Department of Applied Social Science at the University of Stirling. She was previously employed in a social work department, specialising in adoption and fostering. She has carried out research in the field of adoption and disability. Recent publications include work on post-adoption support and disabled students in higher education.

**Janet Read** is Lecturer in Applied Social Studies at the University of Warwick. She teaches social policy and social work students as well as social workers at a postqualifying level. Her main areas of teaching and research are related to community care and the provision of services to disabled children, adults and those close to them. The experiences and perspectives of service users have always been a major focus of her work. In recent years she has been substantially involved in research and development on conductive education, both in this country and in Hungary. Alongside her academic career, she has held a variety of practice, management and training posts in the public and voluntary sectors.

**Professor Sheila Riddell (BA, Cert Ed, PhD)** following her PhD on *Gender and Option Choice in Two Rural Comprehensive Schools* at Bristol University in 1988, worked as Research Fellow in the Department of Education, University of Edinburgh, on a project investigating the impact of the 1981 Education (Scotland) Act, on children with special educational needs. From 1989 to 1996 she was employed at Stirling University, being awarded a personal chair in 1995. Following a year as Dean of Arts and Social Science at Napier University, Edinburgh, Sheila has recently taken up post as Professor of Social Policy (Disability Studies) at Glasgow University. She has researched and written extensively in the areas of special educational needs, disability and gender and education. Publications include *Gender and the Politics of Curriculum Change* (Routledge 1992) and *Policy, Practice and Provision for Children with Specific Learning Difficulties* (Avebury, 1995).

**Dr Carol Robinson** was formerly a social worker for Essex County Council. She is currently Senior Research Fellow and Project Director at the Norah Fry Research Centre, University of Bristol. Having conducted several research projects on services to disabled children over the last 14 years she has developed a special interest in disabled children's rights. Her current areas of research include services to children with severe and multiple impairments who have additional healthcare needs.

**Tom Shakespeare** is University Research Fellow in the Department of Sociology and Social Policy at the University of Leeds. He has written and broadcast widely on disability and related subjects, and is co-author of *The Sexual Politics of Disability* (Cassell, 1996) and *The Disability Reader* (Cassell, 1998). He is the principal investigator of a study entitled *Life As a Disabled Child,* part of the Economic and Social Research Council Research Programme, *Children 5–16: Growing into the Twenty-First Century.* He is father of two disabled children, and an active member of the disability movement.

**Linda Shaw** has, since 1988, been Co-director of the Centre for Studies on Inclusive Education (CSIE), an independent educational charity fully committed to working towards an end to segregated education. Linda has also worked as a support worker with people moving out of long-stay 'mental handicap' hospitals and as a radio and print journalist in this country and overseas.

**Dr Kirsten Stalker (BA, CQSW, PhD)** is Senior Research Fellow at the Social Work Research Centre, University of Stirling, where she has worked since 1991. She is currently joint grant holder of studies investigating the meaning of the 'learning society' for adults with learning difficulties, the resettlement of people with learning difficulties from Scottish hospitals and the exercise of choice by people with learning difficulties and dementia. From 1988 to 1991 Kirsten was a research associate at the Norah Fry Research Centre, University of Bristol, where she worked with Carol Robinson on a national study of short-term care for disabled children. In 1998 Kirsten will be undertaking a study for the Scottish Office exploring disabled children's perceptions of disability.

**Dr June Statham** is a researcher at the Thomas Coram Research Unit, Institute of Education, London University, and Honorary Research Fellow in the Department of Social Policy and Applied Social Studies at the University of Wales, Swansea. She lives in mid Wales and specialises in research on the provision of pre-school services, support for young children and their families, the inclusion of children with special needs in mainstream provision and the needs of children in rural areas. Recent and current work includes an evaluation of the impact of the Children Act 1989 on services for children under eight, a study of open-access family centres, the availability of bilingual education for children with physical impairment and learning difficulties in Wales, and an investigation of the use of sponsored places in voluntary and private daycare services to support children and families in need.

**Dr Carol Thomas** is Lecturer in the Department of Applied Social Science at Lancaster University. She is also heavily involved in Lancaster University's Institute for Health Research. A sociologist of health and illness, she has published in the areas of informal care, domestic labour and health, disability and motherhood, and other health issues. Carol is currently writing a book on women and disability. She is also a grant holder in an ESRC-funded research project in the Health Variations Programme, and is the principal investigator in a research project on the psycho-social needs of cancer patients and their main carers, funded by the NHS Executive North West.

**Nick Watson** is Lecturer in Sociology in the Department of Nursing Studies, University of Edinburgh. Prior to this he worked as a health promotion officer, youth worker and in biomedical research. His current research interests include a study into life as a disabled child (funded by the Economic and Social Research Council) and information needs of patients and their carers (funded by the management executive of the NHS). He is active within the disabled people's movement and is the convenor of AccessAbility, Lothian.

**Dr Helen Westcott** is Lecturer in Psychology at the Open University, and was formerly Research Officer with the NSPCC in London. Helen has worked in the field of child protection and disability for the past six years, with her original research on this topic promoting professional and public awareness of the problem. Helen was a member of the advisory group to the training and resource pack *ABuse and Children who are Disabled* (ABCD pack) and in 1996 her widely acclaimed book with Merry Cross, *This Far and No Further: Towards Ending the Abuse of Disabled Children*, was published by Venture Press. She has presented and published widely on issues relating to child protection and disabled children. Her other research interests centre on the investigative interviewing of children and children's perceptions of social work intervention.